1000

DETAILS IN ARCHITECTURE
CONSEILS D'ARCHITECTURE
ARCHITEKTURELEMENTE
DETAILS IN ARCHITECTUUR

Godefriduskaai 22
2000 Antwerp
Belgium
Tel.: +32 3 226 66 73
Fax: + 32 3 226 53 65
www.booqs.be
info@booqs.be

ISBN: 978-94-60650-390
WD: D/2010/11978/040
(Q058)

Editorial coordinator: Simone K. Schleifer
Editorial coordinator assistant:
Aitana Lleonart
Editor & texts: Àlex Sanchez Vidiella
Art direction: Mireia Casanovas Soley
Design and layout coordination:
Claudia Martínez Alonso
Layout: Cristina Simó
Translation: Cillero & de Motta
Cover photos:
© Andy Ryan

Editorial project:

LOFT publications
Via Laietana, 32, 4.º, of. 92
08003 Barcelona, Spain
Tel.: +34 932 688 088
Fax: +34 932 687 073
loft@loftpublications.com
www.loftpublications.com

Printed in China

1000

DETAILS IN ARCHITECTURE
CONSEILS D'ARCHITECTURE
ARCHITEKTURELEMENTE
DETAILS IN ARCHITECTUUR

014
268
380

426
544

The 1,000 architectural details presented in this book provide a visual and theoretical analysis of detail in contemporary architecture. Construction details are shown in photographs and drawings (plans, elevations, sections, isometric views, sketches, etc.) which, together with their description, assist with understanding and make reading easy.

This book is designed as five sections that correspond to main areas in the architectural process: equipment, environment and sustainability, horizontal and vertical communication, structures and enclosures, and, finally, finishes. These sections also include basic architectural features such as columns, beams, façades, roofing, stairs, railings, doors, windows, elevators, parking garages, swimming pools, landscaping, joinery, glazing, and lighting, among others. Special importance is given to materials, which are highlighted in photographs reflecting details in wood, concrete, metal, stone, steel, glass, wrought iron, etc.

Environment and sustainability deserve a whole chapter to themselves. An architecture that is both sustainable and ecological has been developing since the 1980s as a result of social awareness acquired about the effects of human activity on environmental resources. In contemporary architecture, technology has become an essential part in the design of any construction project and has enabled veritable feats of engineering and architectural marvels to be created that are truly works of art.

Les 1 000 détails architecturaux présentés dans ce livre, montrent une analyse visuelle et théorique du détail dans l'architecture contemporaine. Les détails de construction sont présentés à travers des photographies et des dessins (étages, élévations, sections, axonométries, croquis...) qui, au côté d'un texte descriptif, aident à la compréhension et en facilitent la lecture.

D'un point de vue conceptuel, le livre se compose de cinq grands chapitres qui correspondent à de grandes sections au sein du processus architectural : équipements, environnement et durabilité, communication horizontale et verticale, structure et cloisons et, enfin, finitions. Ces sections incluent à la fois des éléments propres essentiels à l'architecture, tels que les colonnes, les poutres, les façades, les toits, les ponts, les escaliers, les rambardes, les portes, les fenêtres, les ascenseurs, les places de parking, les piscines, le paysagisme, la menuiserie, la verrerie et l'éclairage. Les matériaux utilisés et affichés sur les photos sont particulièrement importants car ils présentent des détails en bois, béton, métal, pierre, acier, verre, fer forgé, etc.

La section de l'environnement et de la durabilité mérite un chapitre spécial. Depuis les années quatre-vingt, une architecture durable et écologique s'est développée, fruit de la conscience sociale issue des effets de l'activité humaine sur les ressources environnementales. Dans l'architecture contemporaine, la technologie est devenue indispensable dans la conception de tout projet de construction et a permis de créer des vraies prouesses d'ingénierie et des bijoux architecturaux, bref, de vrais chefs-d'œuvre.

Die in diesem Band vorgestellten 1.000 architektonischen Details bilden eine visuelle und theoretische Analyse der Details in der zeitgenössischen Architektur. Die Details werden anhand von Fotos und Zeichnungen (Grundrissen, Aufrissen, Querschnittzeichnungen, Axonometrien, Skizzen...) dargestellt, die in Verbindung mit begleitenden Texten das Verständnis erleichtern.

Dieser Band umfasst fünf Kapitel, die den wichtigsten Bereichen innerhalb des architektonischen Prozesses entsprechen: Ausstattung, Umwelt und Nachhaltigkeit, horizontale und vertikale Verbindungen, Struktur, Wände und Decken sowie Finishs. Die einzelnen Kapitel behandeln grundlegende architektonische Elemente wie z. B. Säulen, Träger, Fassaden, Dächer, Decken, Treppen, Geländer, Türen, Fenster, Aufzüge,

Parkgaragen, Swimmingpools, Landschaftsgestaltung, Tischlereiarbeiten, Verglasung, Beleuchtung usw. Besondere Bedeutung kommt den in den Fotografien gezeigten Materialien zu: Details aus Holz, Beton, Metall, Stein, Stahl, Glas, Schmiedeeisen...

Dem Thema Umwelt und Nachhaltigkeit wurde ein eigenes Kapitel gewidmet. Seit den achtziger Jahren hat sich dank des gestiegenen Umweltbewusstseins und des Wissens über die Auswirkungen des menschlichen Handelns auf die Natur eine nachhaltige und ökologisch orientierte Architektur herausgebildet. Die Technologie ist in der zeitgenössischen Architektur beim Entwurf eines jeden Bauprojekts unentbehrlich und hat die Schaffung grandioser architektonischer Schmuckstücke, beeindruckender Ingenieurleistungen und wahrhaftiger Kunstwerke möglich gemacht.

De 1.000 architectonische details die in dit boek voorgesteld worden geven een visuele en theoretische analyse weer van het detail in de hedendaagse architectuur. De bouwdetails worden getoond door middel van foto's en tekeningen (plattegronden, opstanden, secties, axonometrieën, schetsen...) die, samen met een descriptieve tekst, het begrip en de interpretatie ervan vergemakkelijken.

Het boek bestaat conceptueel uit vijf grote hoofdstukken die overeenstemmen met de grote onderdelen van het architectonisch proces: voorzieningen, milieu en duurzaamheid, horizontale en verticale communicatie, structuur en kappen en ten slotte, afwerkingen. Deze onderdelen omvatten op hun beurt, belangrijke elementen die eigen zijn aan de architectuur zoals zuilen, balken, gevels, daken, dakbedekkingen, trappen, leuningen, deuren, vensters, liften, parkeergarages, zwembaden, landschapsarchitectuur, houtwerk, glaswerk, verlichting, enz. Er wordt speciale aandacht besteed aan de materialen in foto's die details in hout, beton, metaal, steen, staal, glas, smeedijzer, enz. weergeven.

Het onderdeel milieu en duurzaamheid verdient een apart hoofdstuk. Sinds de jaren tachtig ontwikkelde zich namelijk langzamerhand een duurzame en ecologische architectuur dankzij het groeiende sociale bewustzijn over de effecten van de menselijke activiteit op de natuurlijke rijkdommen. In de hedendaagse architectuur is technologie voor het ontwerp van gelijk welk bouwproject onmisbaar geworden en heeft gezorgd voor ware technische hoogstandjes en architectonische juweeltjes, kortom echte kunstwerken.

EQUIPMENT

EQUIPEMENTS
AUSSTATTUNG
VOORZIENINGEN

0001

0002

0003

0004

0005

0006

A "house inside a house", composed mainly of steel, glass and aluminum panels with LED lights, was installed in the lobby of the Börsenhalle, the historic seat of the Hamburg Stock Exchange. The new space houses offices, meeting rooms, and a social club, among others.

Dans le vestibule de la Börsenhalle, le siège historique de la Bourse de Hambourg, a été créée une «maison à l'intérieur de la maison», composée principalement d'acier, de verre et de panneaux en aluminium dotés de LED. Le nouvel espace accueille des bureaux, des salles de réunion et un club social, entre autres.

Im Foyer der Börsenhalle, dem altehrwürdigen Sitz der Hamburger Börse, schuf man ein „Haus im Haus", das im Wesentlichen aus Stahl, Glas und Aluminiumpaneelen mit LED-Leuchten besteht. Die neuen Räume beherbergen u. a. Büros, Sitzungssäle und einen Gesellschaftsclub.

In de hal van de Börsenhalle, de historische zetel van de Hamburgse beurs, werd een «huis in een huis» gecreëerd, voornamelijke opgebouwd uit staal, glas en aluminiumpanelen met leds. De nieuwe ruimte herbergt onder andere kantoren, vergaderzalen en een gezelligheidsvereniging.

0008

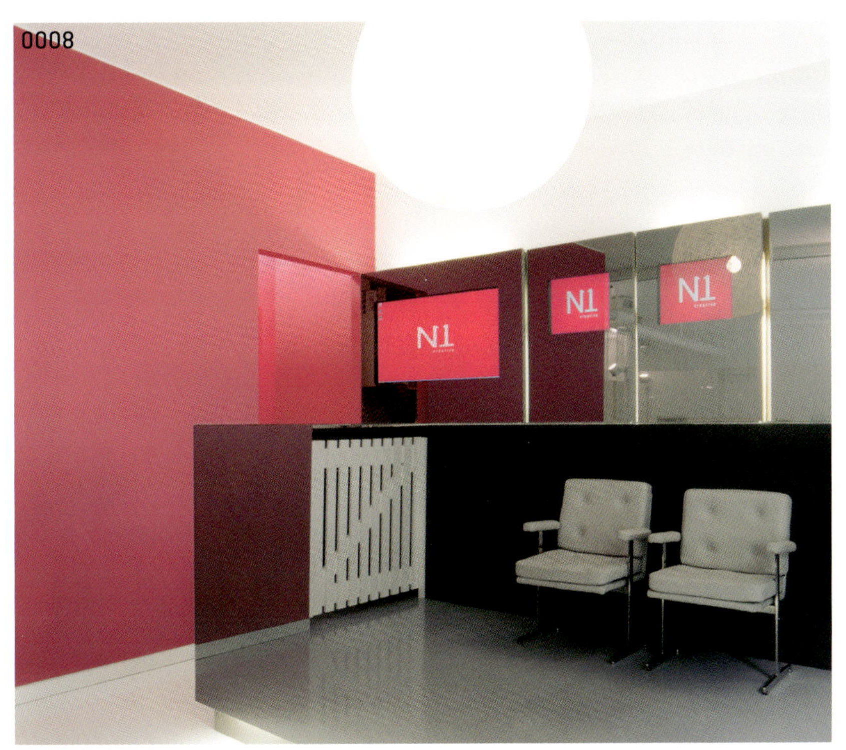

0009

0010

0011

0012

0013

0014

0015

Owing to the function of this building complex – used for cultural, educational, and private research purposes –, the architects created meeting points to facilitate the exchange of knowledge between students and scientists.

Du fait de l'utilisation du complexe par les bâtiments consacrés à la culture, l'enseignement et les sociétés de recherche privées, les architectes ont réfléchi à la création de points de rencontre facilitant l'échange de connaissances entre étudiants et scientifiques.

Da die Gebäude dieses Komplexes der Kultur, der Lehre und privaten Forschungsunternehmen gewidmet sind, entschieden sich die Architekten für die Schaffung von Treffpunkten, die den Austausch von Wissen zwischen Studierenden und Wissenschaftlern erleichtern sollten.

Vanwege het gebruik van het gebouwencomplex voor zowel cultuur, onderwijs als private onderzoeksbedrijven, overwogen de architecten een ontmoetingspunt te creëren dat de uitwisseling van kennis tussen studenten en wetenschappers zou bevorderen.

>

0017

0018

0019

0020

0021

0022

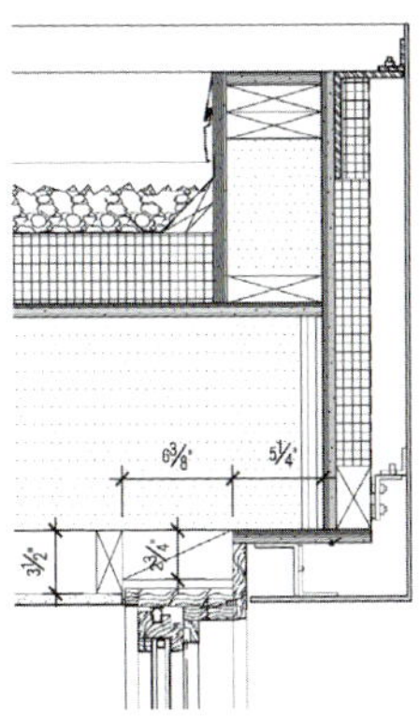

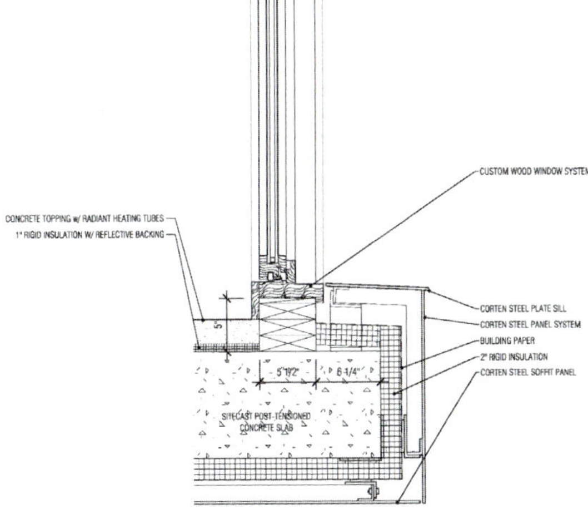
CUSTOM WOOD WINDOW SYSTEM
CONCRETE TOPPING w/ RADIANT HEATING TUBES
1" RIGID INSULATION W/ REFLECTIVE BACKING
CORTEN STEEL PLATE SILL
CORTEN STEEL PANEL SYSTEM
BUILDING PAPER
2" RIGID INSULATION
CORTEN STEEL SOFFIT PANEL
SITECAST POST-TENSIONED CONCRETE SLAB
5 1/2"
6 1/4"
5"

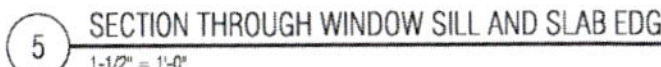
5
SECTION THROUGH WINDOW SILL AND SLAB EDGI
1-1/2" = 1'-0"

0023

0024

The new CriSamar®STEP range by SEVASA offers 8 different designs of anti-slip glass, specially designed for corridors, staircases, walkways, ramps, decking and trafficable roofs, both indoors and outdoors.

La nouvelle gamme CriSamar®STEP, de SEVASA, propose 8 modèles différents de verre antidérapant, tout particulièrement indiqués pour couloirs, escaliers, passerelles, rampes, estrades et toitures accessibles, tant d'intérieur que d'extérieur.

Die neue Produktlinie CriSamar®STEP aus dem Hause SEVASA umfasst rutschfestes Glas in 8 unterschiedlichen Designs, das sich für den Einsatz in Innen- und Außenbereichen und insbesondere in Fluren, auf Treppen, Stegen, Rampen, Podesten und begehbaren Dächern anbietet.

De nieuwe lijn CriSamar®STEP, van SEVASA, biedt 8 verschillende ontwerpen van antislipglas, die vooral geschikt zijn voor gangen, trappen, passerelles, hellingbanen, platformen en betreedbare daken, zowel voor binnen als buiten.

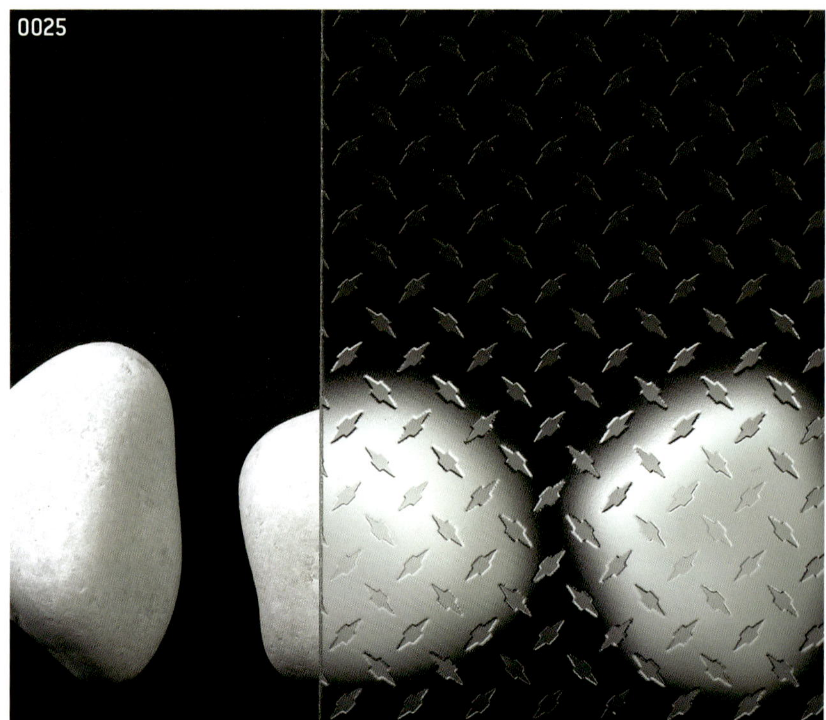

0025

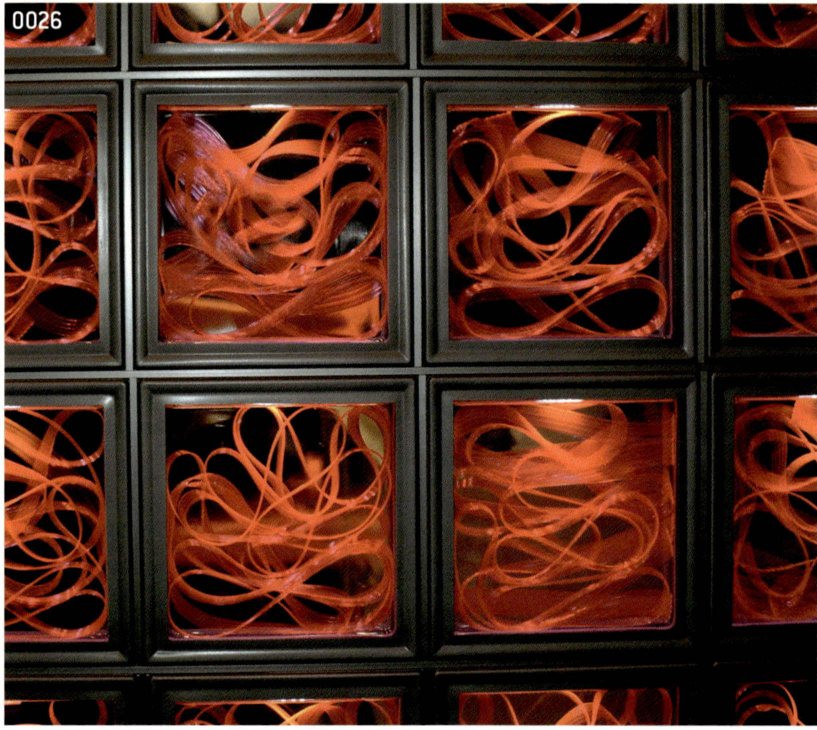

0026

0027

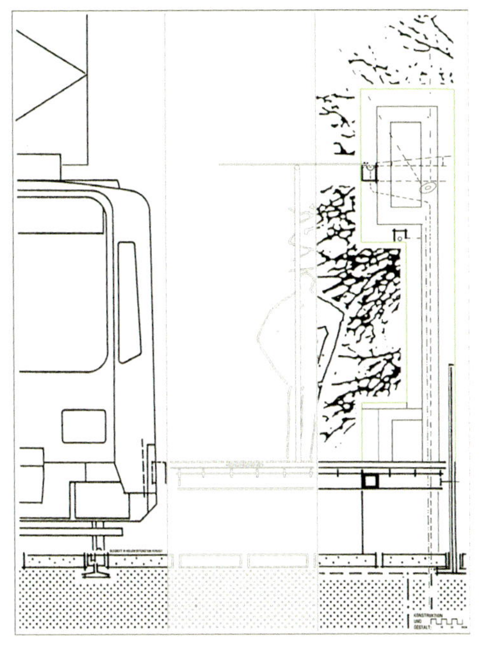

>

>

0028

0029

0030

0031

0032

0033

>

The glass panels in the walls amplify the space in the entrance lobby and maximize the amount of daylighting entering the building through its main entranceway.

Les panneaux en verre de cette enceinte élargissent non seulement l'espace du hall, mais ils laissent également passer une plus grande quantité de lumière dans le bâtiment par la porte principale.

Die Glaspaneele dieser Wandflächen vergrößern nicht nur den Platz in der Eingangshalle, sondern maximieren auch die Lichtmenge, die durch den Haupteingang in das Gebäude strömt.

De glazen panelen van deze kap vergroten niet alleen de beschikbare ruimte van de hal, maar maximaliseren eveneens de hoeveelheid licht dat door de hoofdingang het gebouw binnendringt.

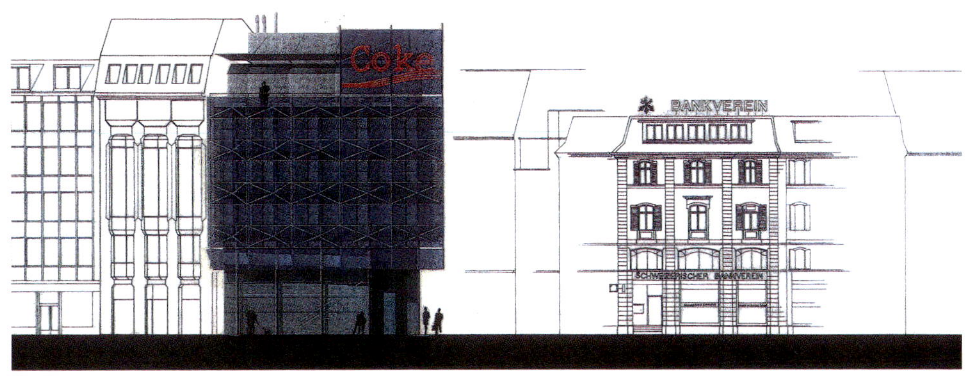
Coke
BANKVEREIN
SCHWEIZERISCHER BANKVEREIN

APOTHEKE
MIGROSBANK
BERNIE'S

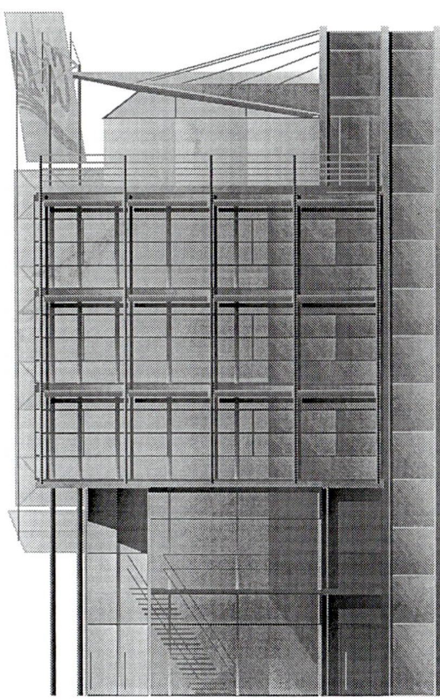

0037

0038

0039

>

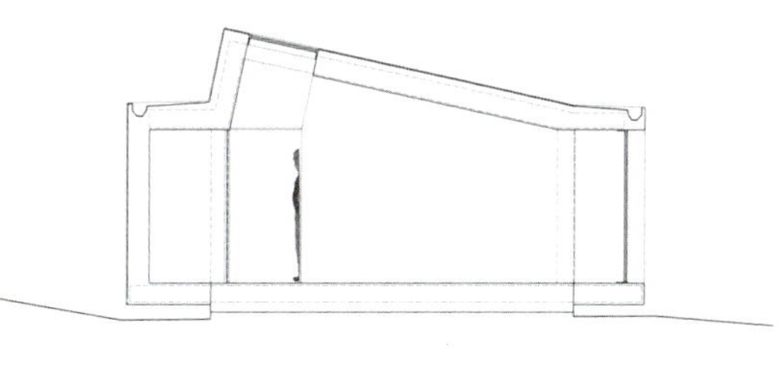

0040

0041

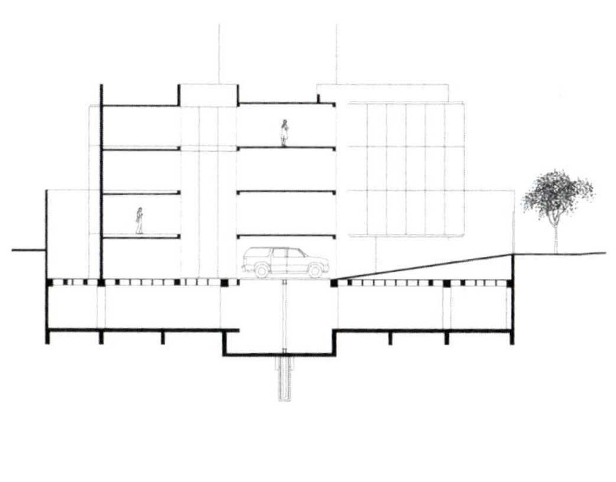

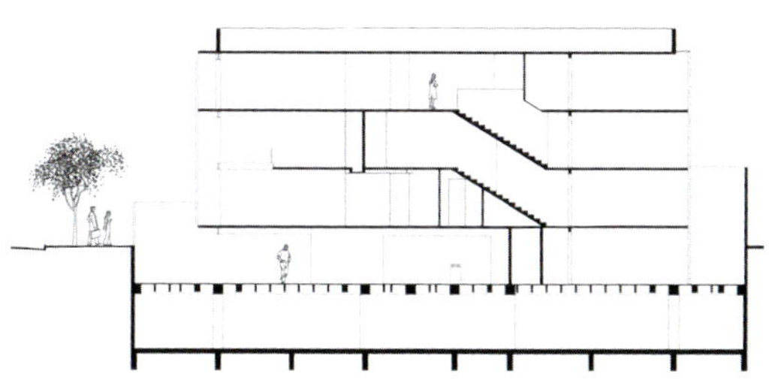

0042

The foyer of this convention center benefits from having a completely transparent roof. The glass sheets are sloped like a gabled roof, with a special feature of having certain sections where the gradient of the structure changes at different heights to make the roof narrower.

Le vestibule de ce palais des congrès dispose de toitures entièrement transparentes. Les panneaux en verre sont inclinés comme un toit à deux pentes, avec toutefois une particularité puisqu'ils sont disposés à différentes hauteurs, sur plusieurs tronçons, l'inclinaison de la structure change, ce qui rend le toit plus étroit.

Das Foyer dieses Kongress- und Konferenzzentrums nutzt vollständig transparente Dachflächen. Die Glaspaneele neigen sich wie Satteldächer, wobei sich die Neigung der Struktur auf verschiedenen Höhen in mehreren Abschnitten ändert und das Dach dadurch schmaler wird.

De hal van dit conventie- en congrescentrum beschikt over een volledig doorzichtige dakbedekking. De glazen panelen lopen diagonaal af zoals bij een puntdak met die bijzonderheid dat op verscheidene hoogten, de hellingshoek van bepaalde structuurdelen verandert waardoor het dak op die plaatsen smaller wordt.

0043

0044

0045

0046

0047

0048

0049

0050

0051

This expanse of skylights features the possibility of pulling open one of the panels to enable air to enter through the space in the open hatch.

Cette verrière offre la possibilité de rabattre l'un des battant vers le bas, ce qui permet de laisser entrer l'air par la rainure qui se forme lorsque la lucarne est ouverte.

Bei dieser Fläche aus Oberlichtern besteht die Möglichkeit, eines der Fenster nach unten zu kippen, um Luft einströmen zu lassen.

Bij deze uit dakramen samengestelde kap kan een vleugel neergelaten worden waardoor lucht kan binnendringen via de spleet van het geopende dakvenster.

0053

0054

0055

0056

0057

0058

0059

0060

0061

0062

The increasingly fashionable design for footbridges and pedestrian transit areas is to cover them with vaulted skylights, which prevents them from becoming claustrophobic tunnels.

Une solution de plus en plus à la mode pour les passerelles et les voies de passage pour piétons réside dans le fait d'insérer dans le plafond des lucarnes, ce qui permet d'éviter les sensations de claustrophobie dans ce type de tunnels.

Eine immer weiter verbreitete Lösung für Fußgängerstege und –brücken besteht in der Verkleidung des Fußwegs mit einem gewölbten Dach aus zahlreichen Oberlichtern. Dadurch wird vermieden, dass derartige Räume als beengende Tunnel wahrgenommen werden.

Een oplossing die steeds meer in trek is voor voetgangerspasserelles en -doorgangen is de bouw van overwelvingen met bovenlichten, waardoor claustrofobische tunnels vermeden worden.

0064

0065

0066

0067

0068

0069

The stairwell of this residential building is spanned along its length by a broad skylight made of wide glass panels, barely broken by the fine lines of the metal frame holding it up.

La cage d'escalier de ce bâtiment résidentiel est parcourue longitudinalement par une large verrière dotée de longs panneaux en verre à peine entrecoupées par les fines brides de la structure métallique qui les supporte.

Das Treppenhaus dieses Wohngebäudes wird in Längsrichtung von einem breiten Dachfenster aus großen Glaspaneelen überspannt, die nur durch die schmalen Leisten der stützenden Metallstruktur unterbrochen werden.

Het trapgat van dit residentiële gebouw wordt in de lengte overkoepelt door een breed bovenlicht met grote glazen panelen, amper onderbroken door de smalle banden van de metalen ondersteunende structuur.

0070

0071

0072

0073

0074

0075

0076

0077

0078

0079

0080

The large skylight spanning this atrium is so similar in design to the façade that it seems as if somebody has placed a mirror between the two. This design adds unity to the project, in addition to a sense of continuity.

La grande lucarne qui donne sur ce vestibule présente un design à tel point semblable à celui de la façade que l'on pourrait croire que quelqu'un a placé un miroir sur l'arête qui les sépare. Cette configuration apporte de l'unité au projet et une sensation de continuité.

Das beeindruckende Dachfenster über diesem Foyer ähnelt der Gebäudefassade in einem solchen Maß, dass es fast scheint, als hätte man am Scheitelpunkt beider Flächen einen Spiegel angebracht. Diese Art der Gestaltung macht das Projekt einheitlicher und verleiht den Eindruck von Kontinuität.

Het grote bovenlicht dat zich boven deze hal uitstrekt lijkt in zijn ontwerp zodanig op de gevel dat het wel lijkt of iemand tussen de twee toppen een spiegel aangebracht heeft. Deze configuratie verschaft eenheid aan het project, en een gevoel van continuïteit.

0082

0083

0084

0085

0086

0087

This country house by Tham & Videgård Hansson Arkitekter features windows in both the walls and gabled roof. Folding brise-soleil shutters installed on the windows provide protection from two different angles of sunlight penetration.

Cette maison rurale, œuvre de Tham & Videgård Hansson Arkitekter, est munie de fenêtres aussi bien sur les murs extérieurs que sur les deux pentes de son toit. Ces fenêtres ont été équipées de stores mobiles, des brise-soleil, qui laissent pénétrer la lumière en fonction de deux positions de réglage bien distinctes.

Dieses von Tham & Videgård Hansson Arkitekter entworfene Landhaus verfügt über Fenster in den Außenwänden wie auch in den Satteldächern. Die Fenster wurden mit klappbaren Fensterläden des Typs „Brise Soleil" versehen, die den Lichteinfall in zwei unterschiedlichen Stärken ermöglichen.

Dit buitenhuis, een bouwwerk van Tham & Videgård Hansson Arkitekter, heeft zowel vensters in de buitenmuren als in het puntdak. Voor al die vensters werden neerklapbare zonneblinden brise-de-soleil geïnstalleerd die twee duidelijk verschillende graden van lichtinval mogelijk maken.

0088

0089

0090

0091

0092

0093

0094

0095

0096

Big windows in most of the walls of this coastal house helped minimize the building's visual impact on the environment. As well as in the windows, glass is used as a protective balustrade on the terrace.

L'utilisation de grandes vitres dans la plupart des façades de cet immeuble situé face à la côte a contribué à réduire au maximum l'impact visuel de cette maison sur la nature. Outre son rôle pour les fenêtres, le verre a été utilisé pour la rambarde de protection sur la terrasse.

Der Einsatz großer Glasflächen für die meisten Fassaden dieses an der Küste gelegenen Wohnhauses trug dazu bei, dass die optische Wirkung des Gebäudes in der Natur minimiert werden konnte. Außer für die Fenster wurde das Glas auch für das Geländer auf der Terrasse verwendet.

Het gebruik van grote ramen in de meeste gevels van deze kustwoning beperkt de visuele impact van dit huis op zijn natuurlijke omgeving tot het minimum. Naast de ramen werd ook glas gebruikt voor de balustrade van het terras.

0098

0099

0100

0101

0102

0103

0104

0105

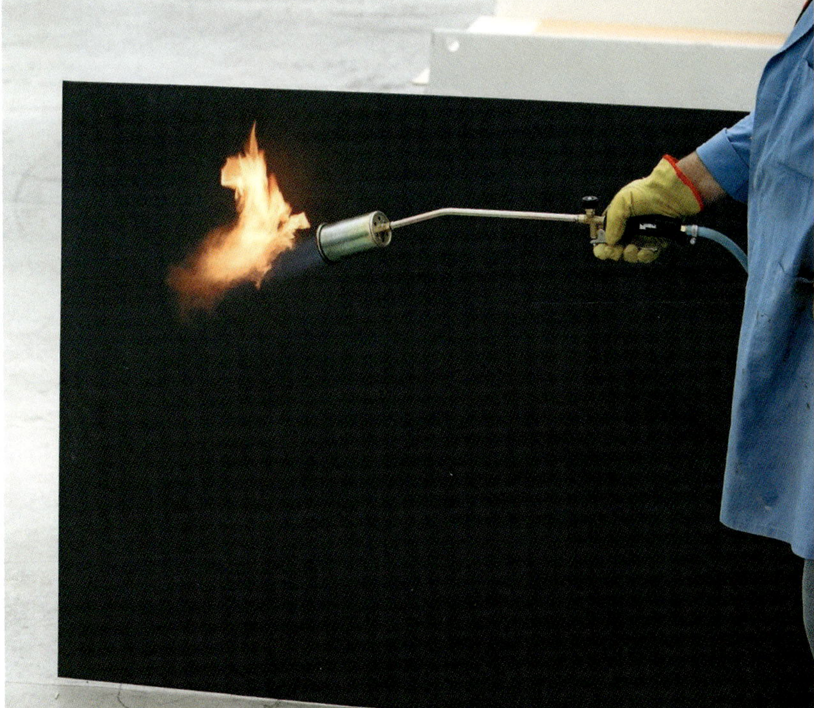

This door solves the problem of having to occupy the entire width of the passageway by opening in a truly inviting way. One wooden panel folds while the remaining one third is a fixed panel with the same covering as the surrounding walls.

Cette porte résout le problème de l'encombrement de la largeur du couloir, sur lequel elle communique de manière très intéressante. Le battant en bois est mobile, tandis que le tiers restant de sa surface est fixe et habillé du même revêtement que les cloisons qui l'entourent.

Diese Tür löst das Problem, die gesamte Flurbreite zu überbrücken, auf besonders ansprechende Art. Eines der hölzernen Türblätter ist aufklappbar, während das übrige Drittel der Tür feststeht und das gleiche Furnier aufweist wie die umgebenden Trennflächen.

Deze deur beslaat de volledige breedte van de gang waartoe ze op een heel aantrekkelijke wijze toegang verschaft. Een houten vleugel is mobiel, terwijl het resterende derde deel van het oppervlak, met dezelfde bekleding als de omringende scheidingswanden, vast staat.

0107

0108

0109

0110

0111

0112

0113

0114

A door may become the focal point of a room. In this case, a striking naïf style floral print not only decorates the surface of the door panel, it even covers the frame.

Une porte peut accaparer le premier plan visuel dans une pièce. Ici, un motif floral voyant de style naïf décore non seulement la surface du battant mais s'étend également jusqu'au cadre.

Eine Tür kann den optischen Mittelpunkt eines Zimmers bilden. In diesem Fall schmückt das auffällige Blumenmuster in naivem Stil nicht nur das Türblatt, sondern auch den gesamten Rahmen.

Een deur kan de visuele trekpleister van een vertrek zijn. In dit geval versiert een opvallend naïef bloemenmotief niet alleen de vleugel maar eveneens de lijst.

0115

0116

0117

0118

0119

0120

0121

0122

0123

0124

0125

0126

A simple door with pale blue acid-etched glass separates the living area from the hallway in this apartment. This material guarantees privacy in the space but also ensures that daylight can enter.

Dans cet appartement, une simple porte en verre poli avec une légère teinte de bleu ciel sépare le salon du couloir. Ce matériau garantit l'intimité de l'espace tout en laissant passer la lumière du jour.

Eine schlichte Tür aus Mattglas mit einer leichten himmelblauen Tönung trennt in dieser Wohnung das Wohnzimmer vom Flur. Das verwendete Material wahrt die Intimsphäre in diesem Raum und sorgt gleichzeitig dafür, dass ausreichend Tageslicht einfallen kann.

De huiskamer wordt in dit appartement van de gang gescheiden door een eenvoudige, lichtblauw getinte, gepolijste glazen deur. Dit materiaal garandeert de intimiteit van de ruimte en verzekert tegelijkertijd de inval van natuurlijk licht.

0127

0128

0129

0130

0131

0132

0133

Exterior door made of wood and wrought iron. The simplicity of the basic structure is in contrast to the wrought iron work on the handle and railing. The malleability of wrought iron enables the creation of spectacular designs that really showcase the craftsmanship, which is reflected in the marks left by the hammer strikes.

Porte extérieure fabriquée avec du bois et du fer forgé. La simplicité de la structure générale contraste avec le travail en fer gorgé réalisé sur la poignée et les barreaux. La malléabilité du fer forgé permet de créer des figures spectaculaires, où prime l'artisanat qui s'exprime à travers les marques laissées par les coups de marteau.

Haustür aus Holz und Schmiedeeisen. Die schlichte Grundstruktur steht im Kontrast zum geschmiedeten Eisen an Griff und Gitter. Die Schmiedbarkeit des Eisens ermöglicht die Schaffung spektakulärer Designs, die in jedem einzelnen der deutlich sichtbaren Hammerschläge die traditionelle Handwerkskunst zeigen.

Buitendeur uit hout en smeedijzer. De eenvoud van de algemene structuur contrasteert met het bewerkt smeedijzer van de knop en het traliewerk. Dankzij de pletbaarheid van het smeedijzer kunnen spectaculaire ontwerpen gecreëerd worden waarbij het ambachtswerk tot uiting komt in de sporen van de hamerslagen.

0134

>

0135

>

∨

0136

0137

0138

0139

0140

>

0141

>

The need to overcome a slope at the entrance was the inspiration for the design of the curved door. As the purpose of the gate was more to block transit rather than to provide security, the designer was able to play with the separations between the different elements.

Le besoin de conserver une pente au niveau de l'accès a inspiré la création des formes courbes de la porte. Étant donné que la clôture avait pour objectif de bloquer le passage, et non de garantir la sécurité, le concepteur a pu jouer avec les séparations entre les différents éléments.

Die Notwendigkeit, an dieser Zufahrt eine Steigung zu überbrücken, ließ die gebogenen Formen des Eingangstors entstehen. Da das Tor vielmehr den Zutritt verwehren sollte als Sicherheit zu gewährleisten, konnte der Designer mit den unterschiedlichen Abständen zwischen den einzelnen Elementen spielen.

De noodzaak een helling aan de ingang te overbruggen diende als inspiratie voor de gebogen vormen van de deur. Aangezien het doel van de omheining er vooral in bestond de toegang te blokkeren en niet zozeer de veiligheid te garanderen, kon de ontwerper spelen met de scheidingen tussen de verschillende elementen.

0142

0143

0144

0145

0146

0147

>

0148

0149

0150

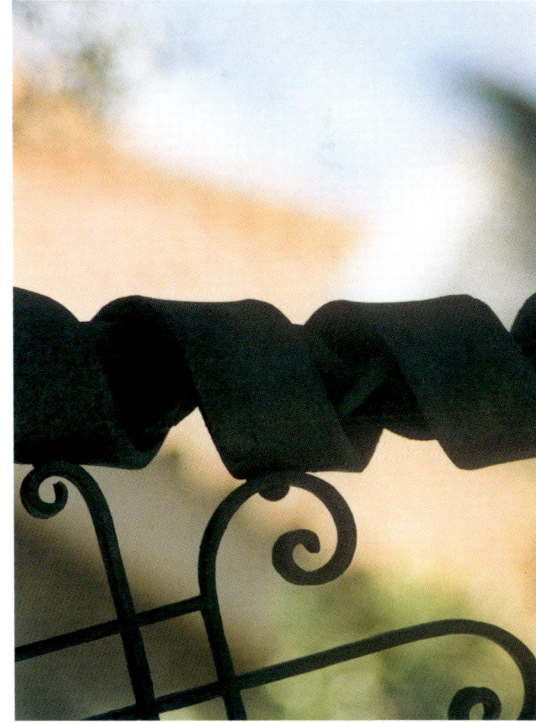

The entrance doors and gates of this project are made from sheet metal painted white and decorated with wrought iron. Design inspired by nature and featuring zoomorphic and floral motifs is very common in this kind of crafted work.

Les portes d'accès et les clôtures réalisées dans le cadre de ce projet ont été fabriquées en tôle métallique peinte en blanc avec des décorations en fer forgé. Le design inspiré de la nature, avec des motifs zoomorphes et floraux, est assez répandu dans ce type d'ouvrages artisanaux.

Eingangstür und Zufahrtstor dieses Projekts bestehen aus weiß lackiertem Stahlblech mit schmiedeeisernen Zierelementen. Das von der Natur inspirierte Design mit zoomorphen und floralen Motiven ist bei derartigen Handwerksarbeiten weit verbreitet.

De toegangsdeuren en omheiningen van dit project werden gebouwd met wit geverfde metalen platen en smeedijzeren versieringen. Het op de natuur geïnspireerde ontwerp, met dier- en bloemmotieven, is heel gebruikelijk in dit soort ambachtswerk.

0151

0152

0153

0154

0155

>

0156

>

∨

0157

0158

0159

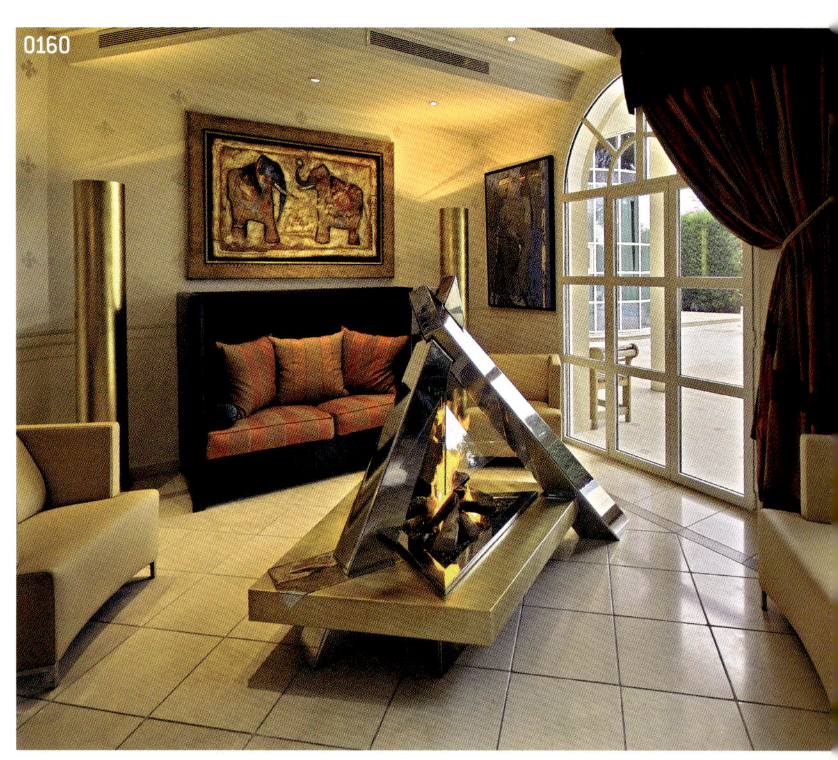

0160

0161

0162

Most glass fireplaces are usually gas-fired. The designs are created using translucent glass so as not to obscure general visibility within the space, since modern fireplaces are usually installed in the center of rooms.

La plupart des cheminées en verre fonctionnent habituellement au gaz. Les modèles sont fabriqués en verre translucide afin de ne pas gêner la vue d'ensemble de l'espace, étant donné que les cheminées contemporaines sont généralement installées au milieu des salons.

Die meisten Glaskamine werden mit Gas betrieben. Die Designer greifen auf durchscheinendes Glas zurück, um die allgemeinen Sichtverhältnisse im Raum nicht einzuschränken, da moderne Kamine mittlerweile für gewöhnlich in der Mitte des Wohnzimmers platziert werden.

De meeste glazen vuurhaarden werken op gas. De ontwerpen worden gerealiseerd uit doorschijnend glas om de algemene zichtbaarheid van de ruimte niet te belemmeren aangezien hedendaagse haarden vaak in het midden van de huiskamer geïnstalleerd worden.

0163

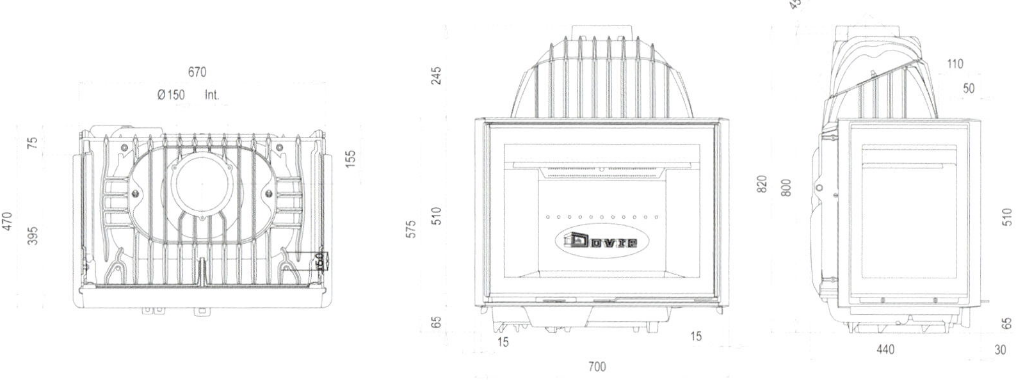
670
Ø150 Int.
75
155
470
395
150
245
575
510
65
15
15
700
DOVRE
45°
110
50
820
800
510
65
440
30

0164

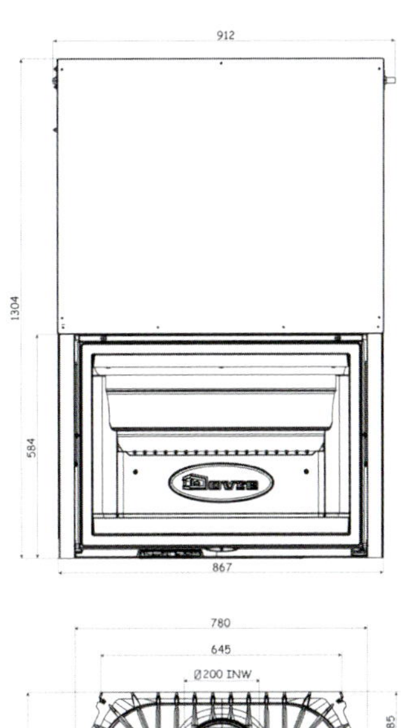

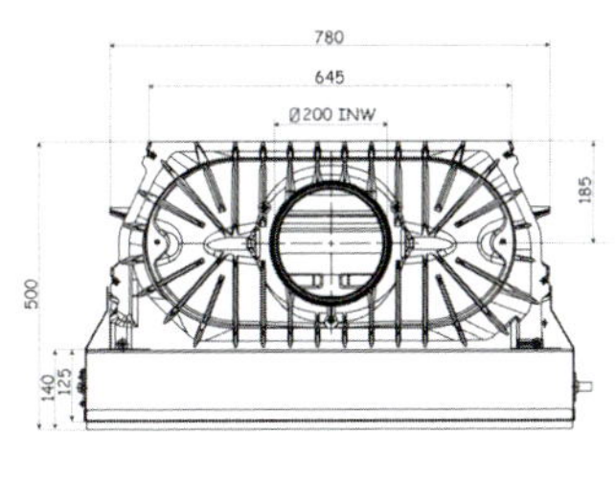

0165

0166

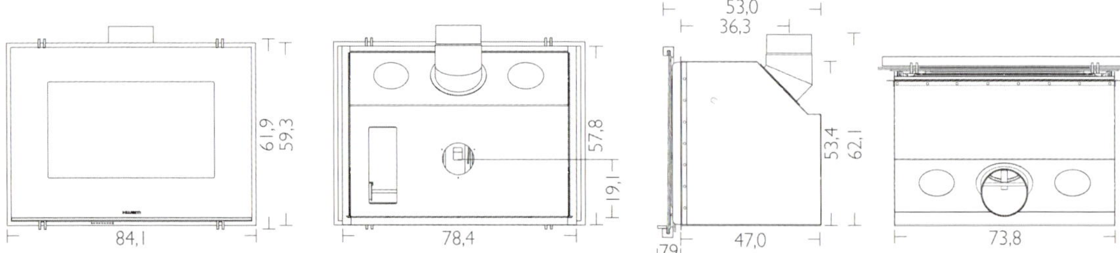

0167

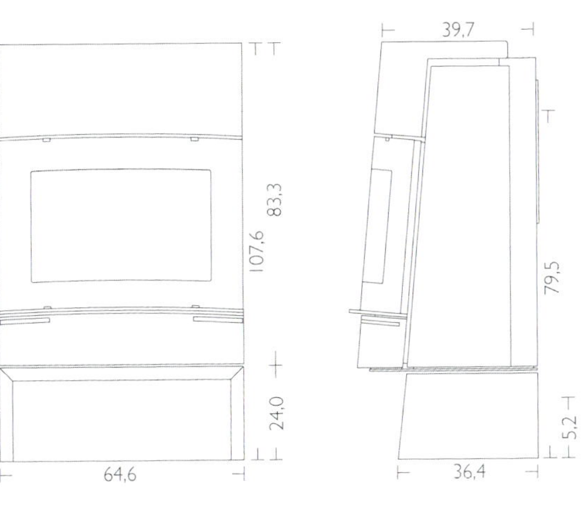
39,7
83,3
107,6
79,5
24,0
5,2
64,6
36,4

0168

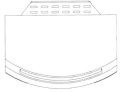

The innovative feature of the Stův 16 is that this fireplace that can be fitted into an existing gap or into a new chimney without major building work so that the user can enjoy efficient additional heating.

L'originalité du modèle Stův 16 réside dans la possibilité d'encastrer cette cheminée dans une ouverture déjà pratiquée ou dans une nouvelle cheminée sans avoir à réaliser de gros travaux, de sorte que l'utilisateur puisse bénéficier d'un chauffage efficace supplémentaire.

Die Originalität des Modells Stův 16 liegt in der Möglichkeit, den Kamin in eine bereits bestehende Nische einzubauen oder in einer neuen Kaminanlage zu installieren. Auf diese Weise kommt der Besitzer in den Genuss einer wirksamen Zusatzheizung.

De originaliteit van het Stův 16-model ligt in de mogelijkheid deze haard zonder grote verbouwingswerken in een reeds bestaande nis of schoorsteen in te bouwen zodat de gebruiker van een efficiënte bijkomende verwarmingsbron kan genieten.

0169

0170

0171

0172

0173

0174

0175

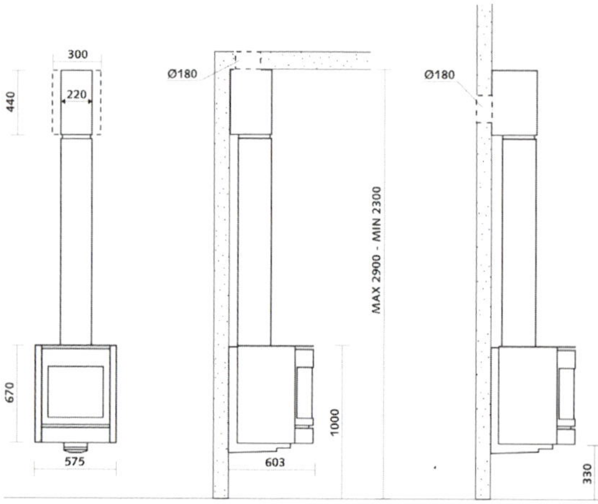

0176

>

0177

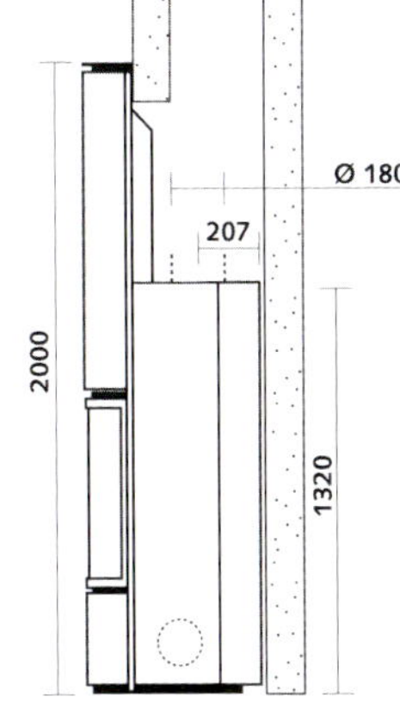
Ø 180
207
2000
1320

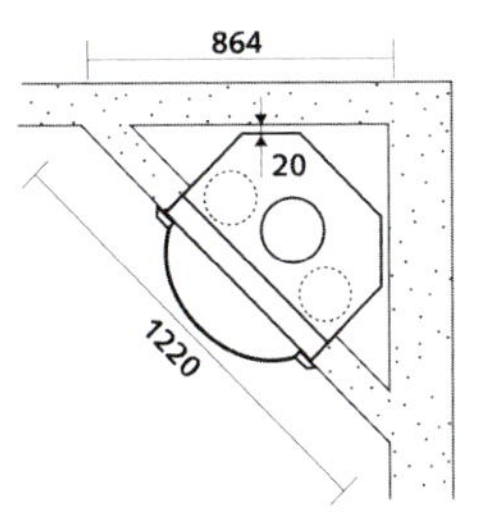
864
20
1220

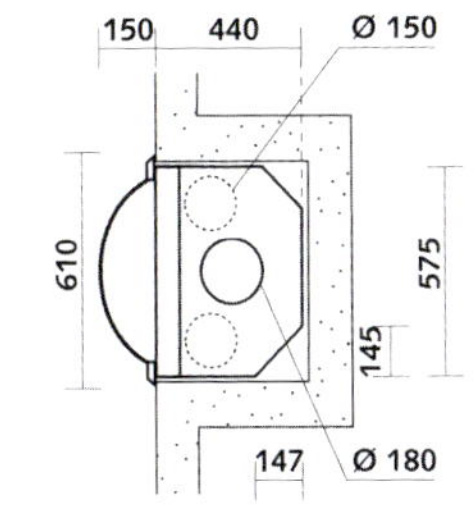
150
440
Ø 150
610
575
145
147
Ø 180

0178

0179

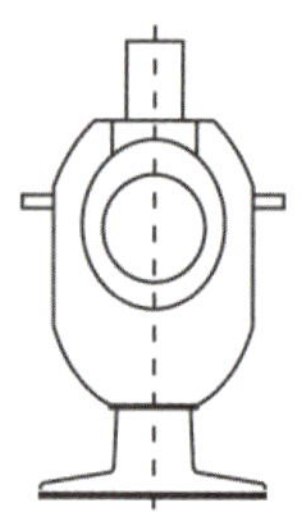

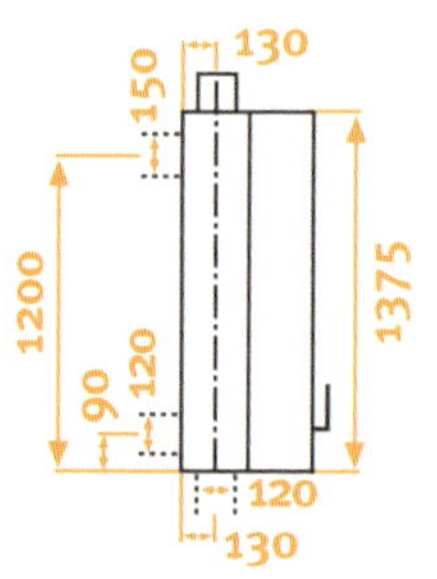

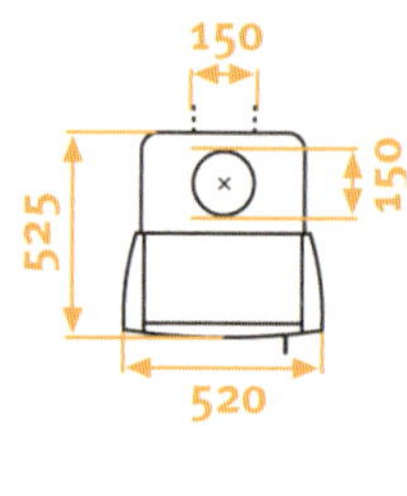

0180

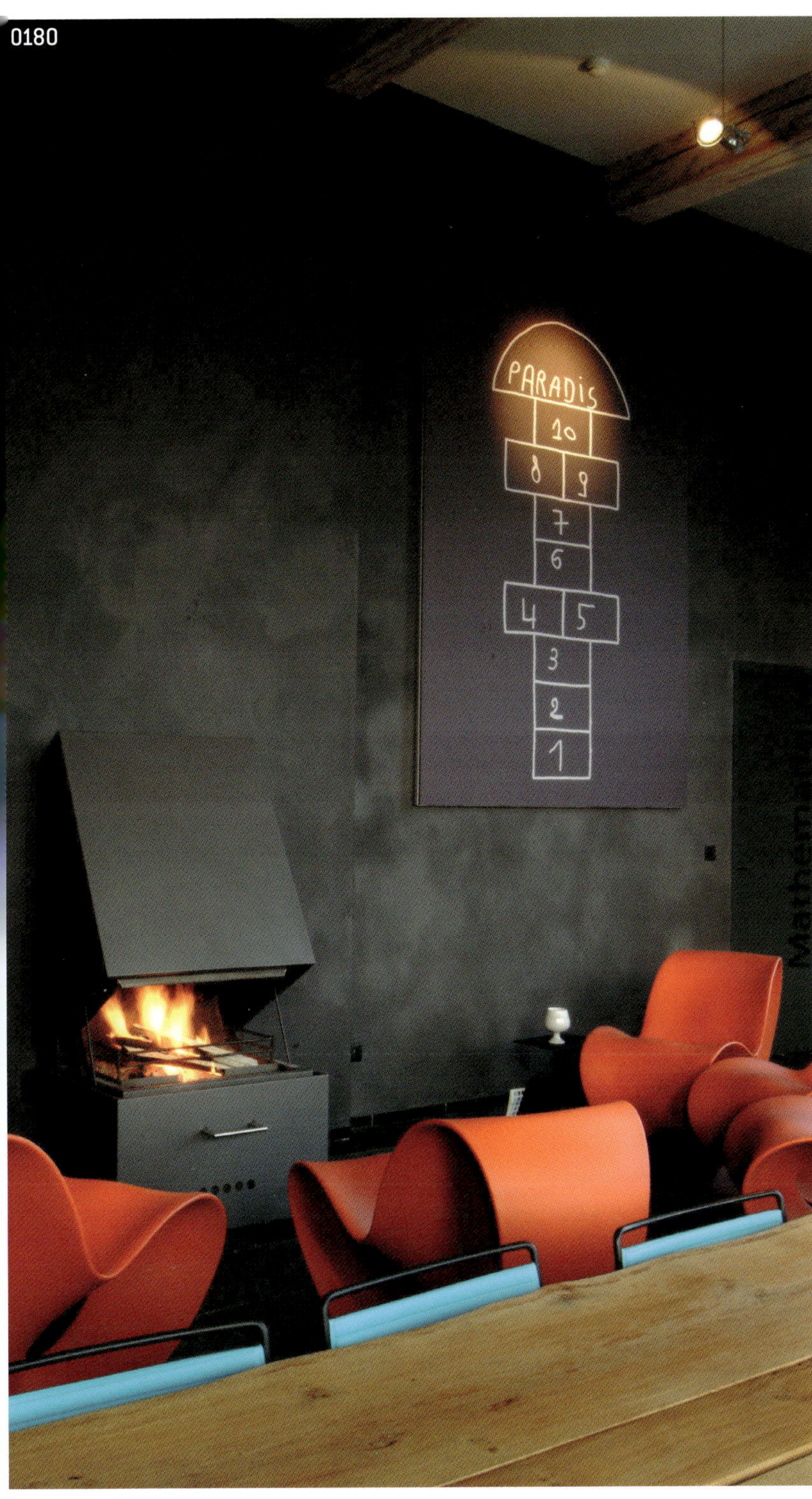

This original stove can be mounted on a wall. It is a closed hearth that performs like the best wood-fired stoves. It operates continuously: it is loaded with firewood at night and relights, even after many hours.

Ce poêle original peut être accroché au mur. Une fois fermé, il est aussi performant que les meilleurs poêles à bois. Il fonctionne en continu : il se recharge la nuit et se rallume même après plusieurs heures.

Dieser originelle Ofen kann an der Wand aufgehängt werden. In geschlossenem Zustand bietet er sämtliche Vorzüge der besten Holzöfen. Außerdem kann er unterbrechungsfrei betrieben werden: Abends wird Brennstoff nachgefüllt, und auch nach vielen Stunden kann das Feuer wieder angefacht werden.

Deze originele kachel kan aan de muur gehangen worden. Gesloten biedt ze even goede resultaten als de beste houtkachels. Ze werkt constant: gedurende de nacht laadt ze bij en ontsteekt probleemloos, zelfs na vele uren.

0181

0182

0183

0184

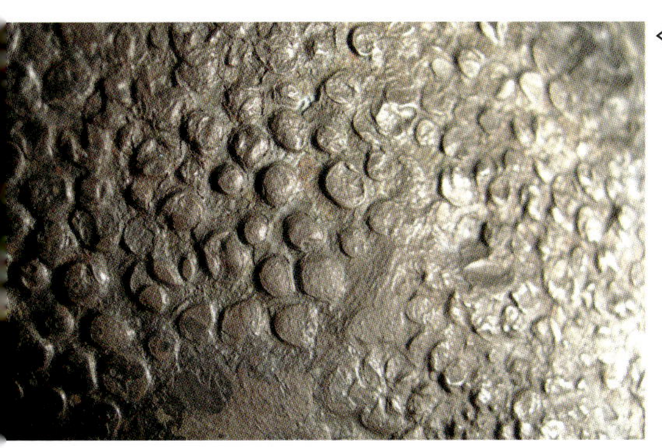

0185

0186

The malleability of wrought iron enables the creation of spectacular and original designs, like this one for example, made from interwoven winding iron pipes, and others imitating a mesh or net. It is a clear example of the way in which architecture sometimes blends with sculpture.

La malléabilité du fer forgé permet de créer des structures spectaculaires et originales, comme par exemple celle-ci formée par des tubes sinueux en fer enchevêtrés entre eux, et d'autres qui imitent un quadrillage ou un filet. Cet exemple montre clairement comment l'architecture se mélange parfois à la sculpture.

Die Schmiedbarkeit des Eisens ermöglicht die Erschaffung spektakulärer und origineller Designs, wie z. B. dieses Tors aus gebogenen, ineinander verschlungenen Metallrohren und Elementen, die ein Netz bzw. Gitter nachahmen. Dies ist ein eindeutiges Beispiel dafür, wie Architektur und Bildhauerei bisweilen miteinander verschmelzen.

Dankzij de pletbaarheid van smeedijzer kunnen spectaculaire en originele ontwerpen gecreëerd worden, zoals deze bijvoorbeeld, bestaande uit in elkaar verstrengelde ijzeren buizen, naast andere die een netwerk simuleren. Dit is een duidelijk voorbeeld van hoe architectuur en sculptuur soms met elkaar versmelten.

0187

0188

0189

0190

>

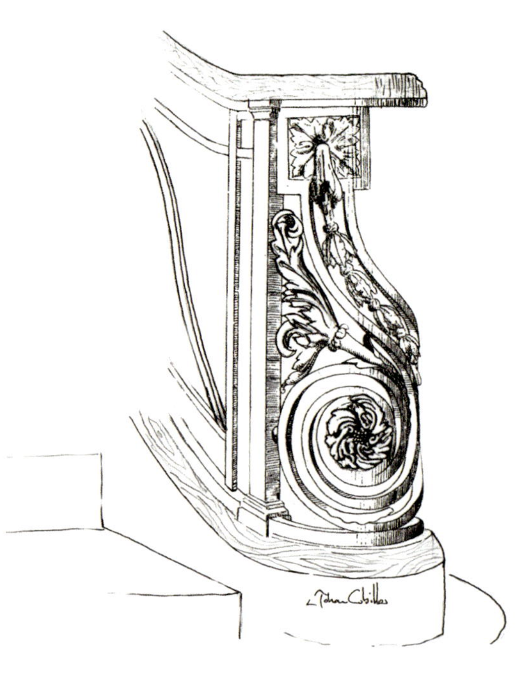

0191

>

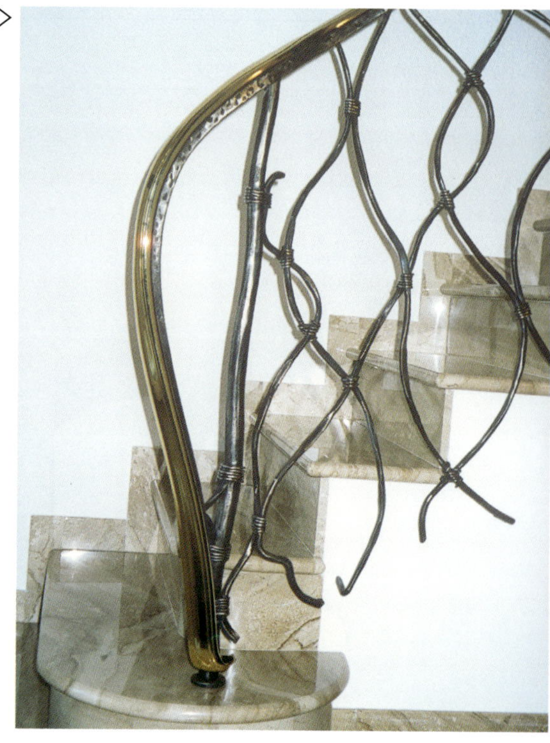

0192

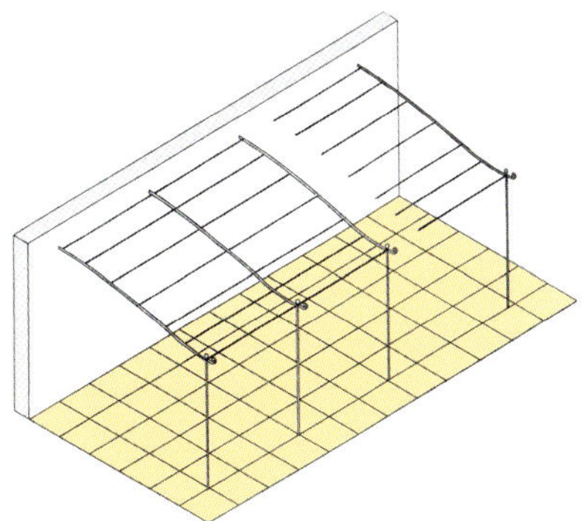

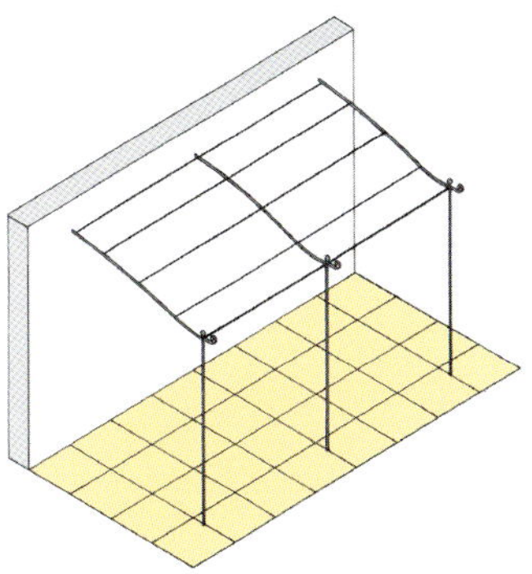

0193

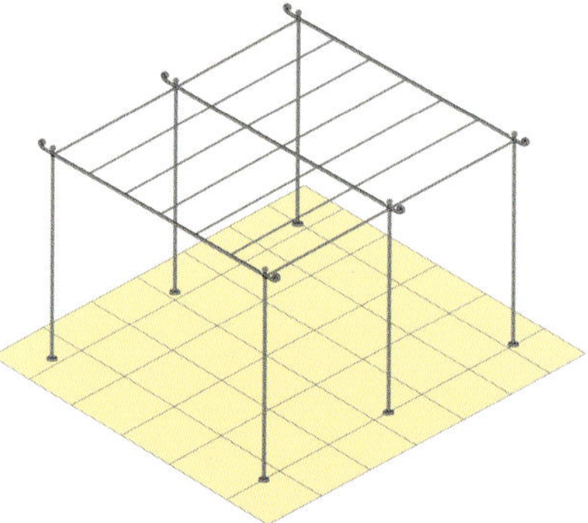

0194

0195

Here is an original and spectacular front entrance to a winery, designed by Miquel Xirau (Spain). The chosen decorative theme is the vine. In this door, the characteristic marks in the wrought iron can be perfectly appreciated.

Porte spectaculaire et originale d'accès à une cave à vin conçue par Miquel Xirau (Espagne). L'élément décoratif choisi est celui de la vigne. Les détails caractéristiques du fer forgé peuvent parfaitement être observés sur la porte.

Diese originelle und besonders außergewöhnliche Eingangstür eines Weinkellers wurde von Miquel Xirau (Spanien) entworfen. Als Motiv wurde der Weinstock ausgewählt. Die Tür zeigt die typischen Merkmale von Schmiedeeisen.

Originele en spectaculaire toegangsdeur van een bodega, ontworpen door Miquel Xirau (Spanje). Het gekozen siermotief is de wingerd. Op de deur zijn de kenmerkende tekens van het smeedijzer perfect zichtbaar.

0196

0197

0198

0199

0200

0201

0202

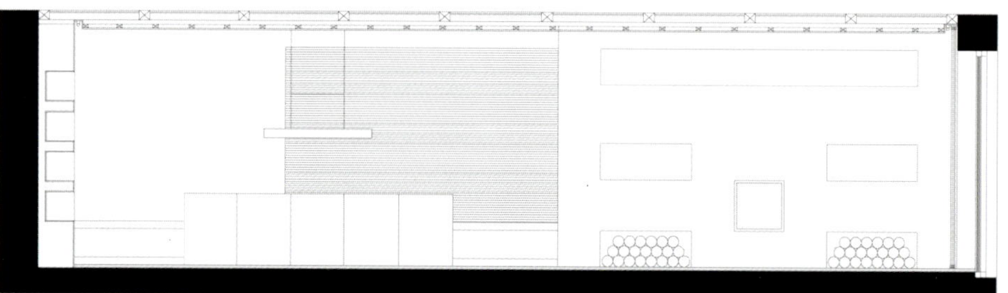

0203

0204

Occupying a small room in a recently remodeled residence, this closet stands out by the intelligent use it makes of space and for the elegance with which the drawers are arranged, enabling the drawer pulls to become a decorative feature.

Cette armoire qui occupe une petite chambre dans une demeure récemment rénovée impressionne de par son astucieuse façon d'exploiter l'espace et par l'élégance avec laquelle les tiroirs se succèdent, avec une poignée qui devient un élément décoratif.

Dieser Einbauschrank, der sich über ein kleines Zimmer einer kürzlich renovierten Wohnung erstreckt, beeindruckt durch die intelligente Raumnutzung und durch die Eleganz der gleichmäßigen Schubladenflächen. Die Griffe stellen gleichzeitig ein Zierelement dar.

Deze kast, in een kleine kamer van een onlangs verbouwde woning, maakt indruk door de intelligente benutting van de ruimte en de elegante schikking van de laden met sierknoppen.

0205

0206

0207

0208

0209

>

0210

0211

0212

0213

The most visually weightless storage system is one that attaches to the wall, particularly if it is in the form of metal or glass shelves. This also allows for uninhibited and original designs like these studio bookshelves designed by Desalto.

Le système de rangement le plus discret visuellement est celui qui s'accroche au mur, surtout s'il s'agit d'étagères en métal ou en verre. De plus, leur design peut être léger et original comme les étagères présentées ici, conçues par Desalto.

An der Wand befestigte Aufbewahrungssysteme wirken besonders leicht und luftig, insbesondere wenn es sich um Metall- oder Glasregale handelt. Außerdem sind moderne und originelle Designs möglich, wie bei diesen Regalen aus dem Hause Desalto.

Het optisch lichtste opbergsysteem is datgene dat aan de muur hangt, vooral als het uitgevoerd werd met metalen of glazen rekken. Bovendien kunnen er informele en originele ontwerpen mee gemaakt worden zoals deze voor een studio ontworpen rekken van Desalto.

0214

0215

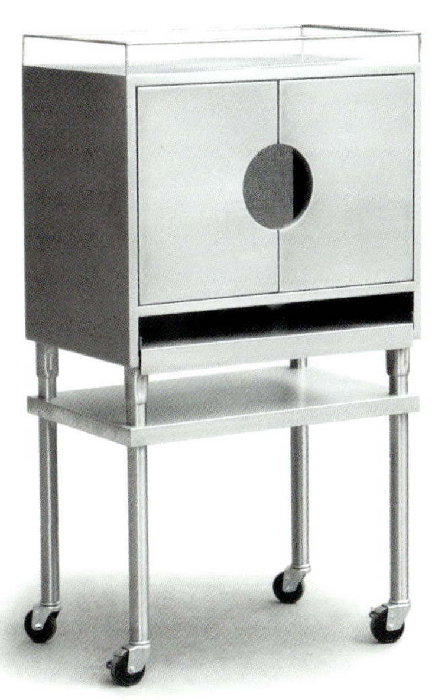

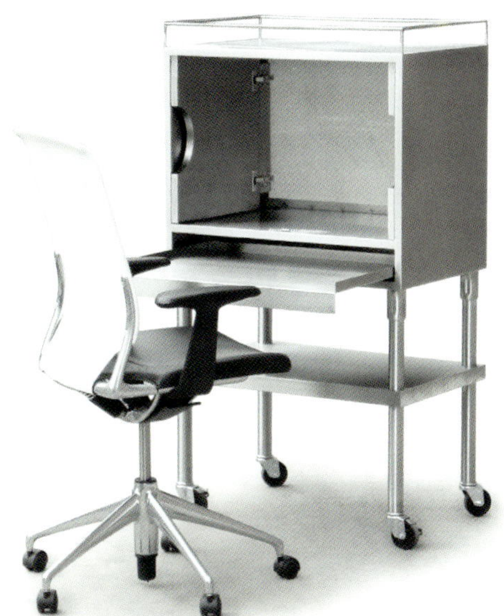

0216

0217

0218

0219

0220

0221

>

0222

0223

Made-to-measure furniture is helpful when adapting to irregularly structured buildings, and provide storage spaces: drawers under a sofa, cabinets making use of setback wall spaces, or which integrate columns, sloping walls, etc.

Les meubles sur mesure peuvent s'adapter aux structures de construction les plus irrégulières et permettent ainsi de gagner de l'espace de rangement. tiroirs sous un canapé, placards qui profitent des retraits du mur ou intègrent des colonnes, un mur incliné, etc.

Maßgefertigte Möbel erlauben die Anpassung an unregelmäßige Baustrukturen und den Gewinn von zusätzlichem Stauraum: Schubladen unter den Sofasitzen, Schränke, die vorhandene Nischen, Säulen oder geneigte Wände nutzen, usw.

Op maat gemaakte meubels kunnen zich aan de meest onregelmatige bouwstructuren aanpassen en creëren extra bergruimte: laden onder de zitting van een sofa, kasten die uitsprongen van de muur benutten, of zuilen, een schuine wand enz. integreren.

0224

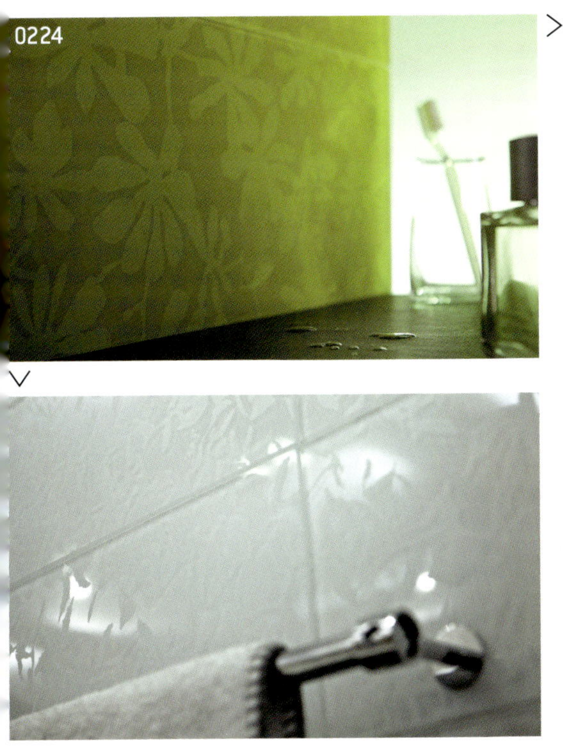

0225

0226

0227

0228

0229

>

0230

>

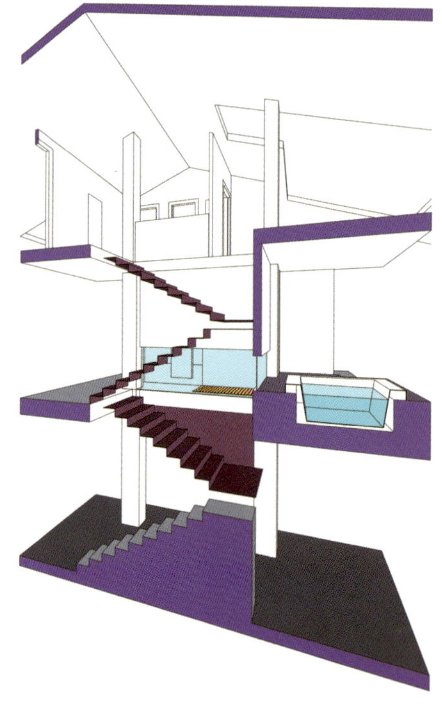

0231

✓

Expanses of mirrored surfaces infuse these marble-covered spaces with light. The golden and neutral tones create a deliberate contrast with the predominance of blue in the rest of the spaces and prevent it from becoming monotonous.

Les vastes miroirs apportent de la légèreté à ces espaces recouverts de marbre. Les tons dorés et neutres présentent un net contraste avec la couleur bleue dominante des autres espaces, rompant ainsi avec la monotonie.

Große spiegelbedeckte Flächen verleihen diesen marmorverkleideten Bereichen Leichtigkeit. Die Goldtöne und neutralen Farben bilden einen wohl überlegten Kontrast zum Blau in den übrigen Räumen und beugen Eintönigkeit vor.

Grote met spiegels bedekte oppervlakken verschaffen lichtheid aan deze met marmer beklede ruimten. De gouden en neutrale tinten bieden een doelbewust contrast met het overheersende blauw in de overige ruimten en vermijden zo de monotonie.

0233

0235

0236

0237

0238

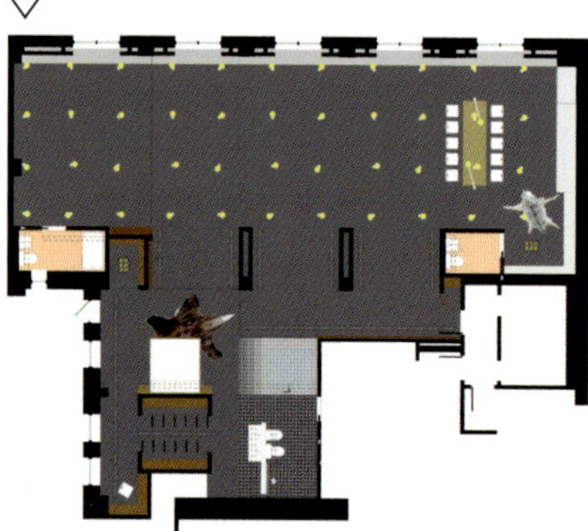

0239

0240

0241

The bathroom walls are covered with Snowflake mosaic tiles by Bisazza, in contrast to the smooth, natural tones of the surfaces of the bathtub and shower recess. The faucets of the hand-basin and shower are industrial-style and have original heart-shaped openings.

Le mur de la salle de bains est revêtu des mosaïques Snowflake de Bisazza, qui contrastent avec les surfaces lisses et les tonalités naturelles de la baignoire et la douche. Les robinets du lavabo et de la douche évoquent un style industriel et présentent la particularité d'avoir un orifice en forme de cœur.

Die Badezimmerwand wurde mit dem Mosaik Snowflake aus dem Hause Bisazza verkleidet und steht im Kontrast zu den glatten Flächen und Naturtönen von Badewanne und Dusche. Die Wasserhähne an Waschbecken und Dusche sind im industriellen Stil gehalten und zeichnen sich durch ihre herzförmigen Öffnungen aus.

De muur van de badkamer is bekleed met het mozaïekmotief Snowflake van Bisazza dat mooi contrasteert met de vlakke oppervlakken en natuurtinten van het bad en de douche. Voor de kranen van de waskom en de douche werd voor een industriële stijl gekozen. Ze vallen op vanwege hun hartvormige openingen.

0242

0243

0244

0245

0246

0247

0248

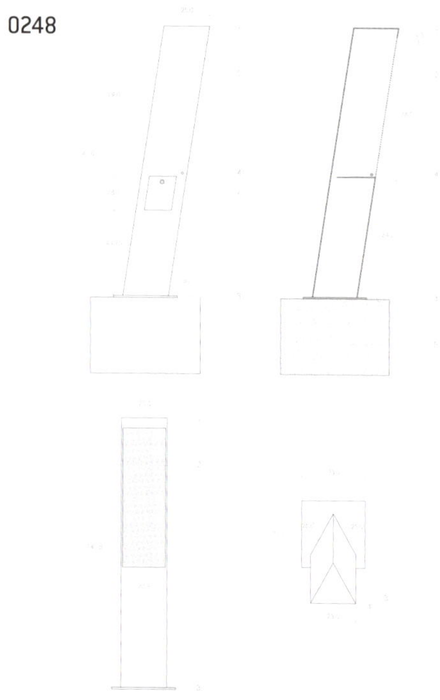

0249

The faceted glass balustrade of this bridge lights up by night. The lighting creates a kaleidoscopic effect of colors on the river down below. The bridge is a symbol that alludes to a Portuguese legend: a crown prince and his beloved who were tragically separated.

La balustrade en verre à facettes de ce pont s'illumine la nuit. Cet éclairage crée un jeu de couleurs kaléidoscopique sur la surface de la rivière. Le pont est un symbole faisant allusion à une légende portugaise : un prince héritier et sa bien-aimée, séparés de manière tragique.

Das facettenartig gestaltete Glasgeländer dieser Brücke wird nachts beleuchtet. Die Beleuchtung sorgt für ein kaleidoskopisches Farbenspiel auf dem Fluss. Die Brücke ist ein Symbol, das auf eine portugiesische Legende anspielt: ein Kronprinz und seine Geliebte wurden auf tragische Weise voneinander getrennt.

De met facetten geslepen glazen balustrade van deze brug wordt 's nachts verlicht. Deze verlichting creëert een caleidoscopisch lichtspel op het wateroppervlak van de rivier. De brug is een symbool dat naar een Portugese legende verwijst: het verhaal van de tragische scheiding van een kroonprins en zijn geliefde.

0250

0251

0252

>

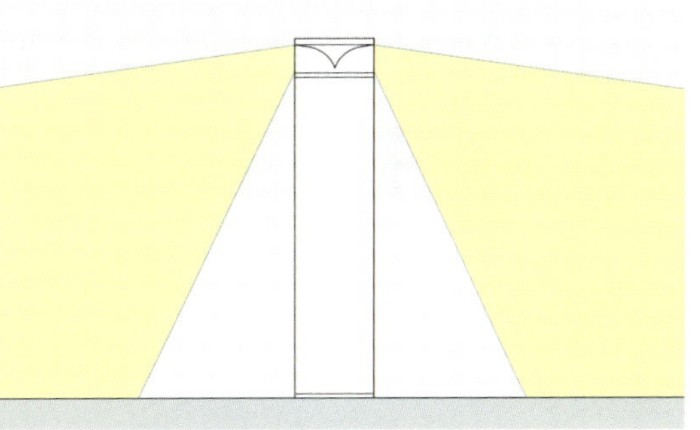

0253

0254

0255

0256

0257

0258

A series of light fixtures are a feature on the exterior of this home. Small spotlights were installed in a line along the entrance structure serving as a porch. Lights were also installed on the plinth on which the house is raised, illuminating the lawn surrounding the building.

Une série de points lumineux est utilisée à l'extérieur de ce logement. De petits points lumineux placés linéairement ont été installés au sein de la structure de l'entrée qui fait office de porche. De plus, des spots éclairant certaines zones du gazon qui entoure le logement ont également été disposés au niveau qui élève le logement.

Im Außenbereich dieses Wohnhauses kommt eine Reihe von Lichtpunkten zum Einsatz. Am Eingangsbereich, der als Veranda fungiert, wurden kleine Scheinwerfer linienförmig angeordnet. Auch in den Sockel des Gebäudes wurden Lichtpunkte integriert, die den Rasen rund um das Haus in Szene setzen.

Op de buitenkant van deze woning werden een reeks lichtpunten aangebracht. Op de ingangsstructuur die dienst doet als veranda, werden op lineaire wijze kleine lichtbronnen geïnstalleerd. Bovendien werden aan de basis van de woning eveneens lichten geplaatst die gericht het omringende gazon verlichten.

0260

0261

0262

0263

0264

0265

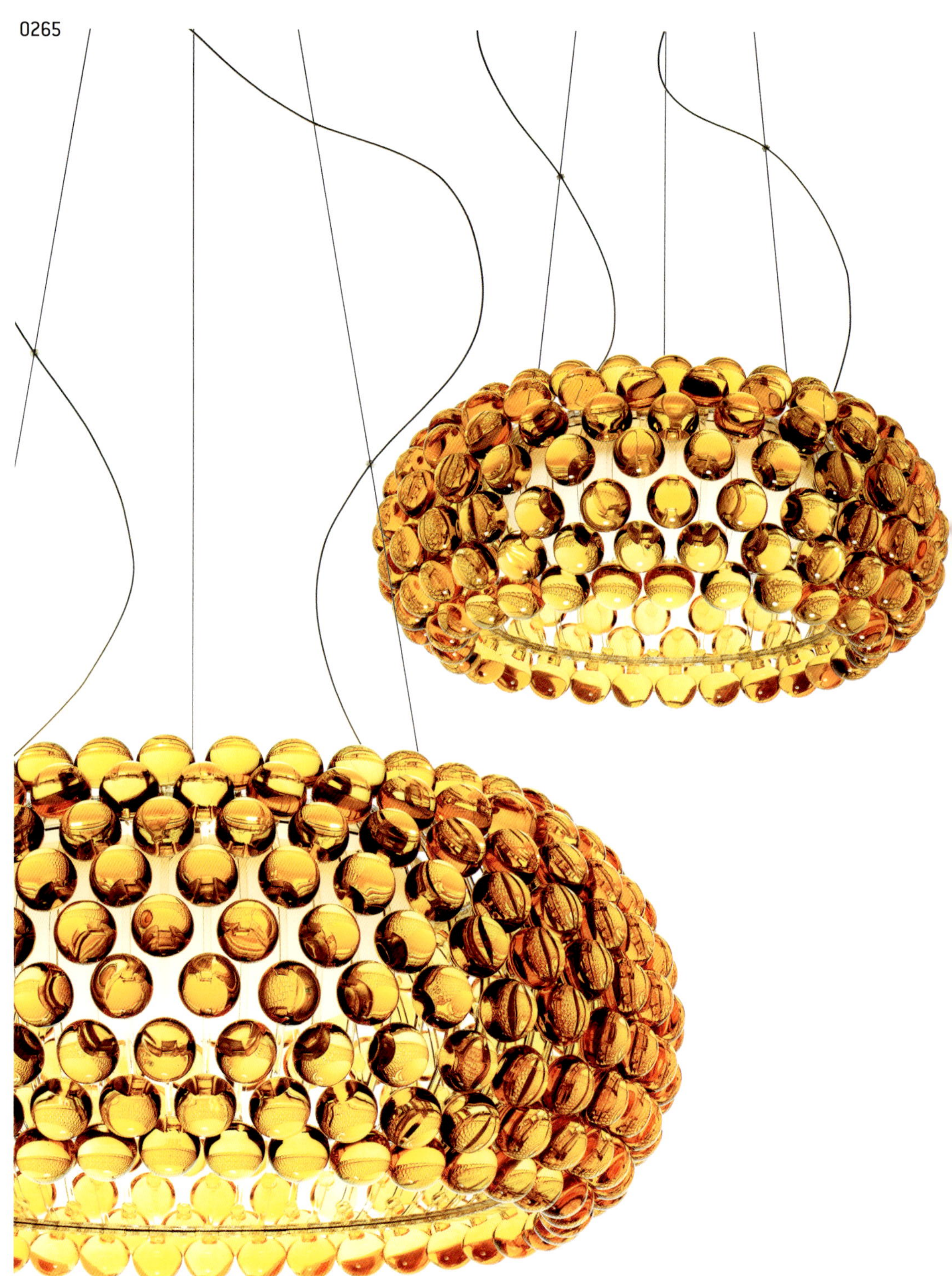

0266

Designed by the Agence Jouin Manku studio, the purpose of these lamps was to bring intensity to the spaces they occupy. Suspended 3 meters in the air, they were made using thin teak strips – to match the wood paneling on the walls, allowing light to filter through their "veins".

En concevant ces lustres, l'Agence Jouin Manku avait pour objectif d'apporter de la vie à l'espace qu'ils occuperaient. Suspendues à 3 m de hauteur, ils ont été construits avec de fines lames de teck (qui s'harmonise avec le bois utilisé pour les revêtements) qui filtrent la lumière à travers leur « veines ».

Diese vom Studio Agence Jouin Manku entworfenen Lampen sollen den Räumen, in denen sie eingesetzt werden, eine gewisse Lebendigkeit verleihen. Die in 3 m Abstand zur Decke aufgehängten Lampen bestehen aus dünnen Teakholzlamellen – passend zum Holz der Verkleidungen – und lassen das Licht durch die „Rippen" scheinen.

Deze lampen, ontworpen door de studio Agence Jouin Manku, hadden als doel de ruimte waarin ze zich bevinden levendigheid te verschaffen. Vervaardigd uit fijne platen van teakhout -passend bij het hout dat voor de wandbekledingen gebruikt werd- en opgehangen op een hoogte van 3 meter, filteren ze het licht door hun «aders».

0267

0268

0269

0270

0271

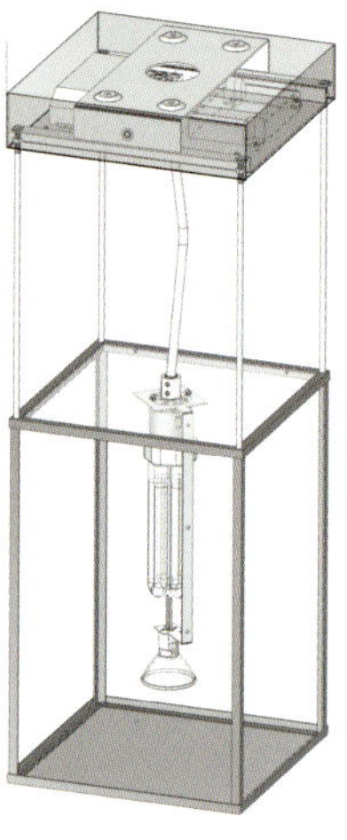

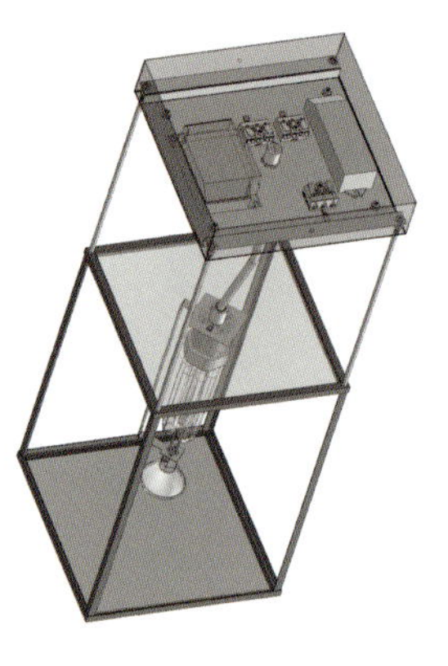

>

0272

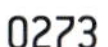

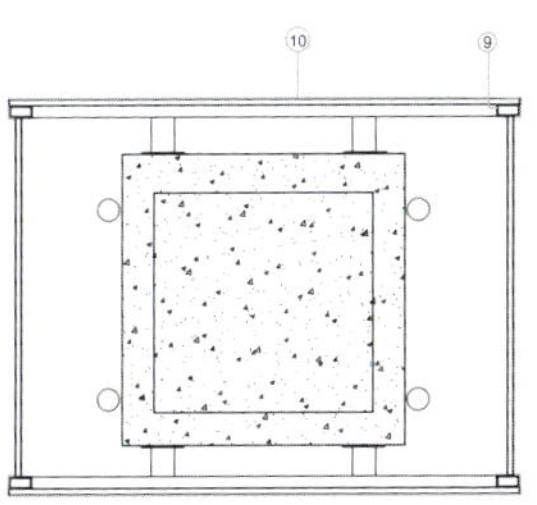

SECCIÓ B B
ESC: 1/10

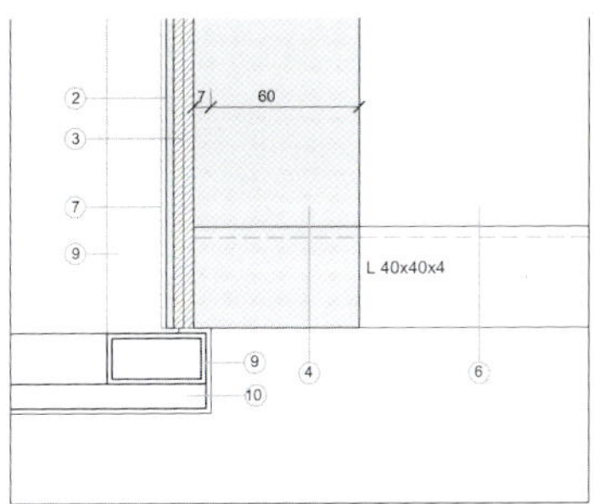

D02.
ESC: 1/2

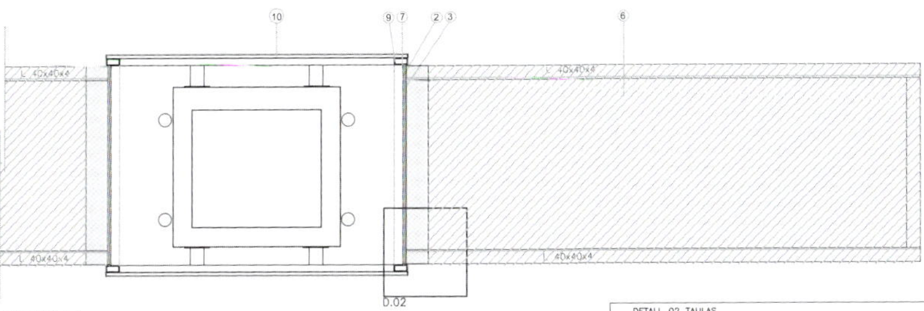

SECCIÓ A A
ESC: 1/10

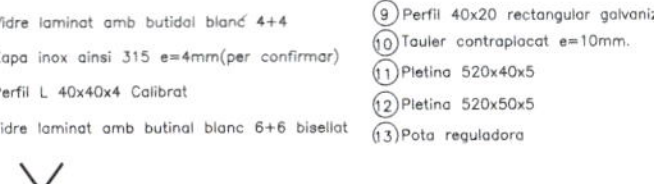

DETALL 02 TAULAS

1. Perfil U 30x15 inox mate
2. Policarbonat 3mm
3. Vidre laminat amb butidal blanć 4+4
4. Xapa inox ainsi 315 e=4mm(per confirmar)
5. Perfil L 40x40x4 Calibrat
6. Vidre laminat amb butinal blanc 6+6 bisellat
7. Perfil U 20x15 inox mate
8. Soldadura
9. Perfil 40x20 rectangular galvanizat
10. Tauler contraplacat e=10mm.
11. Pletina 520x40x5
12. Pletina 520x50x5
13. Pota reguladora

0274

0275

0276

The unsettling interior of this performance space by Daniel Libeskind is forcefully replicated in its lighting design. A number of wider than usual neon tube housings runs over the surface of the suspended ceiling in a somewhat uncontrolled manner, creating sharp angles and breaking off violently.

L'intérieur déconcertant de cet auditorium, œuvre de Daniel Libeskind, trouve indéniablement son pendant dans la conception des sources de lumière. Des conduits pour néons beaucoup plus épais que la normale parcourt le faux plafond de manière aléatoire, donnant lieu à des angles prononcés et des intersections brutales.

Die verblüffende Innengestaltung dieses von Daniel Libeskind entworfenen Auditoriums beeindruckt durch die überzeugende Übertragung des Designs auf die Lichtquellen. Ungewöhnlich breite Leitungen für Neonröhren verlaufen unregelmäßig durch die abgehängte Decke und bilden spitze Winkel und Überschneidungen.

De verbluffende interieurs van dit auditorium, van de hand van Daniel Libeskind, worden weerspiegeld in het ontwerp van hun lichtbronnen. Enkele neonbuizen, veel dikker dan gebruikelijk, lopen kriskras, met uitgesproken en abrupte hoeken over het valse plafond.

0277

0278

0279

0280

0281

0282

A range of acoustic insulation measures are generally used to soundproof office spaces. When combined, these measures provide a high noise absorption capacity as required by new technical building regulations.

Généralement utilisés dans les bureaux afin de les isoler du bruit extérieur, on emploie des isolants acoustiques qui offrent une haute capacité d'absorption acoustique et sont obligatoires dans les nouveaux codes techniques relatifs aux constructions.

Im Allgemeinen werden diverse Schalldämmungen eingesetzt, um Büroräume gegen Lärmeinwirkungen abzuschirmen. Diese Dämmungen müssen gemäß den neuesten Bauvorschriften einen hohen Schallschluckgrad aufweisen.

Om kantoren tegen extern lawaai te isoleren, worden in het algemeen bepaalde geluidsisolatoren gebruikt die het door de nieuwe technische bouwnormen vereiste geluidabsorberend vermogen bieden.

0283

0284

0285

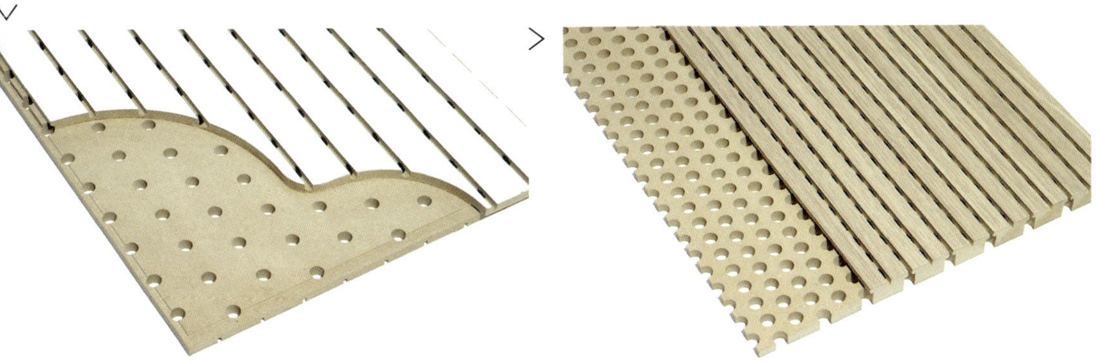

0286

0287

0288

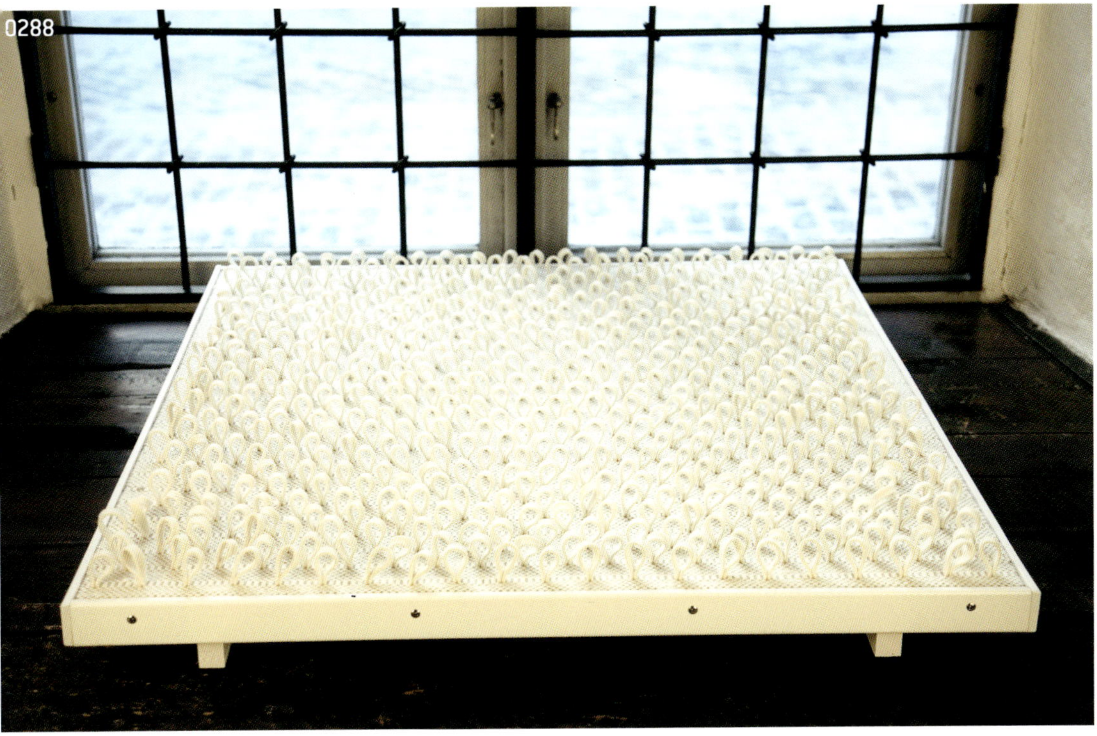

0289

0290

0291

0292

0293

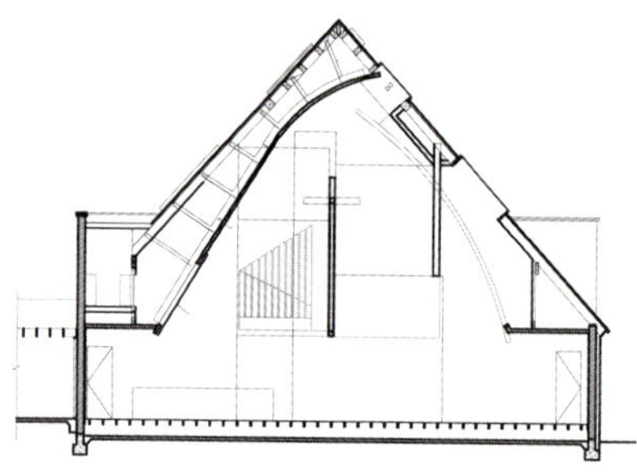

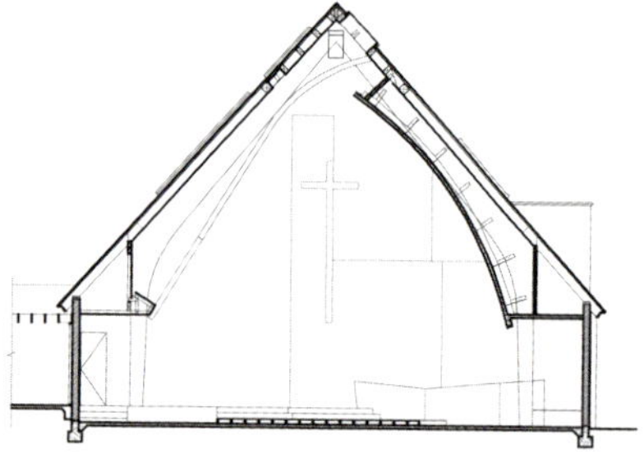

0294

This restaurant was laid out as a series of spaces with differing degrees of privacy. This private room, decorated with a strong Moroccan flavor, features red foam panels that absorb sound from the main restaurant area to create a relaxed atmosphere.

Au sein de ce restaurant, différentes zones avec différents degrés d'intimité ont été recherchées. Dans ce salon privé, au style marocain marqué, des panneaux en mousses de couleur rouge ont été installés qui absorbent le bruit généré dans le restaurant et permettent de créer une atmosphère détendue.

In diesem Restaurant wurden verschiedene Bereiche mit unterschiedlichen Levels an Intimsphäre eingerichtet. Dieser Privatsalon in marokkanischem Stil wurde mit roten Schaumstoffpaneelen ausgestattet, die den im Restaurant herrschenden Lärmpegel dämpfen und die Schaffung einer entspannten Umgebung ermöglichen.

In dit restaurant werd gestreefd naar verschillende zones met diverse niveaus van intimiteit. In dit privésalon, in uitgesproken Marokkaanse stijl, werden rode schuimrubberen panelen geïnstalleerd die het in het restaurant heersende geluid absorberen en daardoor een ontspannen sfeer creëren.

0295

0296

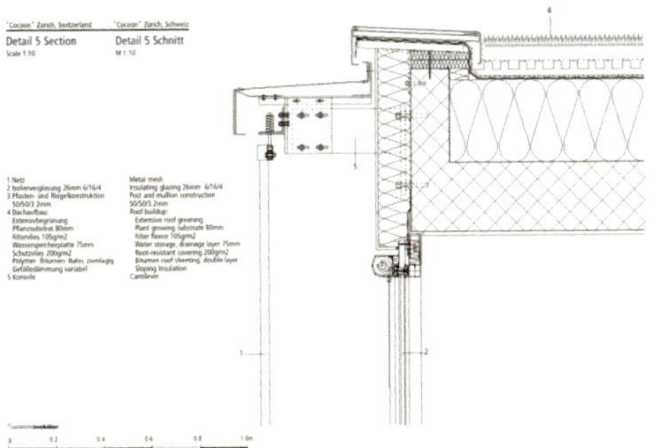
"Cocoon" Zurich, Switzerland
"Cocoon" Zürich, Schweiz
Detail 5 Section
Scale 1:10
Detail 5 Schnitt
M 1:10
1 Netz
2 Isolierverglasung 26mm 6/16/4
3 Pfosten- und Riegelkonstruktion 50/50/3.2mm
4 Dachaufbau:
Extensivbegrünung
Pflanzsubstrat 80mm
Filtervlies 105g/m2
Wasserspeicherplatte 75mm
Schutzvlies 200g/m2
Polymer- Bitumen- Bahn, zweilagig
Gefälledämmung variabel
5 Konsole
Metal mesh
Insulating glazing 26mm 6/16/4
Post and mullion construction 50/50/3.2mm
Roof buildup:
Extensive roof greening
Plant growing substrate 80mm
Filter fleece 105g/m2
Water storage, drainage layer 75mm
Root-resistant covering 200g/m2
Bitumen roof sheeting, double layer
Sloping insulation
Cantilever

0297

0298

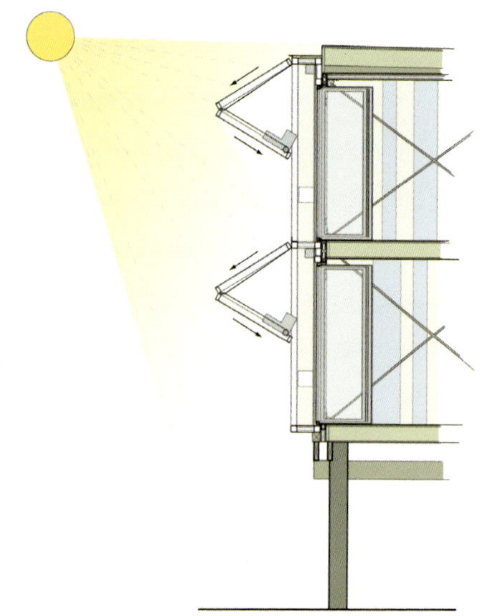

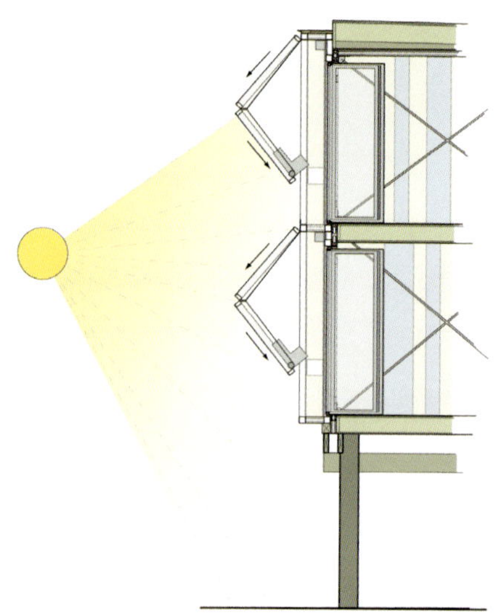

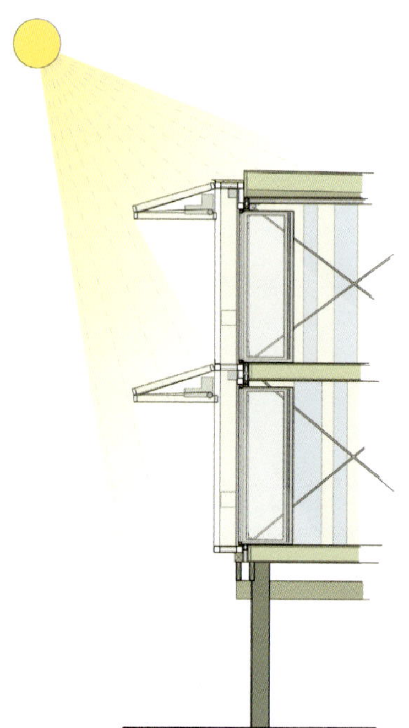

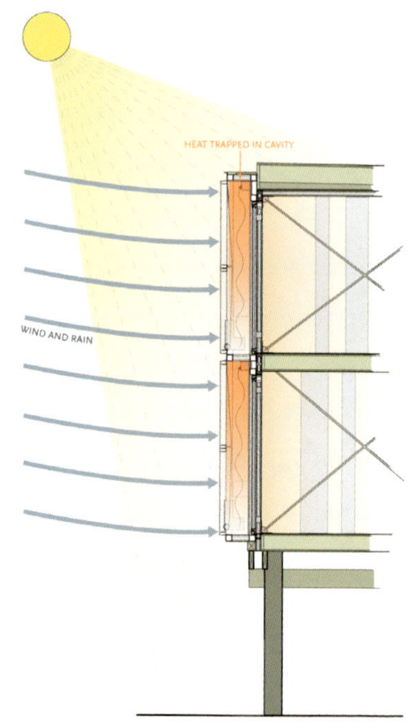

0299

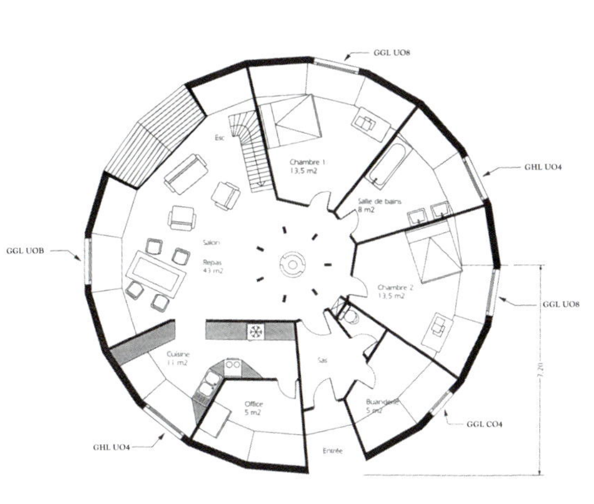
GGL UO8
Esc
Chambre 1
13,5 m2
GHL UO4
Salle de bains
8 m2
GGL UOB
Salon
Repas
43 m2
Chambre 2
13,5 m2
GGL UO8
Cuisine
11 m2
Sas
7,20
Office
5 m2
Buanderie
5 m2
GGL CO4
GHL UO4
Entrée

0300

0301

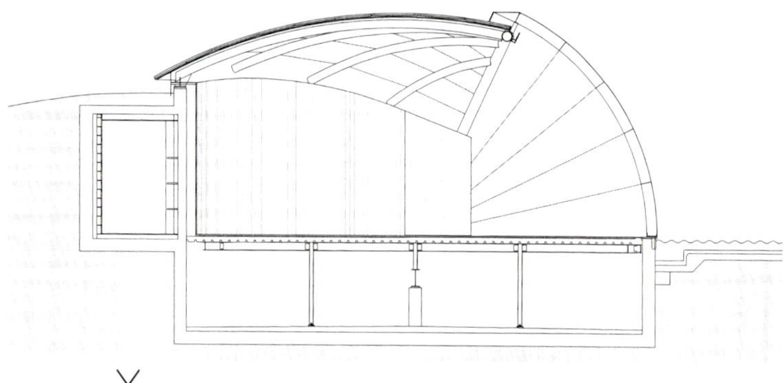

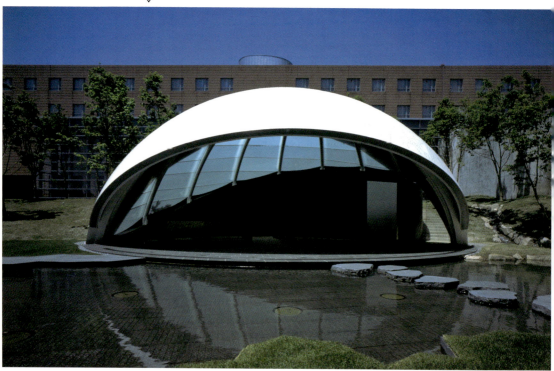

This small wedding chapel in the Kobuchizawa Hotel in Yamanashi is made up of two large panels, one in steel and the other glass. When the groom lifts the bride's veil, the steel structure is raised mechanically to reveal a pool. The panel weighs 11 tons and takes 38 seconds to open.

Cette petite chapelle de cérémonies de mariage de l'hôtel Kobuchizawa, à Yamanashi, est formée de deux grandes feuille : l'une en acier et l'autre en verre. Lorsque le marié découvre le visage de la mariée, la structure en acier se lève mécaniquement et permet de découvrir le bassin. Le poids de la feuille est de 11 tonnes et elle met 38 secondes à s'ouvrir.

Die kleine Hochzeitskapelle des Hotels Kobuchizawa in Yamanashi besteht aus zwei großen Platten: einer Stahl- und einer Glasfläche. Wenn der Bräutigam das Gesicht der Braut enthüllt, wird die Stahlstruktur mechanisch angehoben und gibt den Blick auf den Teich frei. Die Stahlplatte wiegt 11 Tonnen und öffnet sich innerhalb von 38 Sekunden.

Deze kleine trouwkapel in het hotel Kobuchizawa, in Yamanashi, bestaat uit twee grote wandvleugels: een van staal en de andere van glas. Wanneer de bruidegom het gezicht van de bruid ontsluiert, wordt de stalen structuur mechanisch omhoog gebracht en wordt het meer zichtbaar. Het paneel weegt 11 ton en het duurt 38 seconden om het te openen.

0302

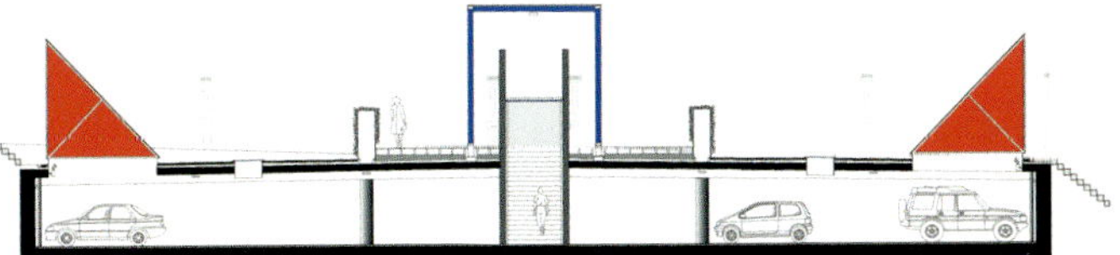

0303

0304

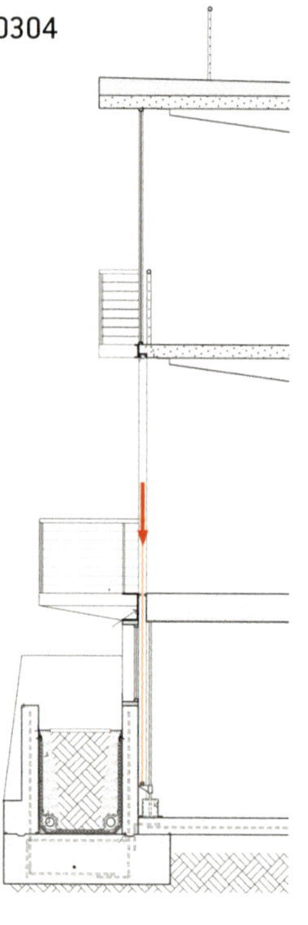

0305

0306

0307

>

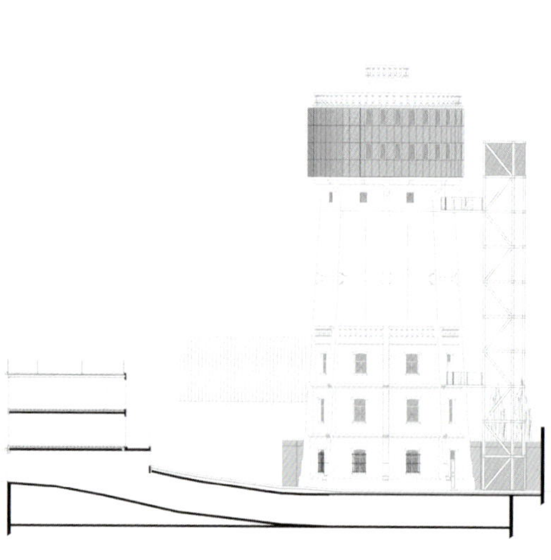

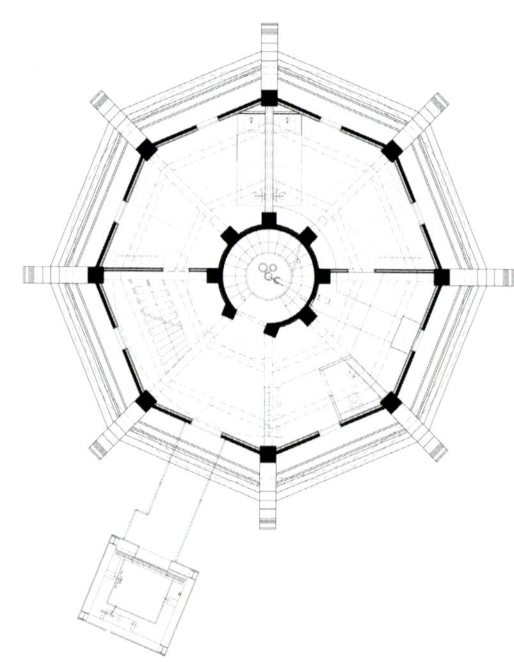

0308

>

0309

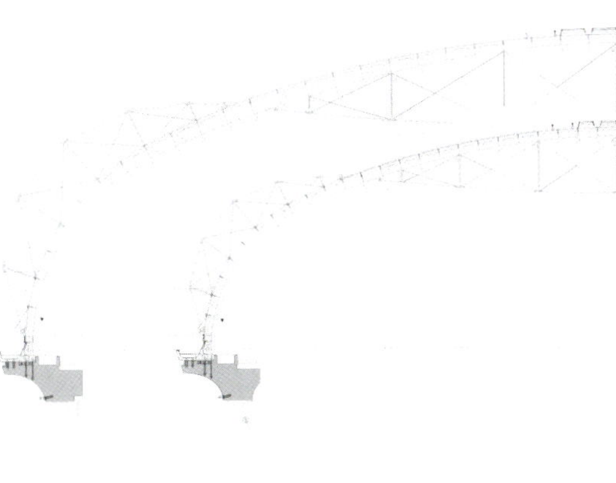

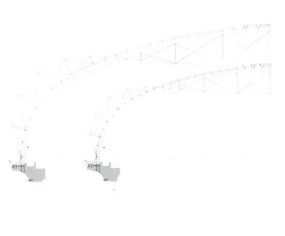

The prefabricated flooring and roof panels come fully incorporated with radiant floor heating, hot and cold water and waste water pipes, and ventilation and electrical systems ducts.

Le chauffage par plancher chauffant, les conduits d'eau froide et d'eau chaude, ainsi que les conduits des eaux usées, de ventilation et d'électricité sont intégrés au revêtement et aux panneaux de toiture préfabriqués.

Die vorgefertigten Boden- und Deckenplatten enthalten eine Fußbodenheizung, die Kalt- und Warmwasserrohre sowie die Abwasser-, Lüftungs- und Stromleitungen.

De geprefabriceerde vloerbedekking en -panelen herbergen stralingsverwarming, leidingen voor koud en warm water, evenals afvalwater, het ventilatie- en elektriciteitssysteem.

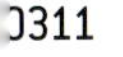
0311

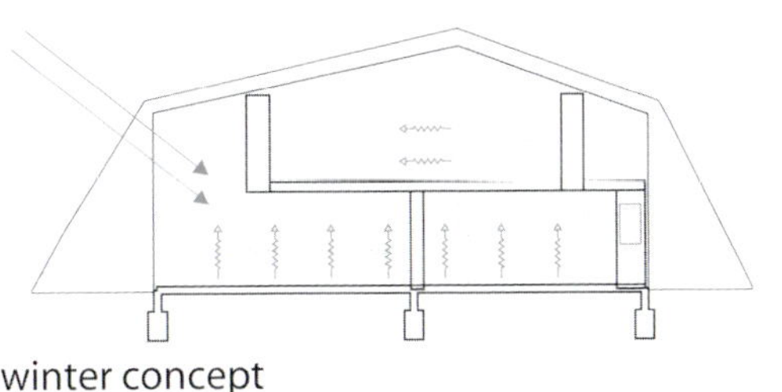
winter concept

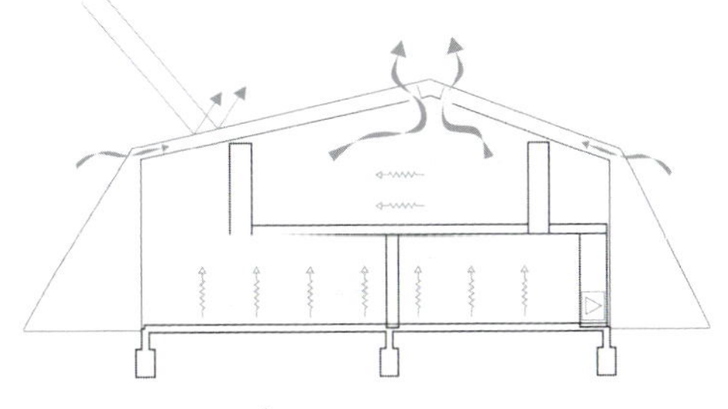
summer concept

0312

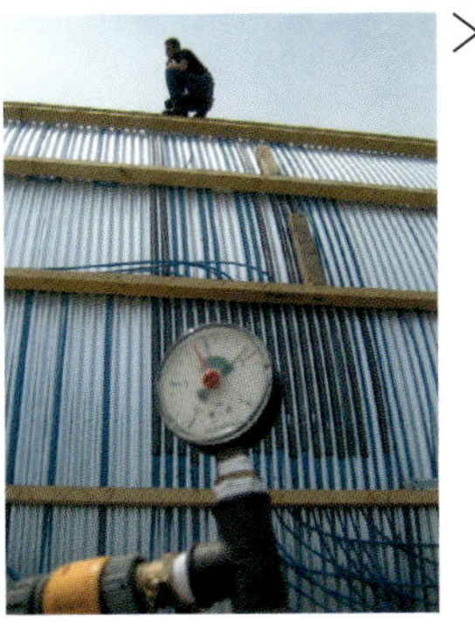

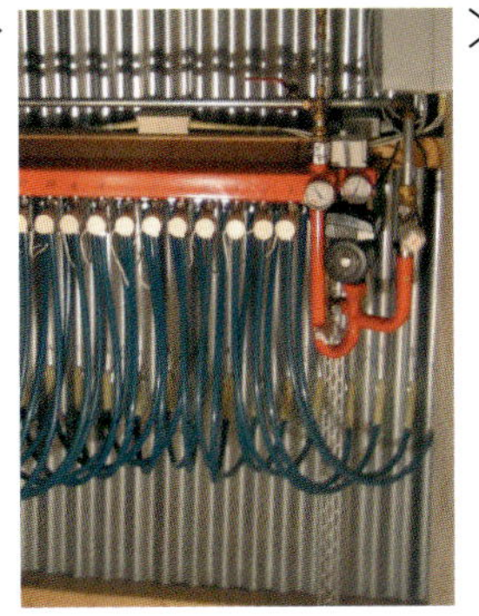

0313

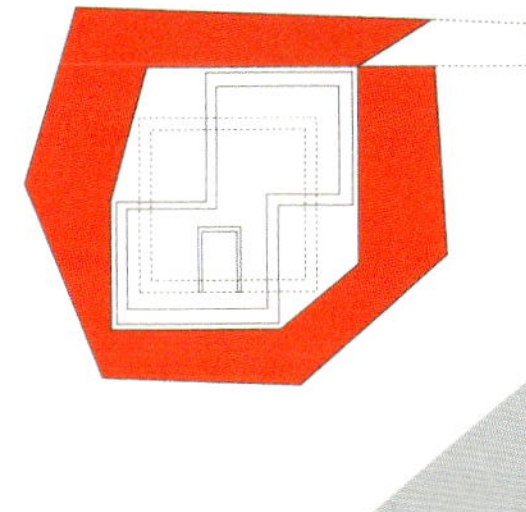

0314

0315

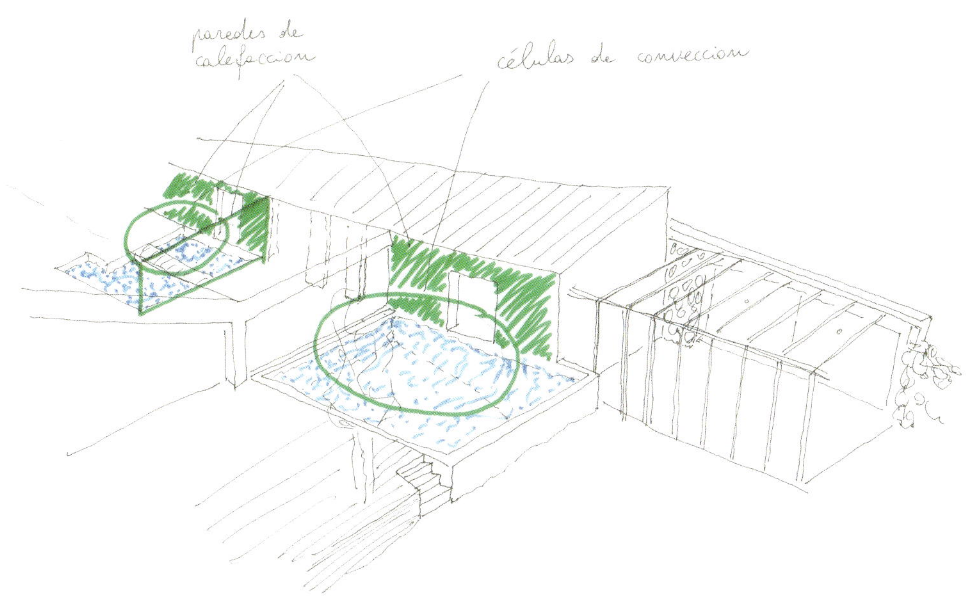
paredes de calefaccion
células de conveccion

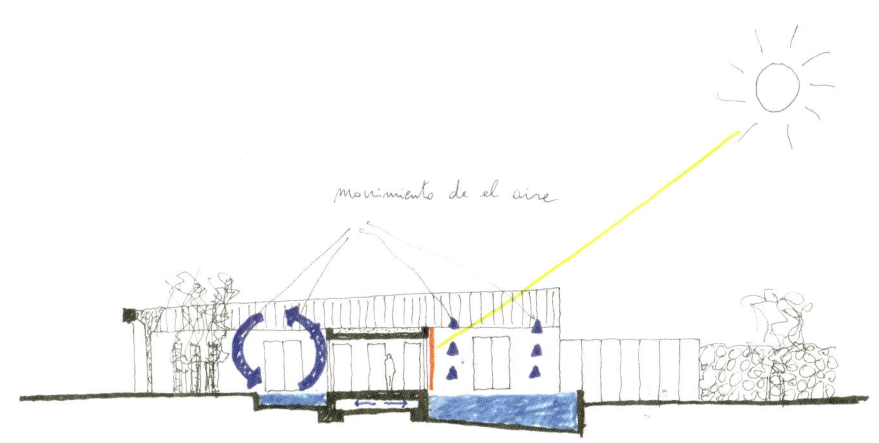
movimiento de el aire

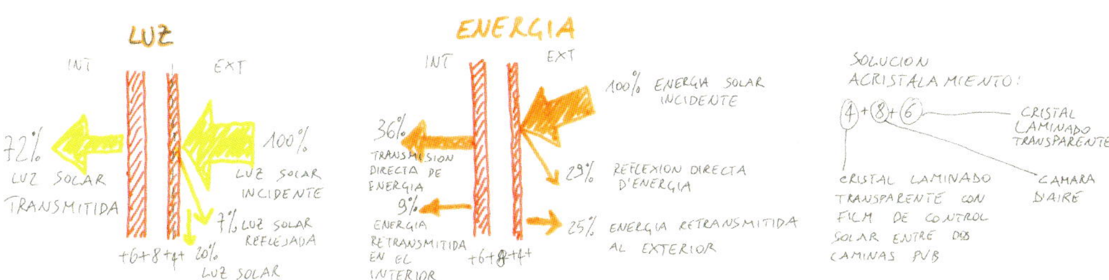
LUZ
INT
EXT
72%
LUZ SOLAR TRANSMITIDA
100%
LUZ SOLAR INCIDENTE
7% LUZ SOLAR REFLEJADA
+6+8+4+
20%
LUZ SOLAR ABSORBIDA
ENERGIA
INT
EXT
100% ENERGIA SOLAR INCIDENTE
36%
TRANSMISION DIRECTA DE ENERGIA
29% REFLEXION DIRECTA D'ENERGIA
9%
ENERGIA RETRANSMITIDA EN EL INTERIOR
25% ENERGIA RETRANSMITIDA AL EXTERIOR
SOLUCION ACRISTALAMIENTO:
4+8+6
CRISTAL LAMINADO TRANSPARENTE
CRISTAL LAMINADO TRANSPARENTE CON FILM DE CONTROL SOLAR ENTRE DOS CAMINAS PVB
CAMARA D'AIRE

0316

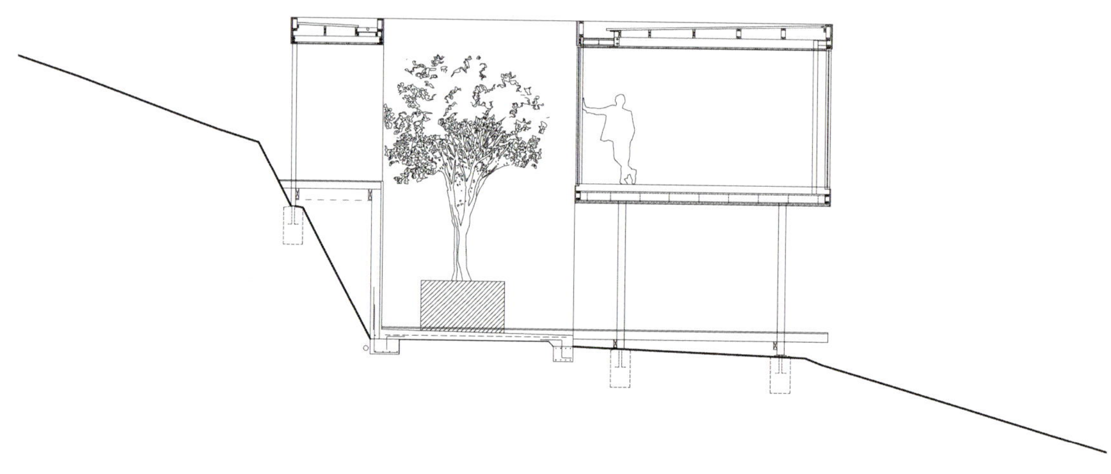

0317

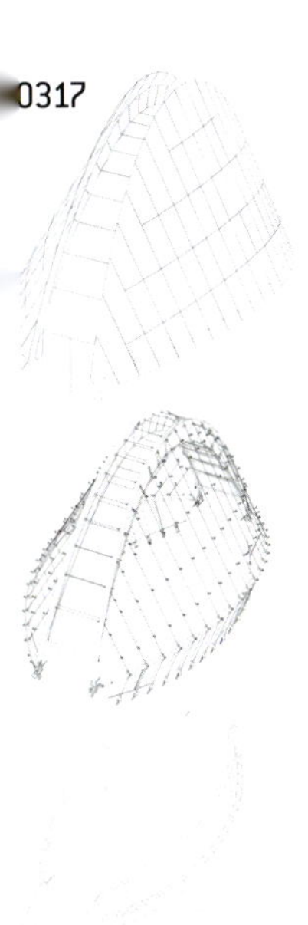

0318

0319

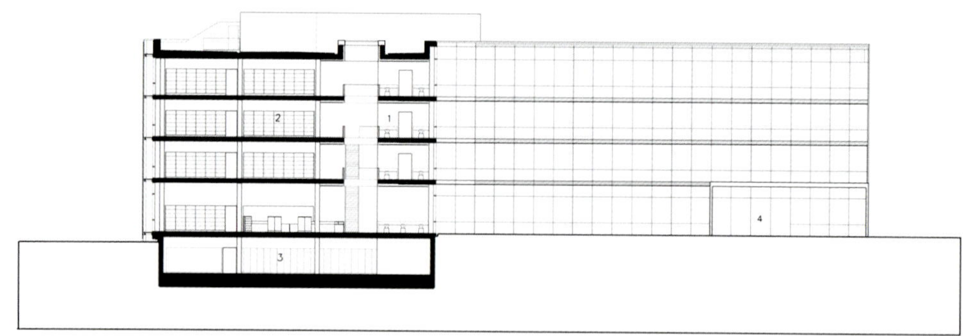

Rostock University library is located at the entrance of the new university campus. The technical concept used, called *bauteilaktivierung* or component activation, consists of water pipes inset in the concrete foundations, which are connected to geothermal sources and thermally regulate the building.

La bibliothèque de l'Université de Rostock se trouve à l'entrée du nouveau campus universitaire. Le concept technique utilisé, appelé *bauteilaktivierung*, se compose de conduites d'eau dans les fondations en béton, reliées à des sources géothermiques et qui régulent thermiquement le bâtiment.

Die Universitätsbibliothek Rostock befindet sich am Eingang des neuen Campus. Das hier eingesetzte Konzept der *Bauteilaktivierung* umfasst Wasserleitungen im Betonfundament, die an Geothermiequellen angeschlossen sind und die Gebäudetemperatur regulieren.

De bibliotheek van de Universiteit van Rostock ligt aan de ingang van de nieuwe universiteitscampus. Het gebruikte technische concept, *bauteilaktivierung* genaamd, bestaat uit een samenstel van waterleidingen in de betonnen funderingen, aangesloten op geothermische bronnen die het gebouw thermisch regelen.

0320

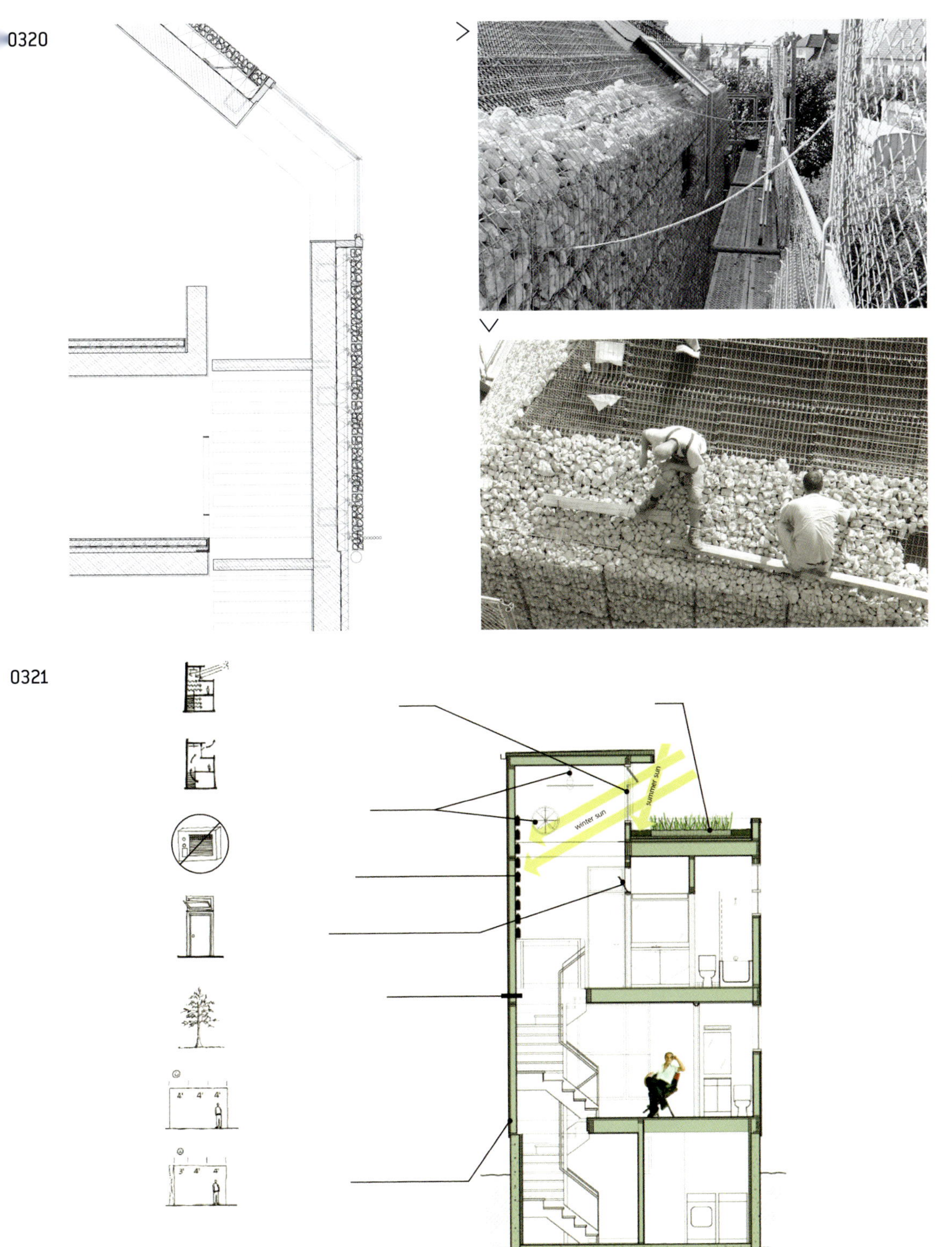

0321

0322

0323

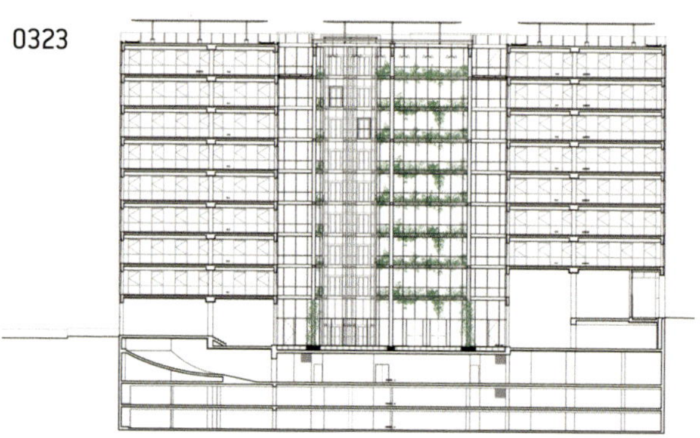

0324

0325

0326

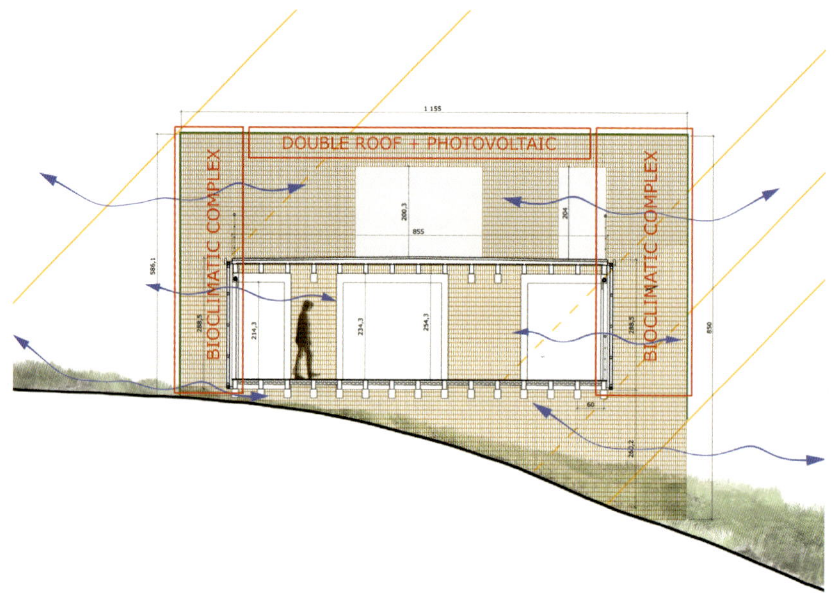

1 155
DOUBLE ROOF + PHOTOVOLTAIC
BIOCLIMATIC COMPLEX
BIOCLIMATIC COMPLEX

0327

0328

0329

0330

The balconies of this building housing laboratories have depths that vary depending on their orientation. This allowed the designers to control exactly how much shade was produced at each part of the building, drastically reducing the cost of cooling systems.

Au sein de ce bâtiment pour laboratoires, la profondeur de chaque balcon varie en fonction des points cardinaux. Cela permet aux concepteurs de contrôler avec exactitude l'ombre qui est générée au sein de chaque partie de l'immeuble, ce qui réduit drastiquement les frais en matière de système de réfrigération.

In diesem Laborgebäude variiert die Tiefe der einzelnen Balkons je nach Himmelsrichtung. Auf diese Weise können die Konstrukteure exakt den Schatten bestimmen, der in den verschiedenen Bereichen des Gebäudes entsteht, wodurch die Kosten für die Gebäudekühlung wesentlich reduziert werden.

In dit laboratoriumgebouw varieert de diepte van elk balkon in functie van de windstreken. Op die manier kunnen de ontwerpers nauwkeurig de schaduw controleren die in elk deel van het gebouw ontstaat, wat drastisch de kost in koelsystemen beperkt.

0331

0332

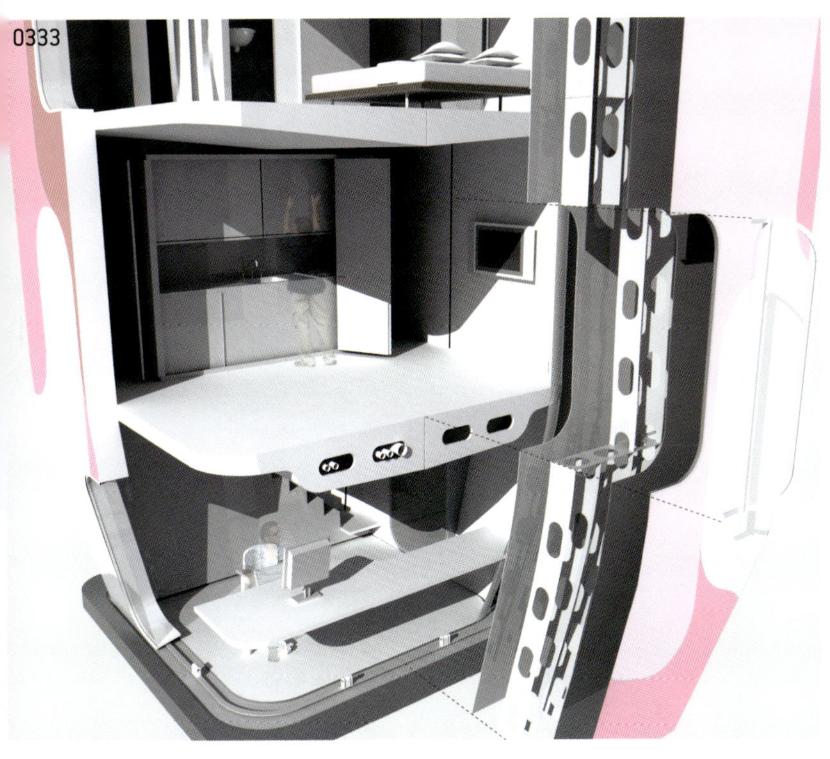
0333

0334

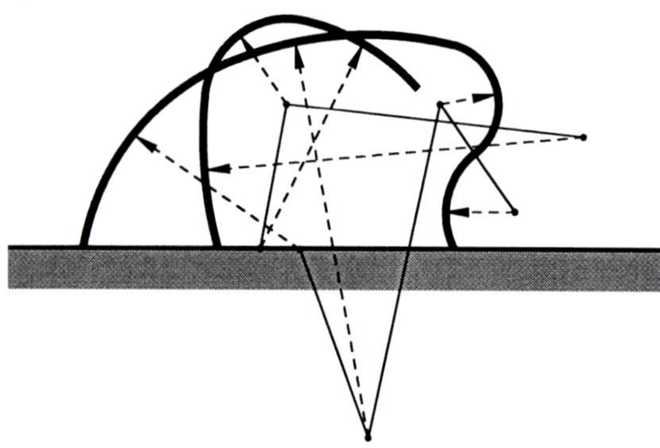

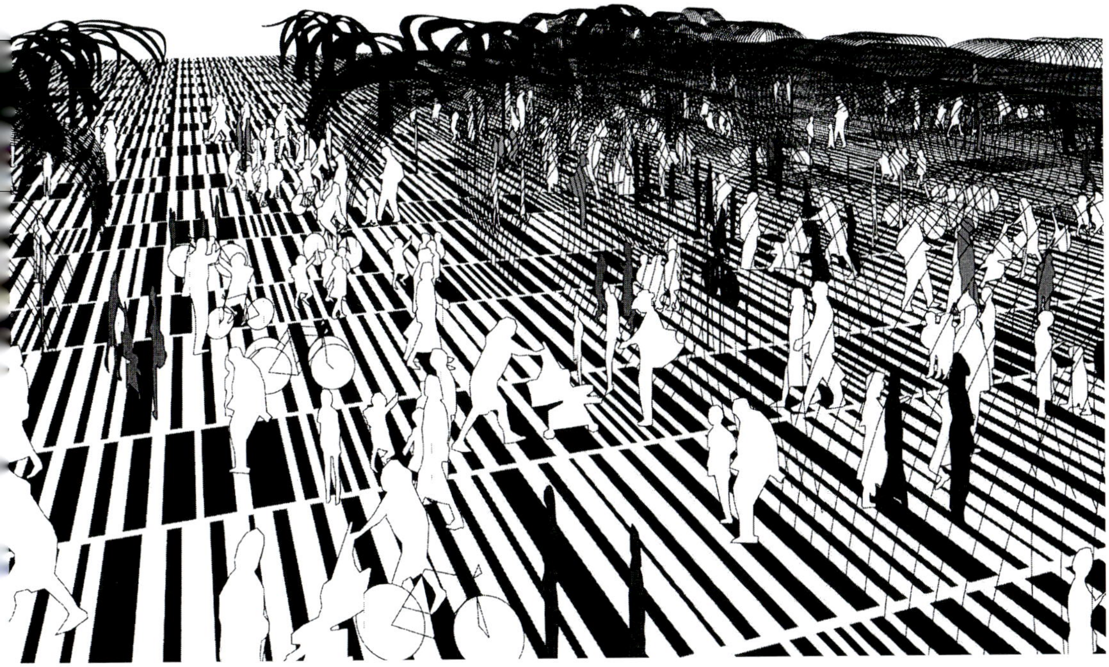

0335

0336

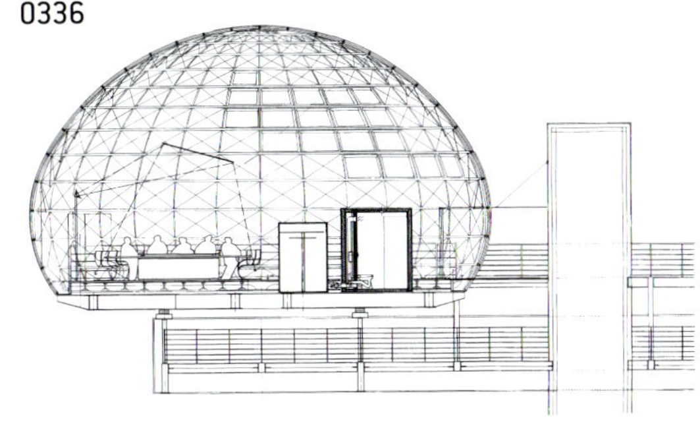

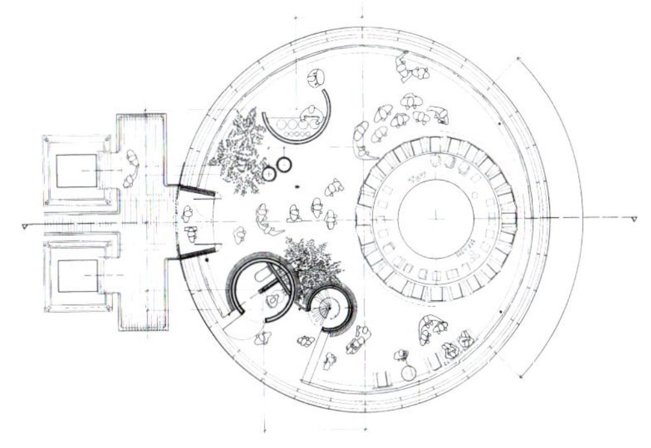

Advanced glass construction techniques were used to construct this shell greenhouse in Malmö. The glass skin is suspended by steel arches. The completely untreated glass covers a surface area of 120 m^2 (1,290 sq ft), a volume of 890 m^3 (31,430 cu ft), with a length of 22 m (72 ft), and a height of 10.5 m (34.5 ft).

Pour la construction de cette serre en forme de coquille à Malmö, des techniques avancées de construction en verre ont été employées. La même peau de verre est autoportante grâce à des arcs en acier. Le verre, qui n'a pas été traité, présente une surface de 120 m^2, un volume de 890 m^3, une longueur de 22 m et une hauteur de 10,5 m.

Beim Bau dieses muschelförmigen Gewächshauses in Malmö wurden die neuesten Verfahren im Glasbau angewendet. Die Glashaut wird von Stahlbögen gehalten. Das völlig unbehandelte Glas bedeckt 120 m^2 Fläche und 890 m^3 Rauminhalt auf 22 m Länge und 10,5 m Höhe.

Voor de bouw van deze schelpvormige serre in Malmö, werden geavanceerde glasbouwtechnieken toegepast. De glazen huid werd over stalen bogen gespannen. Het glas, dat geen enkele behandeling onderging, bestrijkt een oppervlakte van 120 m^2 en creëert een volume van 890 m^3, met een lengte van 22 m en een hoogte van 10,5 m.

0337

0338

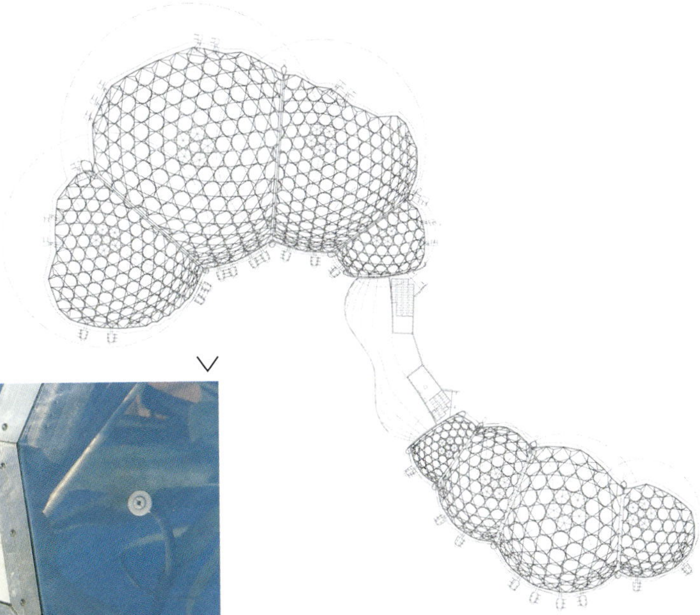

0339

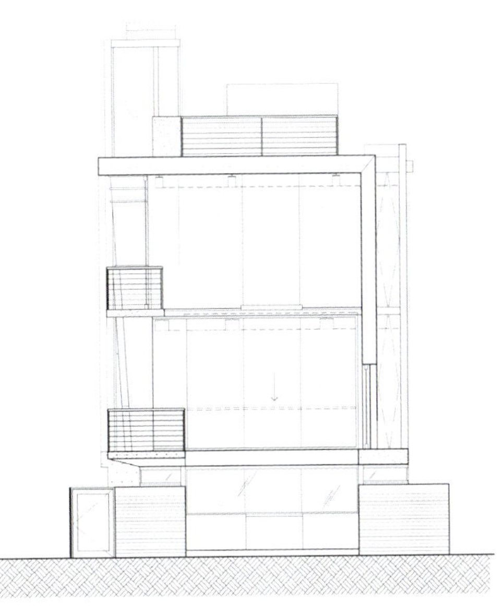

0340

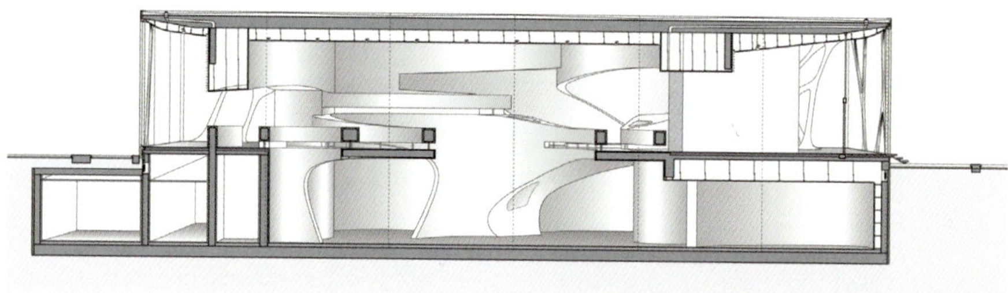

0341

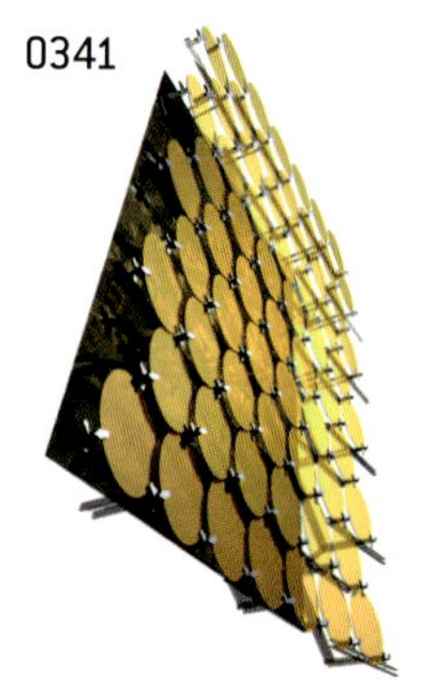

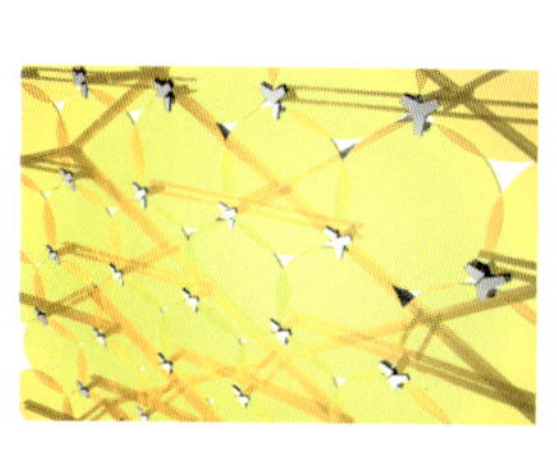

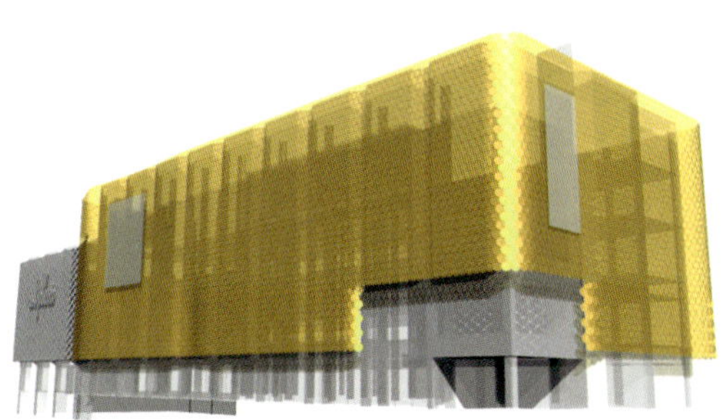

0342

0343

0344

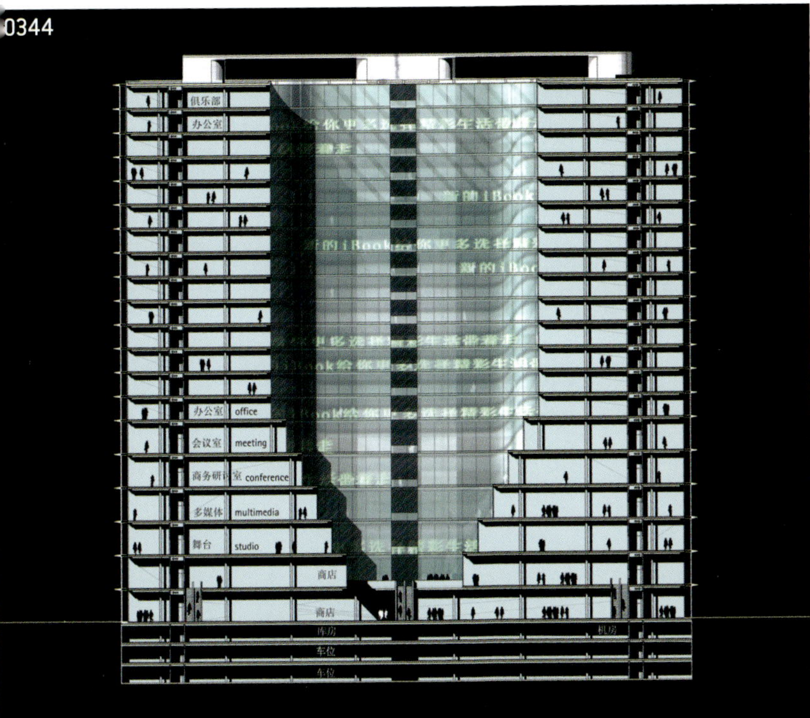

俱乐部
办公室
办公室 office
会议室 meeting
conference
多媒体 multimedia
舞台 studio
商店
商店
库房
机房
车位
车位

0345

For this luxury hotel in the heart of the Rioja Alavesa wine district, Frank O. Gehry designed a building full of undulating forms, made possible by the use of the titanium plates that form part of the overhanging roof. Some of the walkways are surrounded by the steel structure and glass divider walls.

Frank O. Gehry a projeté pour cet hôtel de luxe en pleine ville de La Rioja d'Alava un bâtiment aux formes ondulées, grâce aux plaques de titane qui forment partie des saillies. Certaines des passerelles sont entourées par la structure en acier et les cloisons correctrices en verre.

Frank O. Gehry entwarf für dieses Luxushotel in der spanischen Region Rioja Alavesa ein Gebäude mit wellenförmigen Vorsprüngen aus Titanblech. Einige Stege sind von der Struktur aus Stahl und Glaswänden umgeben.

Frank O. Gehry ontwierp voor dit luxehotel te midden van de Riojastreek in Alava een gebouw met golvende vormen dankzij de titaniumplaten die gebruikt werden om de uitspringende delen samen te stellen. Bepaalde passerelles worden door de stalen structuur omgeven, in combinatie met glazen wanden.

0347

0348

0349

0350

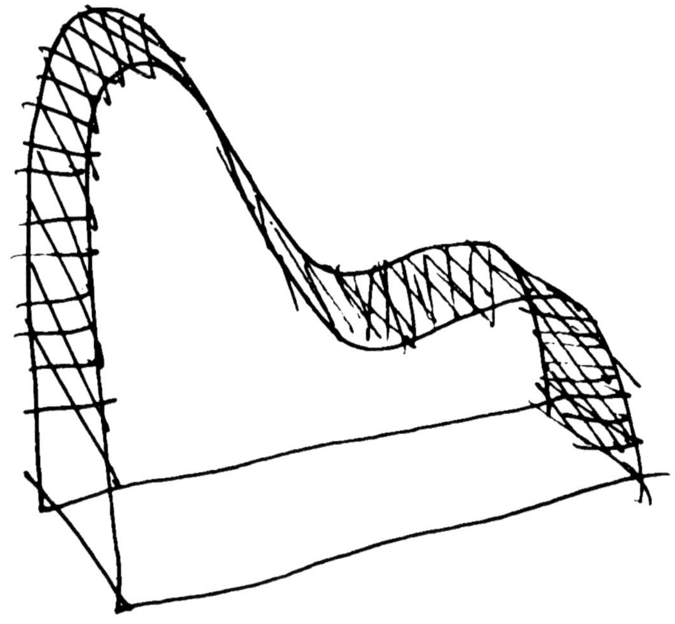

0351

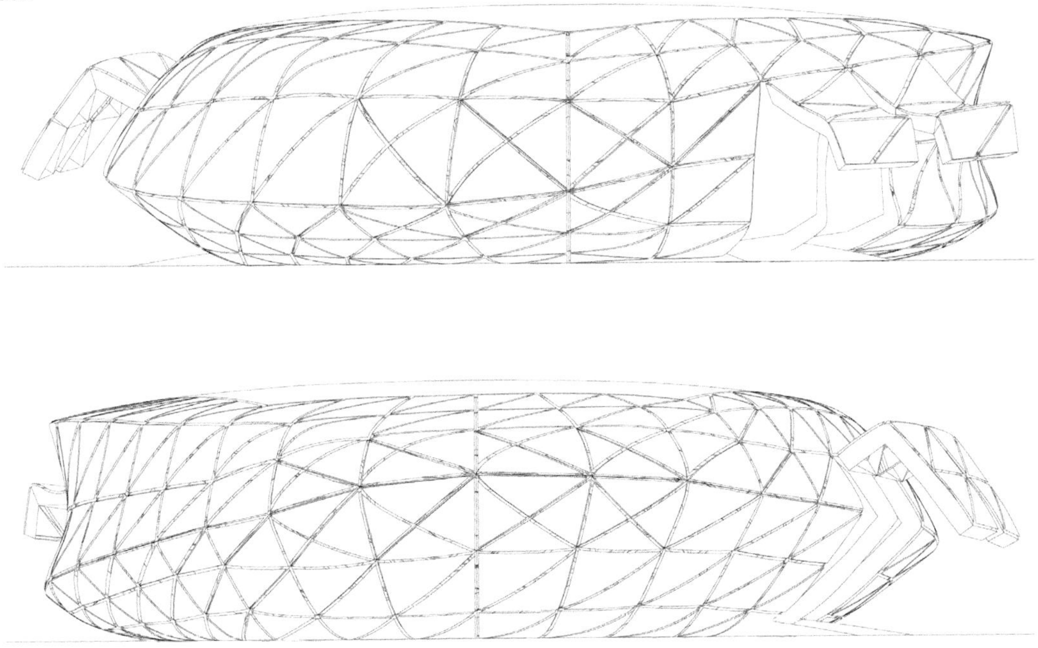

0352

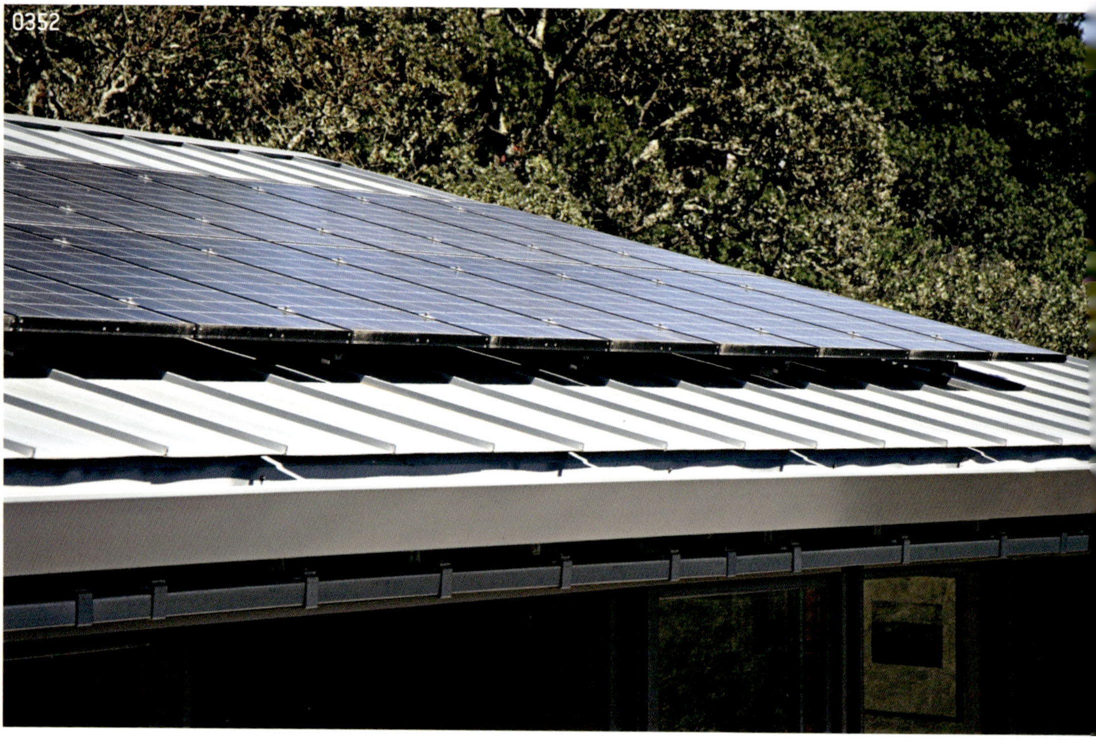

0353

354

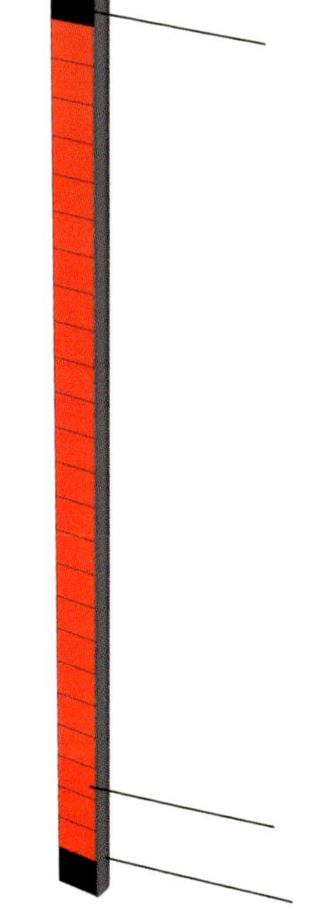

The exterior cladding and interior finishes are inspired by the technology applied to the wings of a plane; the skin is rigid, compact, and light at the same time. The smallest module of the house was created by assembling 8 aluminum panels 2.43 m x 9.14 m (8 ft x 30 ft). Each module provides 24 m^2 (260 sq ft) of floor space.

Le revêtement extérieur et les finitions intérieures puisent leur inspiration dans la technologie utilisée pour les ailes des avions ; l'enveloppe est rigide, compacte et légère. L'assemblage de 8 panneaux en aluminium (2,43 x 9,14 m) permet de créer le plus petit module de logement. Chaque module occupe 24 m^2 de niveau.

Die Außenverkleidung und die Finishs im Inneren sind von der Technologie inspiriert, die beim Bau von Flugzeugtragflächen zum Einsatz kommt. Die Außenhaut ist starr, kompakt und gleichzeitig leicht. Die Verbindung von 8 Aluminiumpaneelen (2,43 x 9,14 m) ermöglicht die Schaffung des kleinsten Wohnmoduls. Jedes Modul erstreckt sich über eine Fläche von 24 m^2.

De buitenbekleding en de binnenafwerking zijn geïnspireerd op de technologie die gebruikt wordt voor de vleugels van een vliegtuig; de huid is onbuigzaam, compact en tegelijkertijd licht. De assemblage van 8 aluminium panelen (2,43 x 9,14 m) maakt de creatie van een uiterst kleine woningmodule mogelijk. Elke module beslaat een grondvlak van 24 m^2.

0355

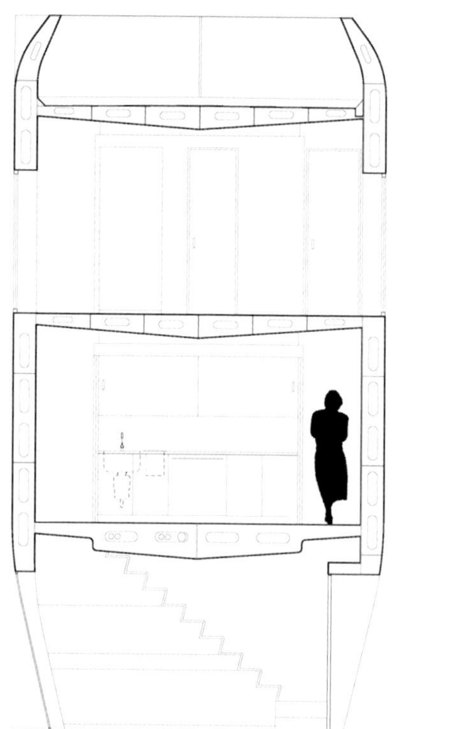

0356

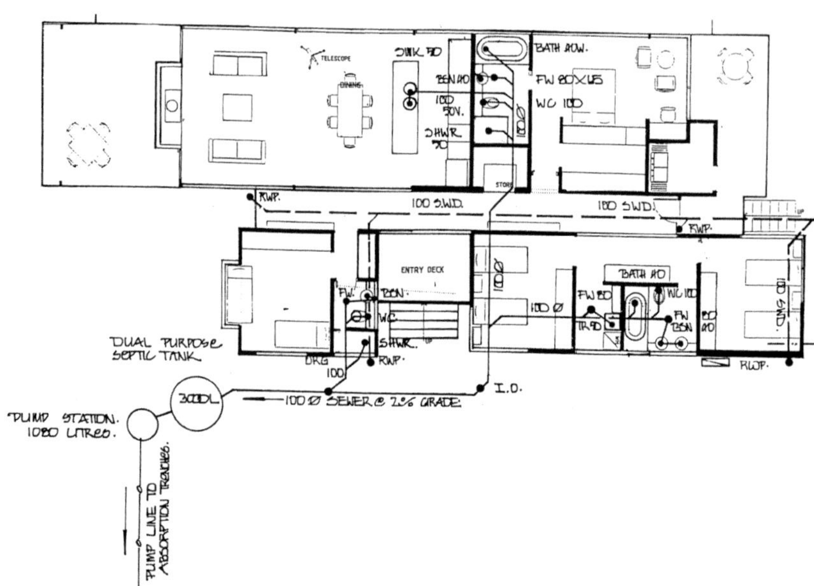

0357

0358

0359

0360

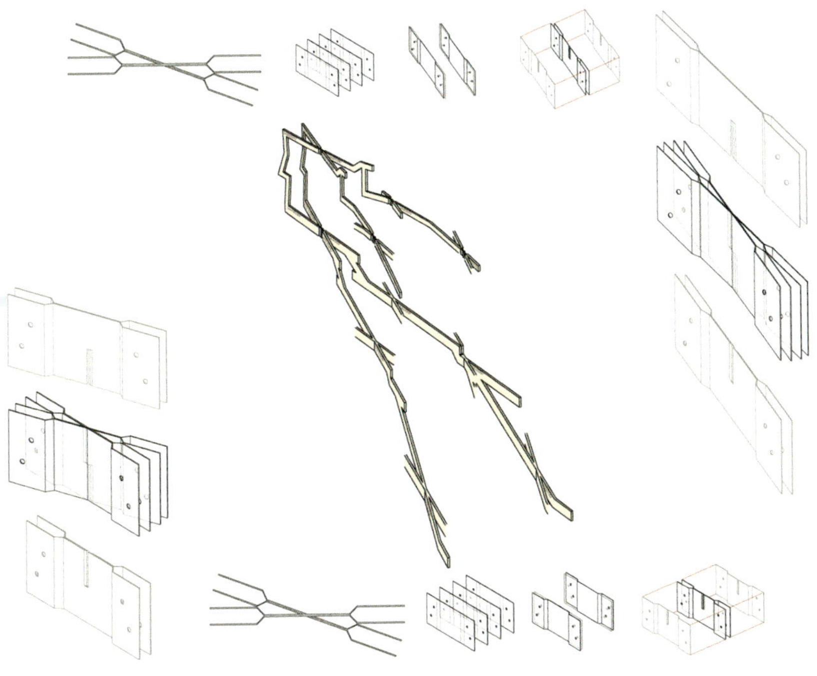

0361

0362

0363

0364

Chris Bosse is a specialist in projects connecting architecture with the virtual world. Paradise Pavilion, designed for the Entry 06 exhibition in Germany, features biomorphic forms created with different software systems. Natural forms inspire his design of architectural structures.

Chris Bosse est spécialiste dans les projets qui connectent l'architecture avec le monde virtuel. Le Paradise Pavilion, conçu pour l'exposition Entry 06 en Allemagne, présente des formes biomorphiques conçues à l'aide de divers systèmes de software. Il puise son inspiration dans les formes naturelles pour créer des structures architecturales.

Chris Bosse ist auf Projekte spezialisiert, die die Architektur und die virtuelle Welt verbinden. Der für die Ausstellung Entry 06 in Deutschland entworfene Paradise Pavilion weist biomorphe Formen auf, welche mithilfe unterschiedlicher Softwaresysteme gestaltet wurden. Natürliche Formen regen Bosse zur Schaffung architektonischer Strukturen an.

Chris Bosse is specialist in projecten die de architectuur in verband brengen met de virtuele wereld. Het Paradise Pavilion, ontworpen voor de tentoonstelling Entry 06 in Duitsland, vertoont biomorfe vormen die ontworpen werden met behulp van diverse softwaresystemen. De natuurlijke vormen inspireren hem om architectonische structuren te genereren.

0365

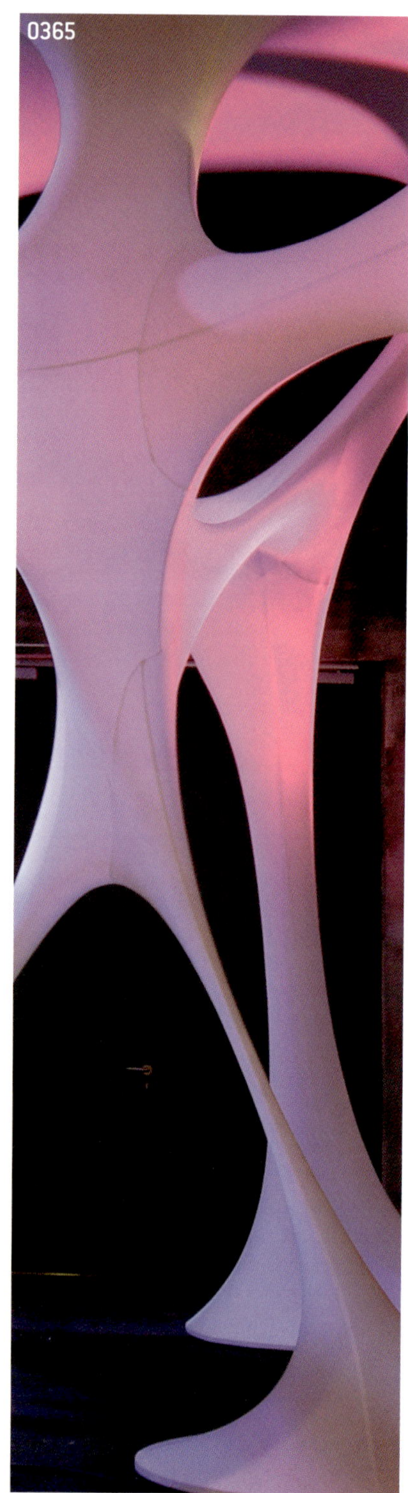

0366

0367

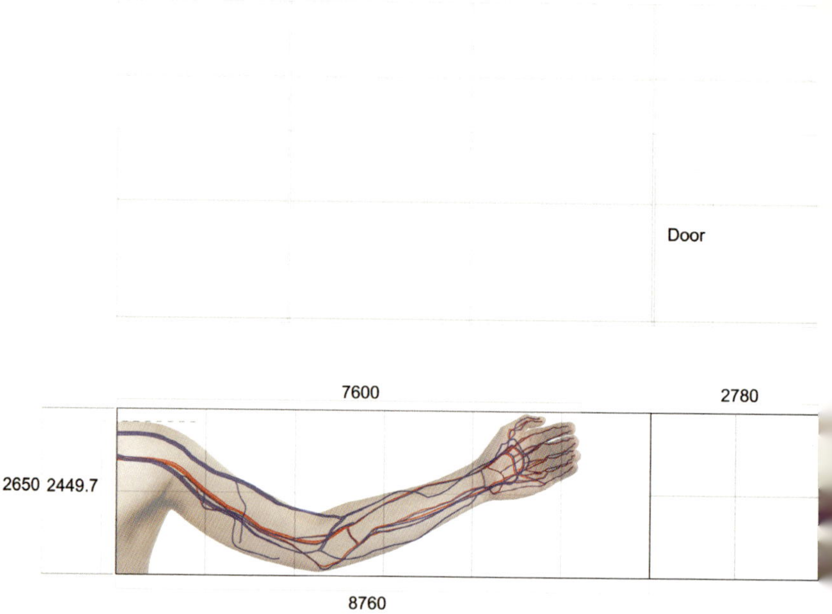

0368

Door

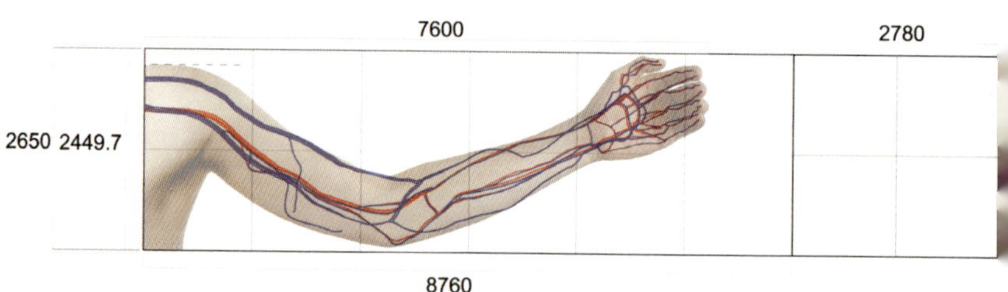

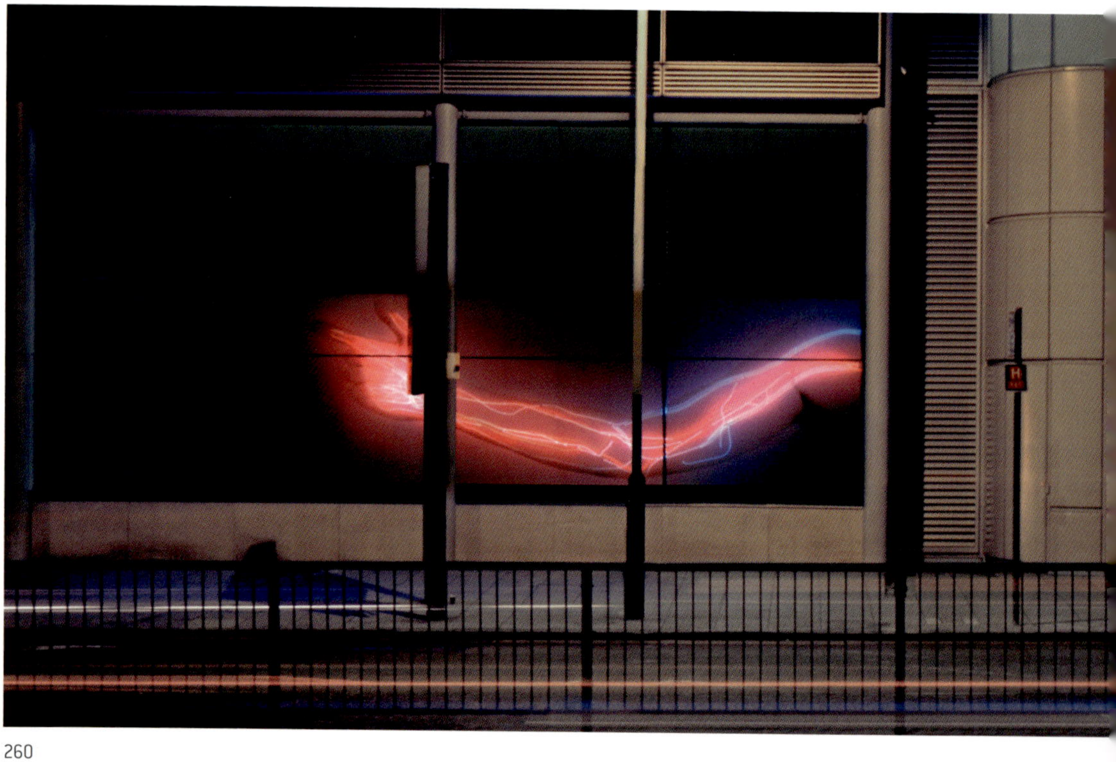

0369

0370

0371

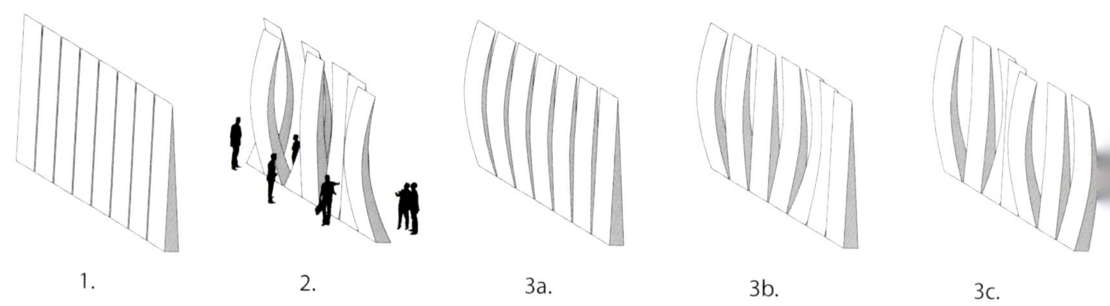

0372

0373

This wall responds to people's movements. It consists of 7 panels curving independently forwards or backwards, with LED lights that illuminate more or less depending on proximity. The wall also produces sounds: the sounds are more paused when movements are more synchronized.

Ce mur répond au mouvement des personnes. Il est formé de 7 panneaux qui s'incurvent indépendamment vers l'avant ou vers l'arrière et dont les LED sont plus ou moins allumées en fonction de la proximité des personnes. Le mur émet également des sons : plus les mouvements sont synchronisés et plus les sons sont pausés.

Diese Wand reagiert auf die Bewegung von Personen. Sie besteht aus 7 Paneelen, die sich unabhängig voneinander nach vorne bzw. hinten biegen und deren LEDs je nach Nähe der Menschen mehr oder weniger hell leuchten. Außerdem gibt die Wand auch Klänge ab: je höher die Synchronisierung der Bewegungen, desto pausierter die Töne.

Deze muur reageert op de beweging van de mensen. Hij bestaat uit 7 panelen die zich op onafhankelijke wijze naar voren of naar achteren buigen, en waarvan de leds meer of minder gaan branden in functie van de nabijheid. De muur brengt ook geluid voort: hoe synchroner de bewegingen, hoe langzamer het geluidsritme.

0374

0375

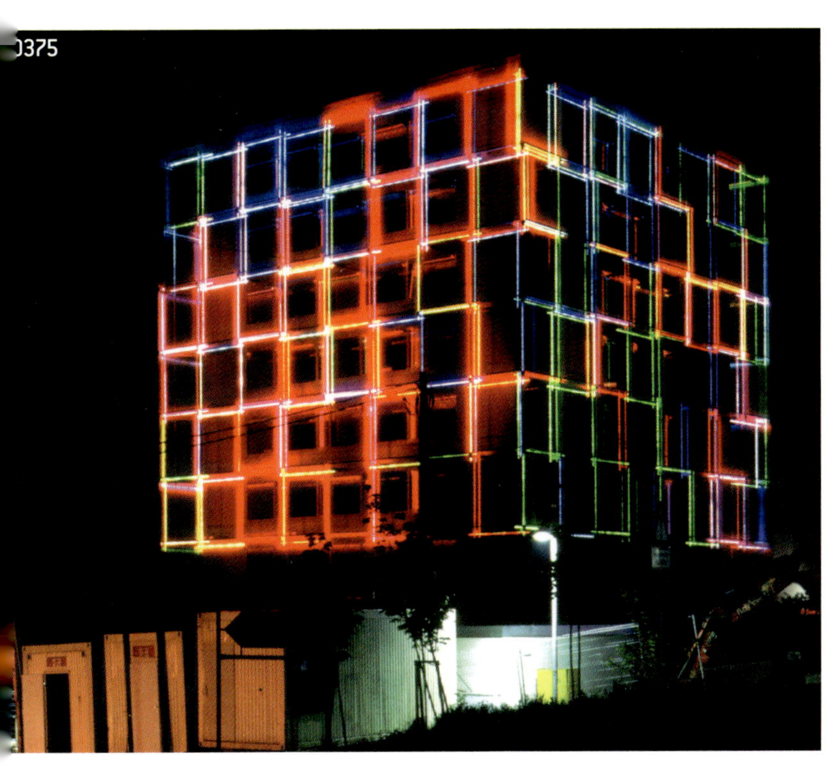

0376

0377

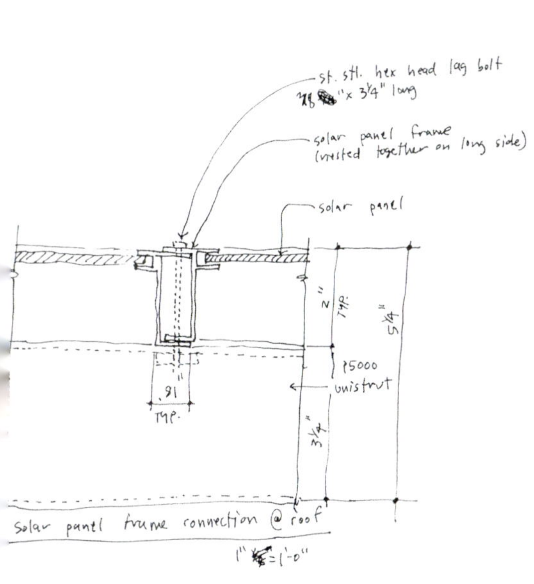
st. stl. hex head lag bolt
"x 3¼" long
solar panel frame
(riveted together on long side)
solar panel
2" TYP.
5¼"
P5000
unistrut
.81
TYP.
3¼"
solar panel frame connection @ roof
1" = 1'-0"

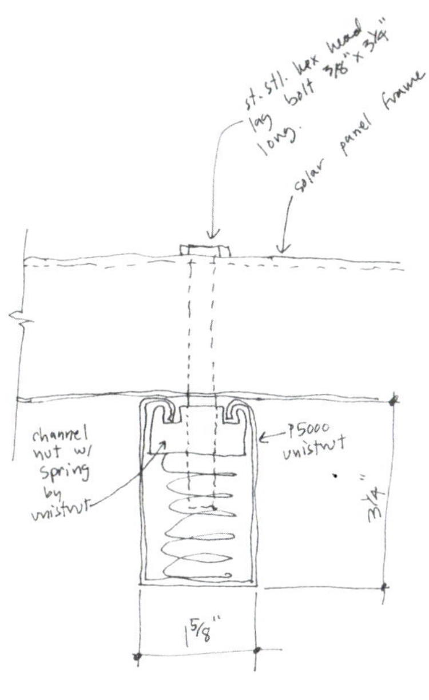
st. stl. hex head lag bolt 3/8" x 3¼" long.
solar panel frame
channel nut w/ spring by unistrut
P5000 unistrut
3¼"
1⅝"
solar panel connection @ unistrut

0378

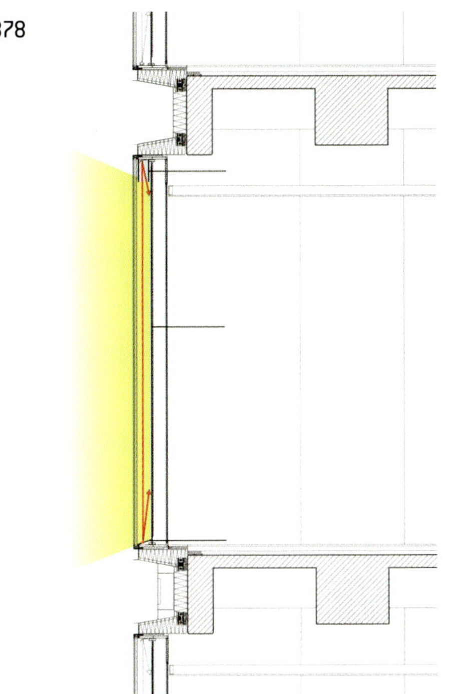

0379

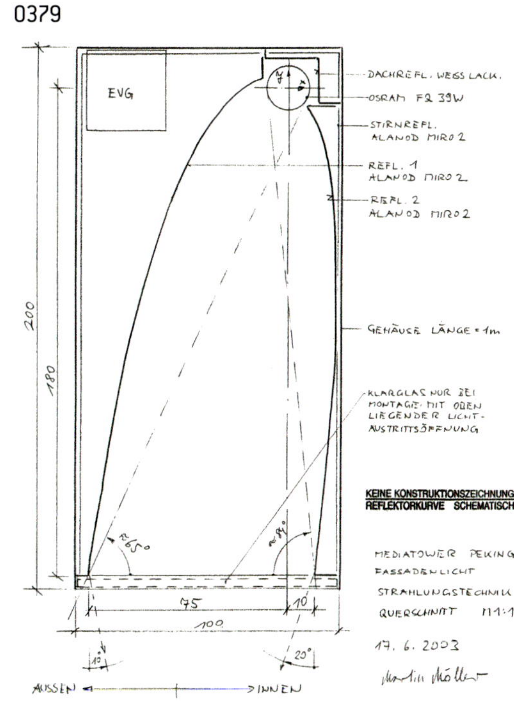
EVG
DACHREFL. WEISS LACK.
OSRAM FQ 39W
STIRNREFL.
ALANOD MIRO 2
REFL. 1
ALANOD MIRO 2
REFL. 2
ALANOD MIRO 2
GEHÄUSE LÄNGE = 1m
KLARGLAS NUR BEI MONTAGE MIT OBEN LIEGENDER LICHT-AUSTRITTSÖFFNUNG
KEINE KONSTRUKTIONSZEICHNUNG
REFLEKTORKURVE SCHEMATISCH
MEDIATOWER PEKING
FASSADENLICHT
STRAHLUNGSTECHNIK
QUERSCHNITT M1:1
17. 6. 2003
200
180
75
10
100
AUSSEN
INNEN

ENVIRONMENT AND SUSTAINABILITY

ENVIRONNEMENT ET DURABILITÉ
UMWELT UND NACHHALTIGKEIT
MILIEU EN DUURZAAMHEID

This installation made from recycled cardboard, forming a total of 3,500 molecules of two different forms, was exhibited by design students from the University of Technology, Sydney. The molecules are plastered on walls, ceilings and each other, and illuminated by neon lights.

Cette installation en carton recyclé, formant un total de 3 500 molécules de deux manières différentes, a été présentée par les étudiants de conception de l'Université de Technologie de Sydney. Les molécules sont plâtrées sur les murs, sur les toits et entre elles, et éclairées par des lumières au néon.

Diese Installation aus Recyclingkarton, die insgesamt 3.500 Moleküle in zwei unterschiedlichen Ausführungen umfasst, wurde von den Design-Studenten der TU Sydney präsentiert. Die Moleküle sind mit Gips mit Wänden und Decken sowie untereinander verbunden und werden mit Neonlicht beleuchtet.

Deze installatie van gerecycled karton, die op verschillende manieren een totaal van 3.500 molecules vormt, werd door de studenten Ontwerp van de Technologische Universiteit van Sydney voorgesteld. De molecules zijn in muren, daken en onderling gepleisterd en worden door neonlichten verlicht.

0381

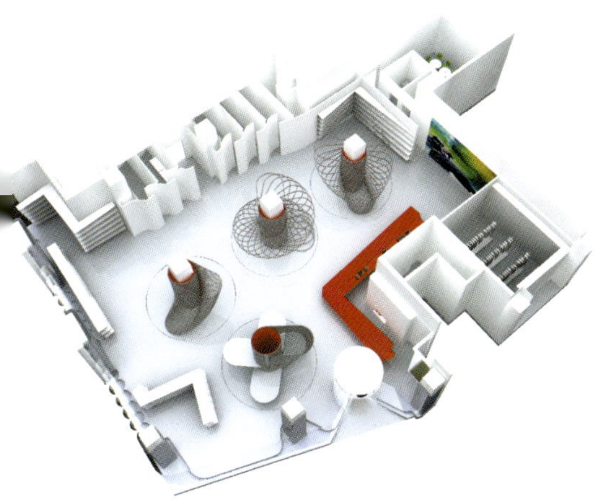

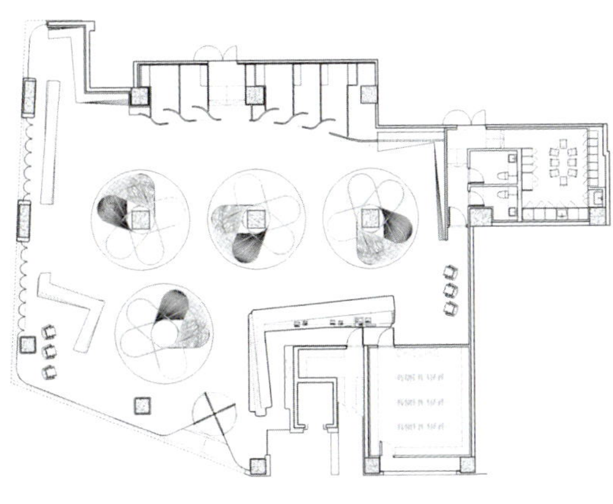

0382

0383

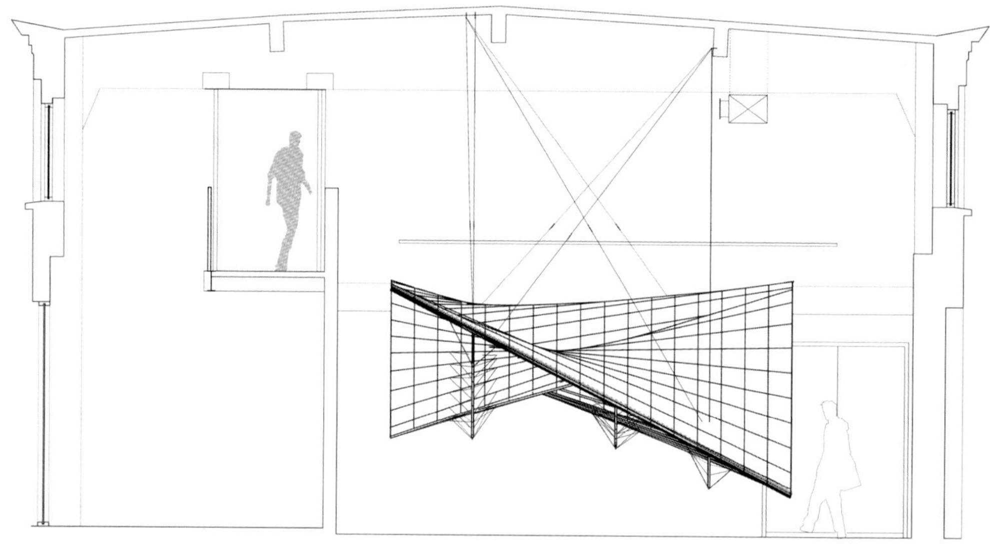

0384

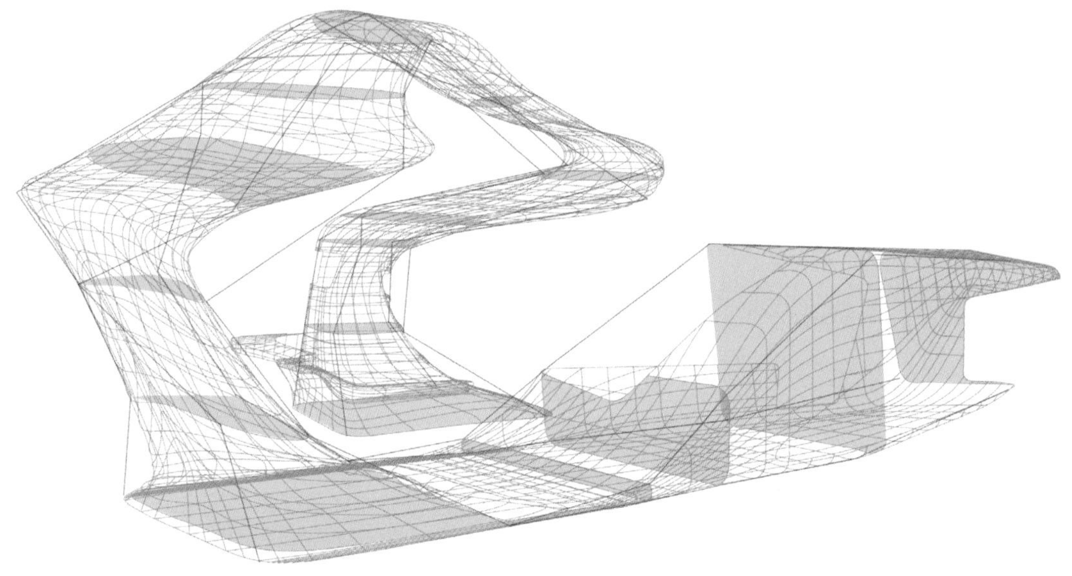

0385

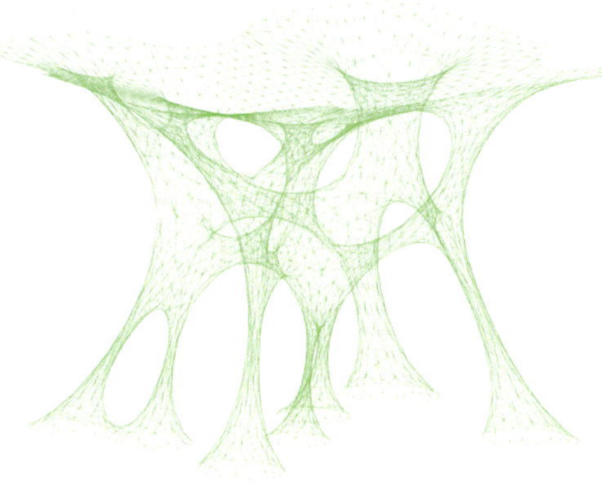

0386

>

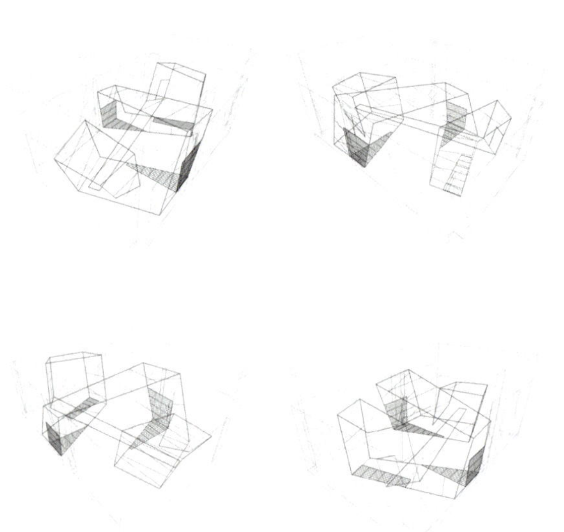

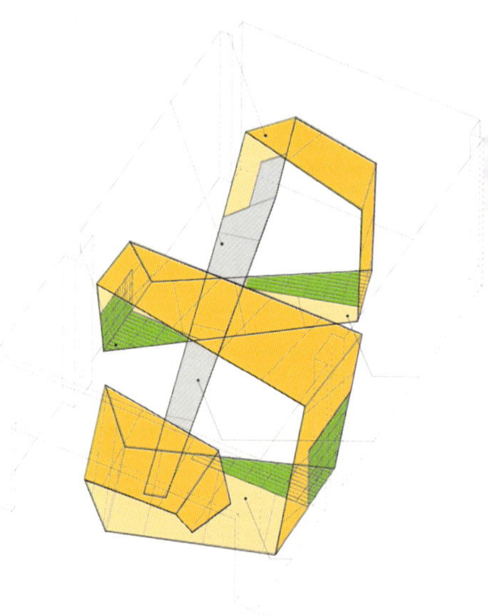

0387

>

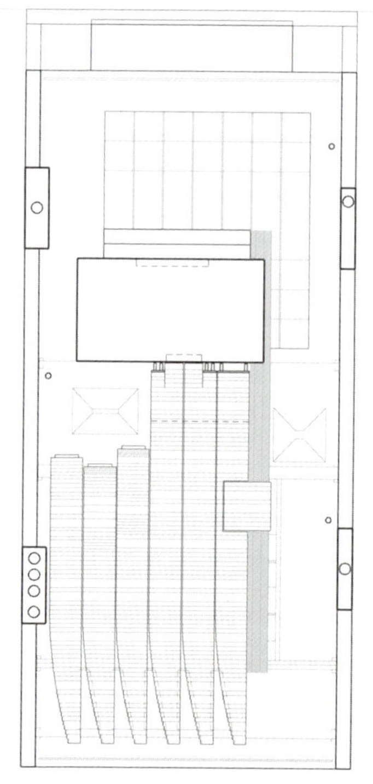

0388

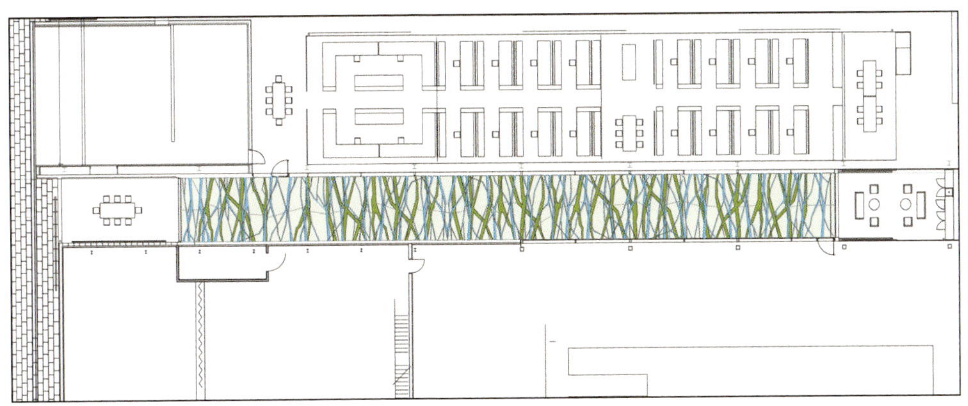

Francis Soler employed three strategies for his Les Bons Enfants government building project in Paris: new lighting, landscaping, and a new skin on the façade. Standing for over 70 years, this building had already undergone remodelling three times. The ornamental tracery of the skin produces shadows and reflections on the façade.

Pour l'immeuble ministériel des Bons Enfants à Paris, Francis Soler a misé sur trois mesures : nouvel éclairage, nouveau jardin et nouveau revêtement au niveau de la façade. Cet immeuble, vieux de plus de 70 ans, avait déjà fait l'objet de trois interventions. L'enveloppe ornementale en acier donne naissance à des ombres et à des reflets sur la façade.

Für das Ministerialgebäude Bons Enfants in Paris setzte Francis Soler auf drei Maßnahmen: Neue Beleuchtung, neuer Garten und neue Fassadenverkleidung. Dieses über 70 Jahre alte Gebäude war bereits drei Mal umgebaut worden. Die Zierhaut aus Stahl erzeugt attraktive Schatten und Lichtreflexe auf der Fassade.

Voor het ministerieel gebouw Bons Enfants in Parijs, koos Francis Soler voor drie maatregelen: nieuwe verlichting, een nieuwe tuin en een nieuwe gevelbekleding. Dit meer dan 70 jaar oude gebouw, werd reeds driemaal verbouwd. Het stalen sieromhulsel genereert schaduwen en weerkaatsingen op de gevel.

0389

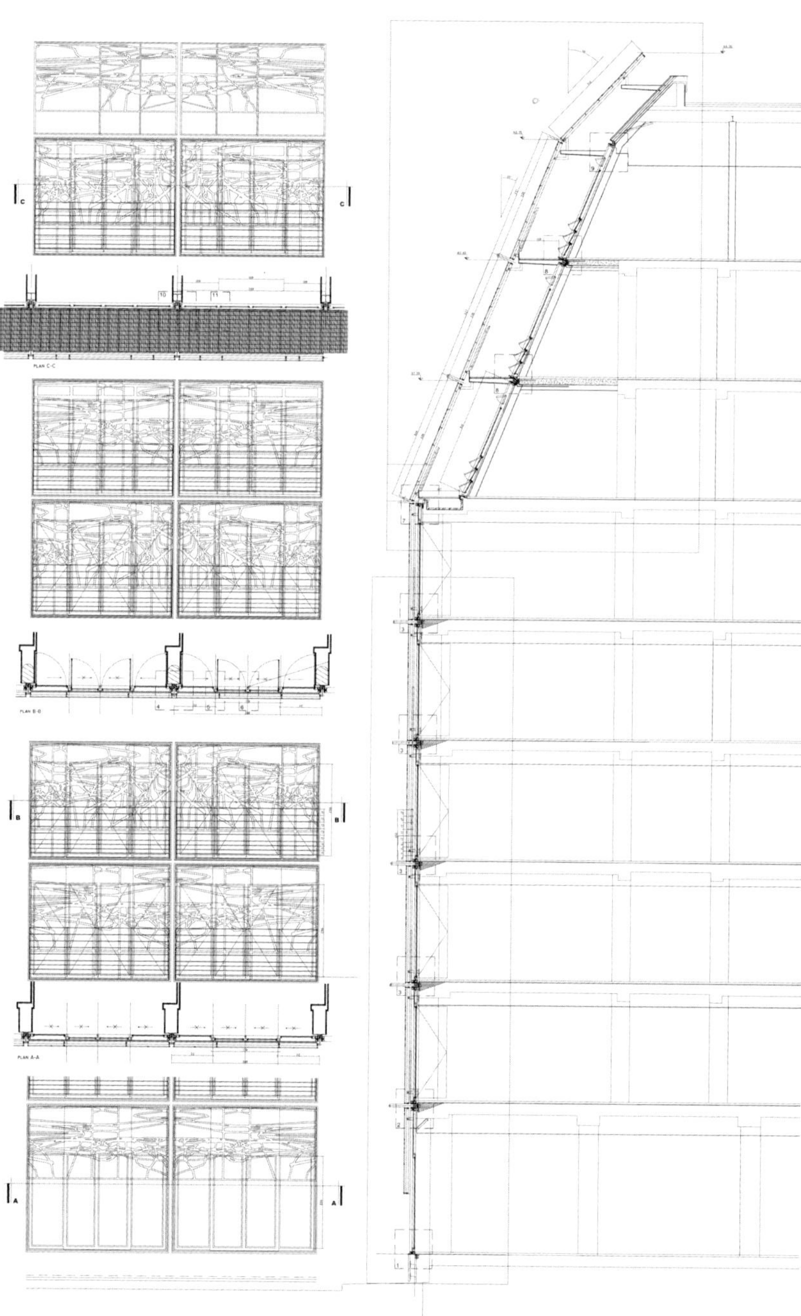

0390

>

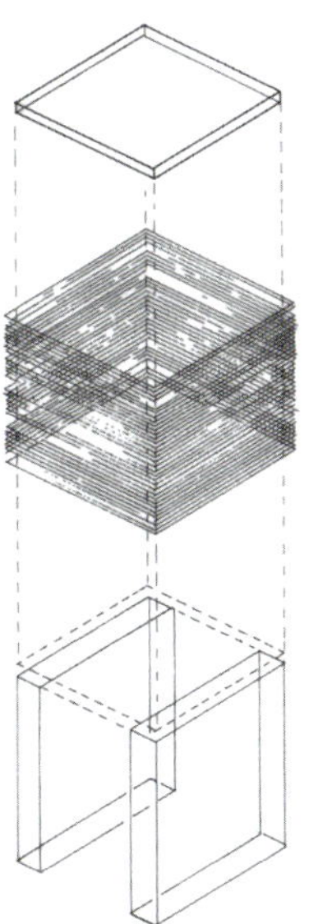

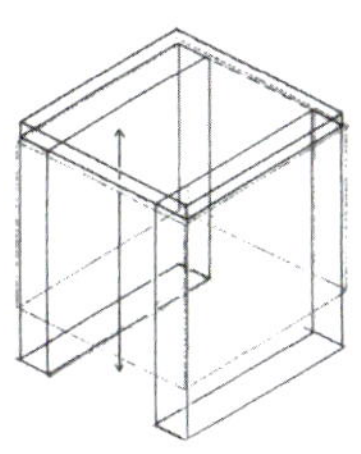

0392

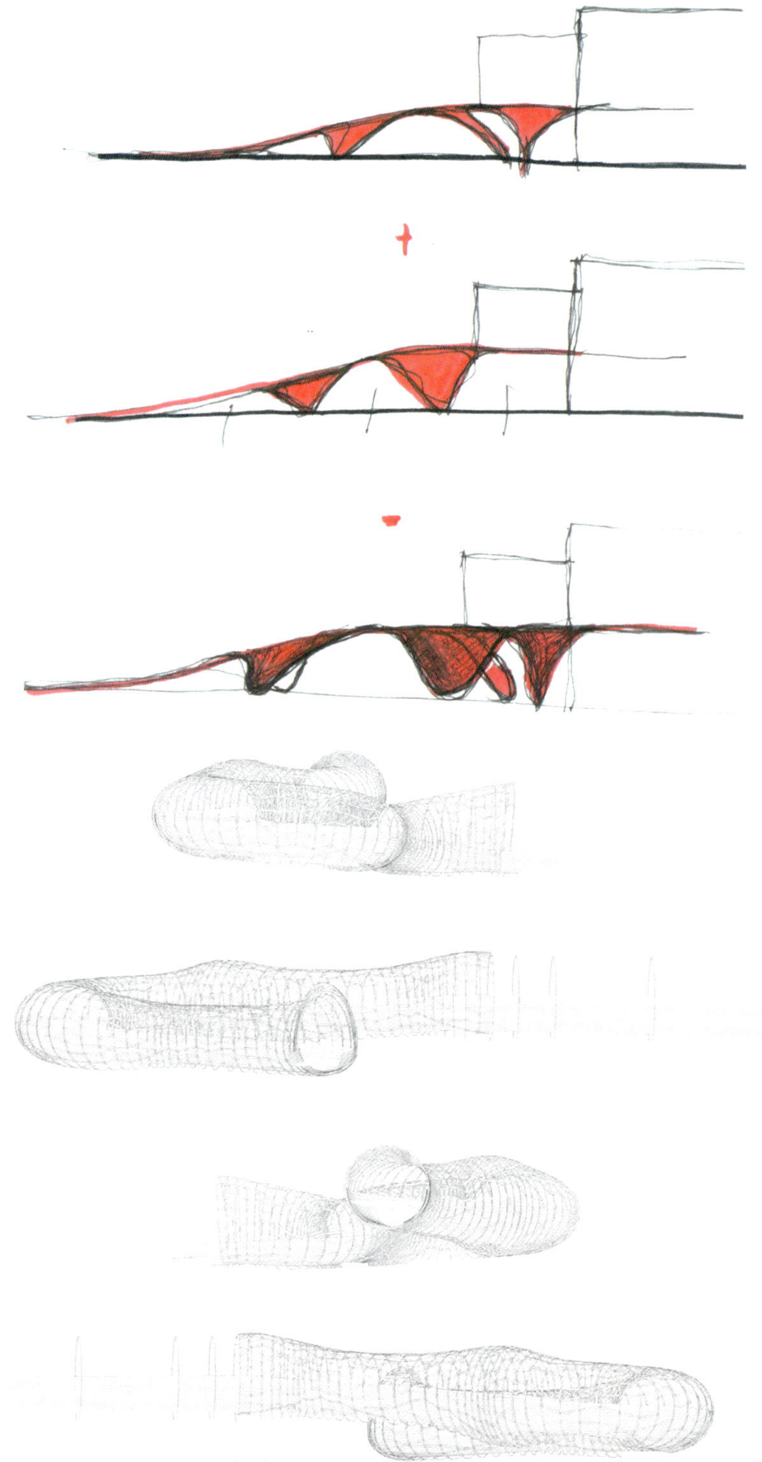

0393

0394

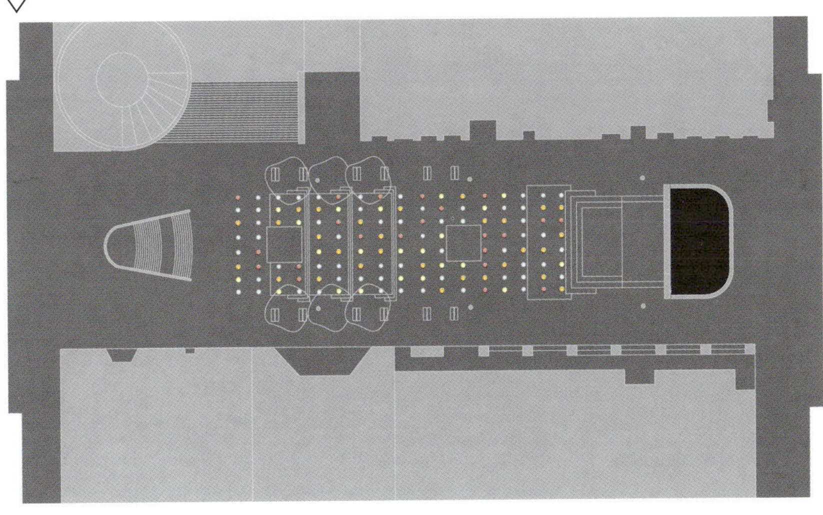

0395

0396

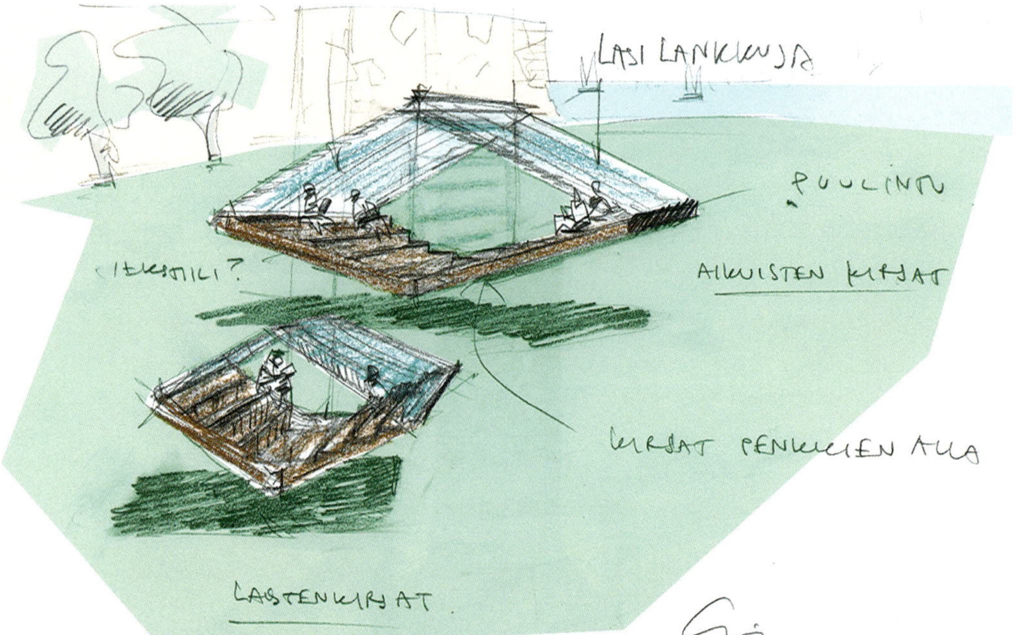

0397

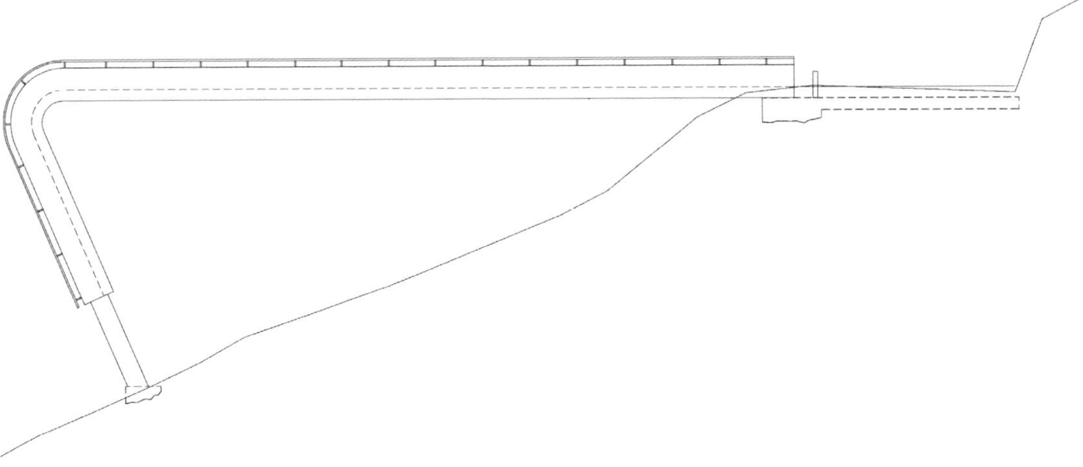

0398

0399

The main façade of this house has passive and active strategies: skylights for convection and natural lighting, four greenhouse areas for capturing heat during the winter, thermal solar panels in the roof, and a solar dryer for clothes.

La façade principale de cette habitation propose des stratégies passives et actives : aux lucarnes pour la convection et l'éclairage naturel, viennent s'ajouter quatre zones de serres pour emmagasiner la chaleur solaire pendant l'hiver, les panneaux solaires thermiques de la toiture, ainsi qu'un séchoir solaire pour le linge.

Die Hauptfassade dieses Wohngebäudes zeigt passive und aktive Baustrategien: Zu den Dachfenstern für Wärmekonvektion und natürlichen Lichteinfall kommen vier verglaste Bereiche, die im Winter die Sonnenwärme auffangen, Solarpaneele auf dem Dach und ein Bereich zum Wäschetrocknen.

De hoofdgevel van deze woning omvat passieve en actieve strategieën: naast de dakramen voor convectie en natuurlijke verlichting, werd gezorgd voor vier serrezones om tijdens de winter de zonnewarmte op te vangen, thermische zonnepanelen op het dak en een zonnedroger om de was te drogen.

Bioclimatic operation

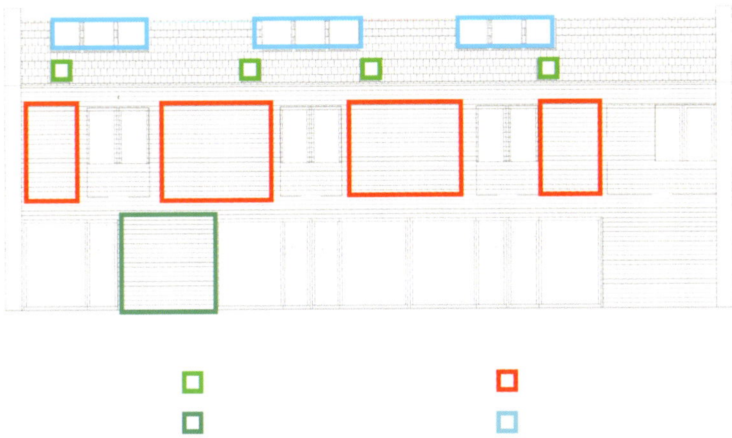

0401

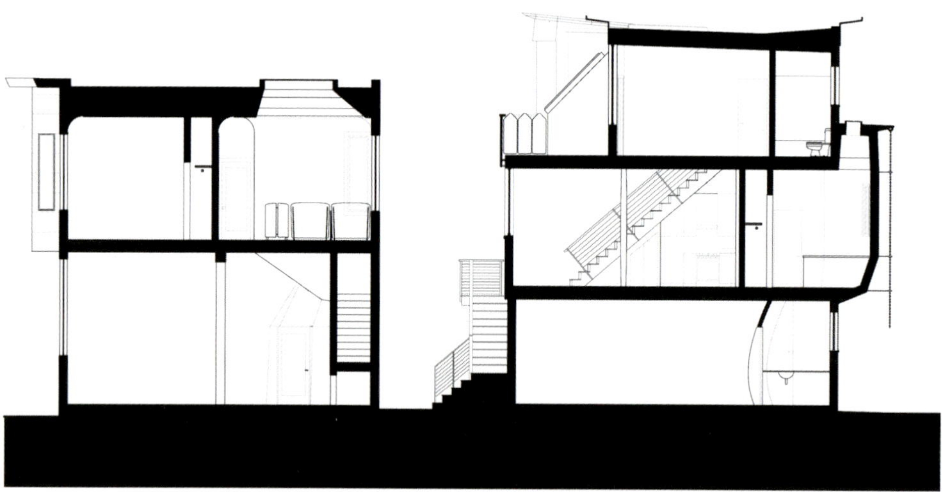

0402

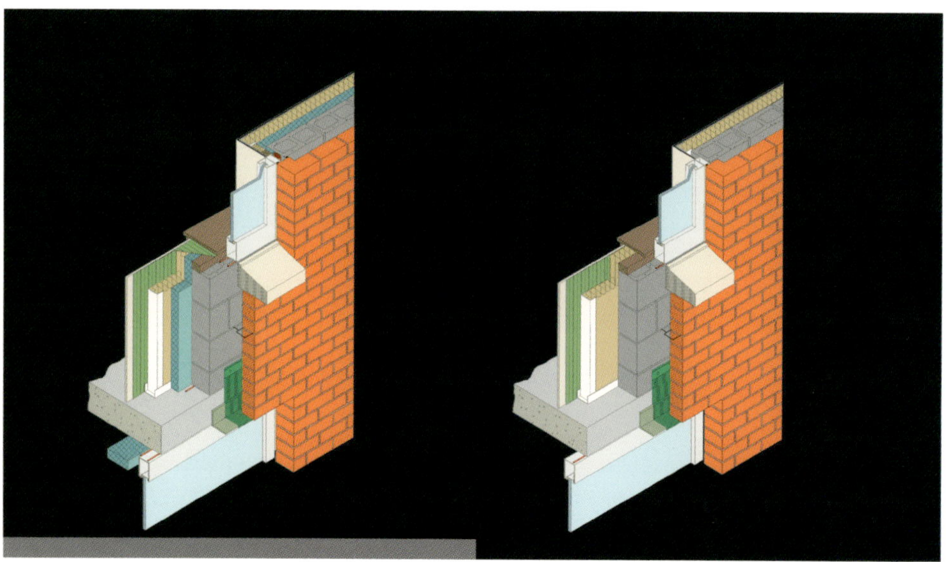

0403

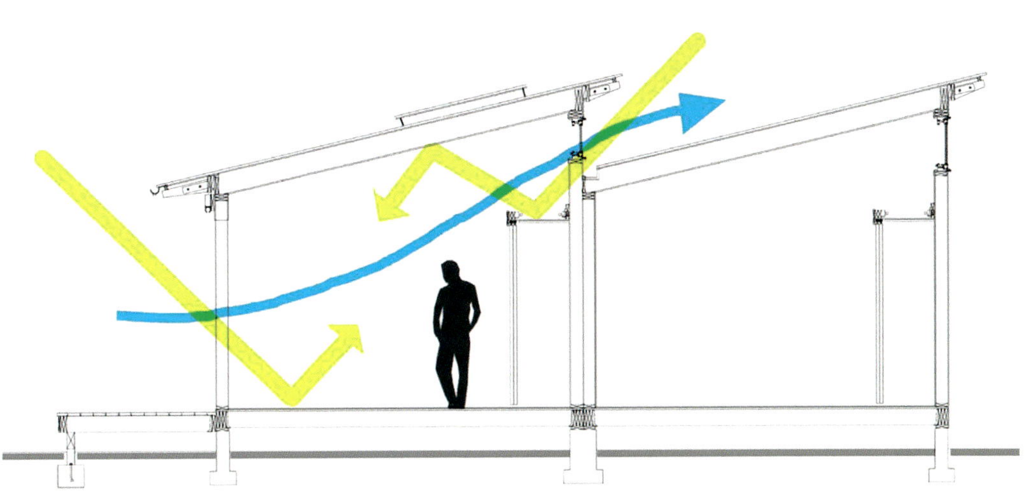

0404

0405

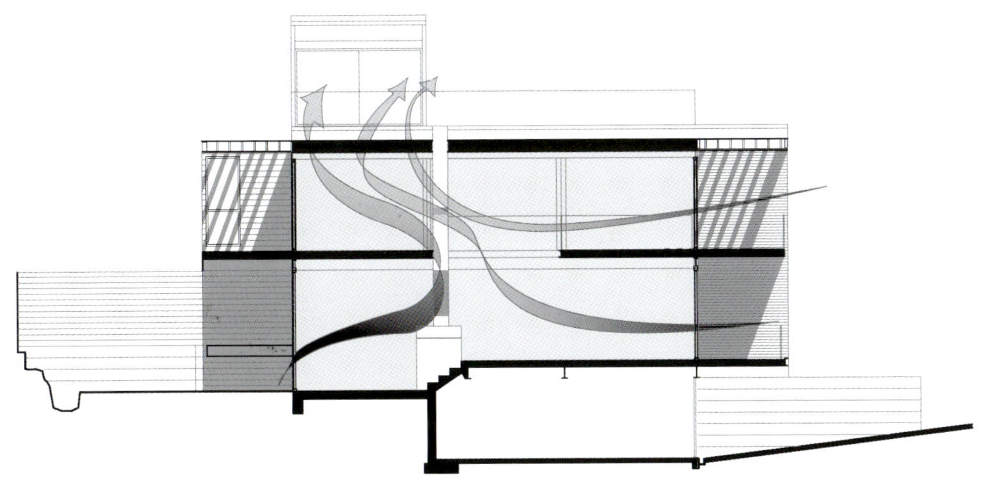

SECTION : NATURAL VENTILATION AND SOLAR SHADING DIAGRAM

0406

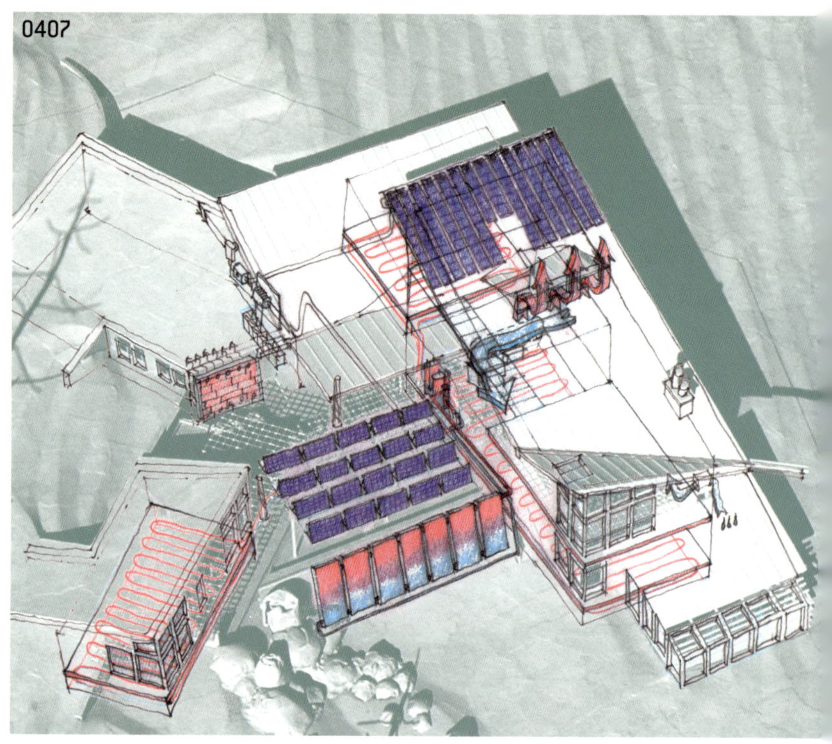

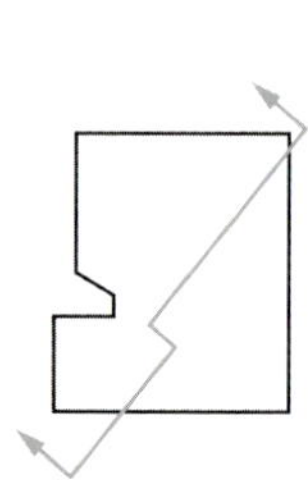

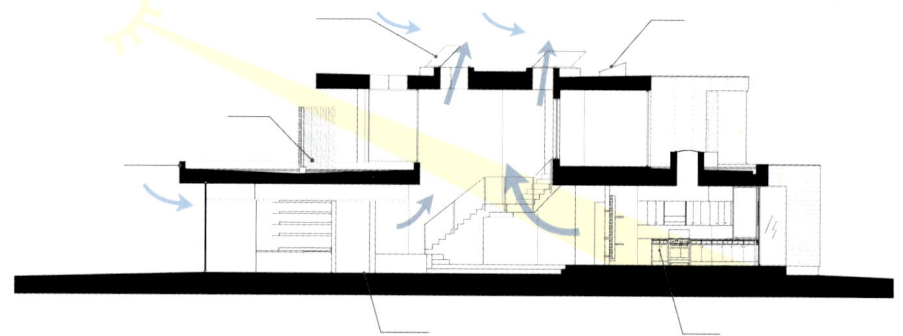

The bioclimatic section indicates the methods for cooling during the summer, such as cross-ventilation and the solar chimney effect caused by motorized skylights in the roof, which expel warm air from the dwelling.

La section bioclimatique indique les méthodes de génération de fraîcheur pendant l'été, telles que la ventilation croisée et l'effet de cheminée solaire obtenu grâce aux lucarnes à moteur de la toiture, qui expulsent l'air chaud de l'habitation.

Die Bioklimatik-Skizze verdeutlicht die Verfahren zur Erzeugung kühler Belüftung im Sommer, wie z. B. durch Kreuzlüftung und den Kamineffekt dank der motorbetriebenen Dachfenster, die die warme Luft aus dem Gebäude leiten.

De bioklimatische sectie duidt op de methoden voor de opwekking van koelte tijdens de zomer, zoals de kruisventilatie en het zonnehaardeffect dat veroorzaakt wordt door de gemotoriseerde dakramen die de warme lucht van de woning afvoeren.

0409

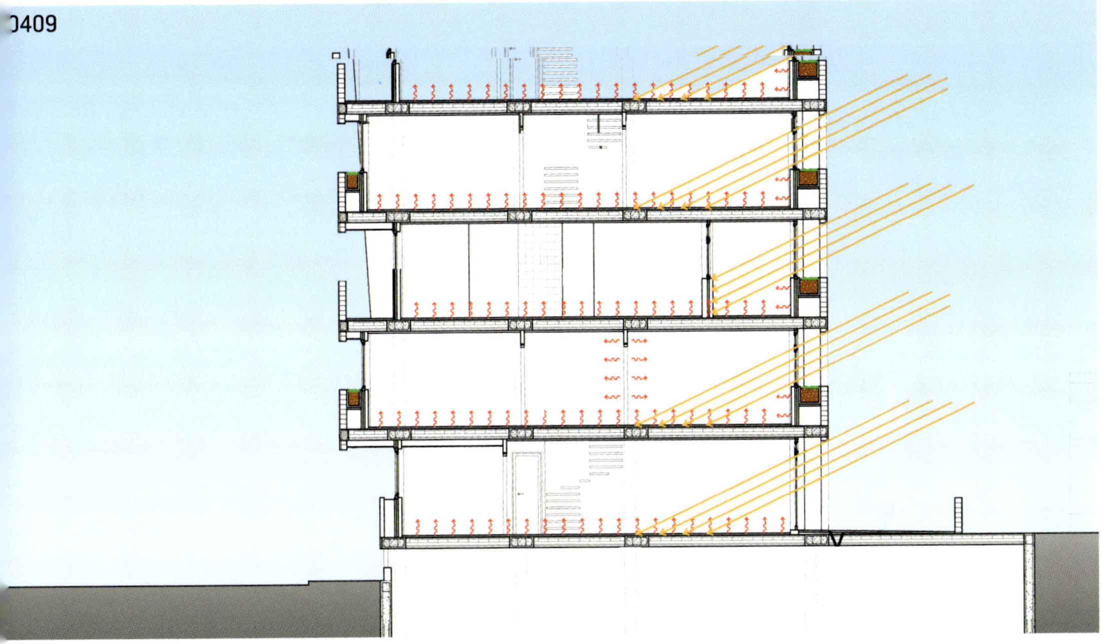

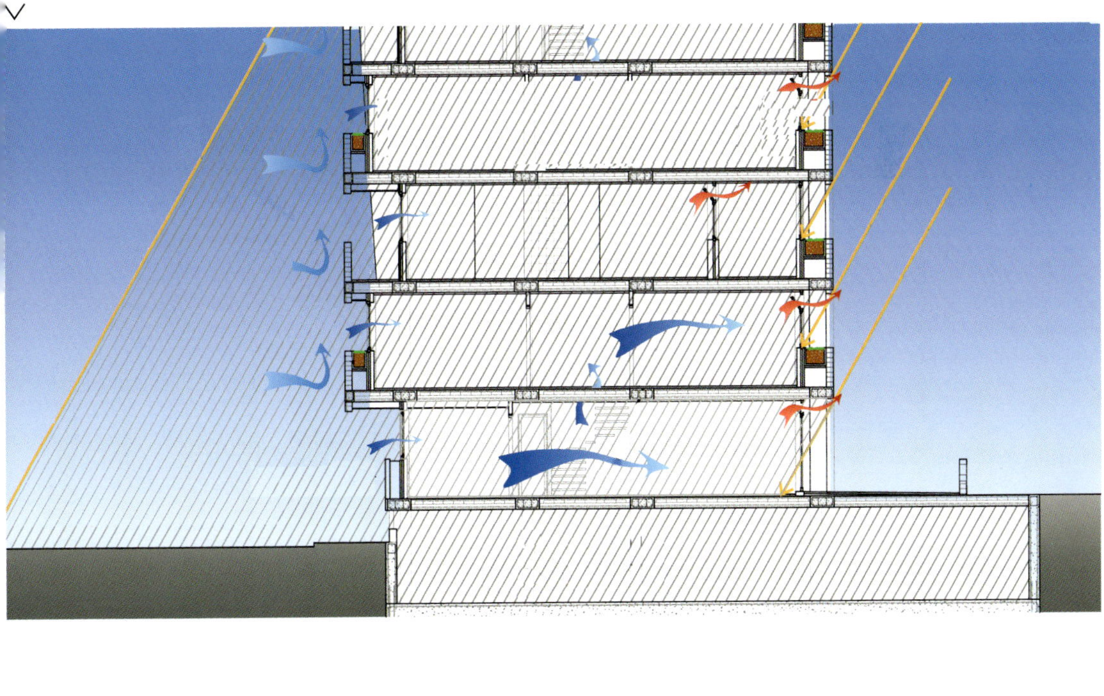

0410

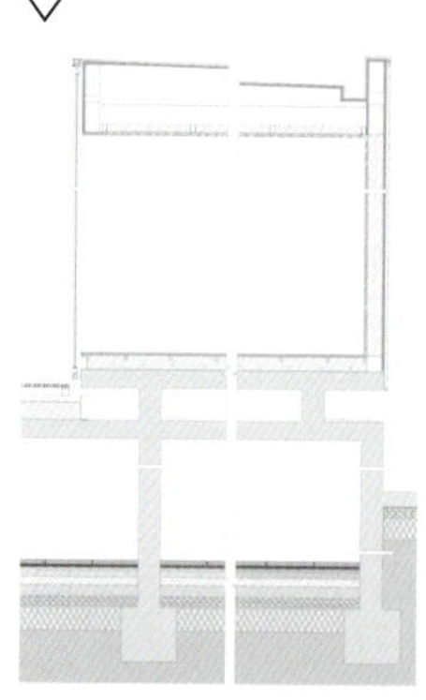

0411

0412

0413

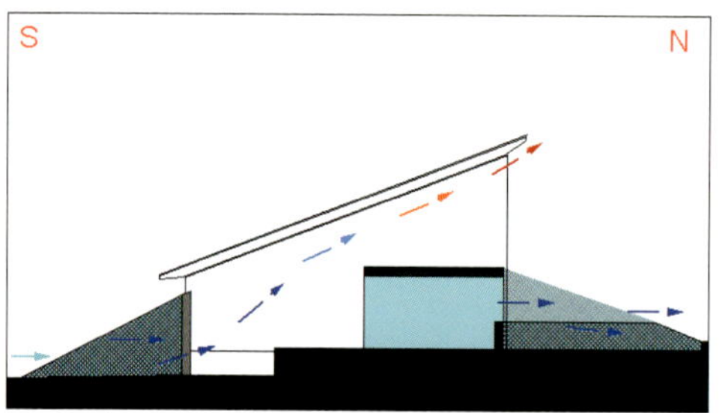

section

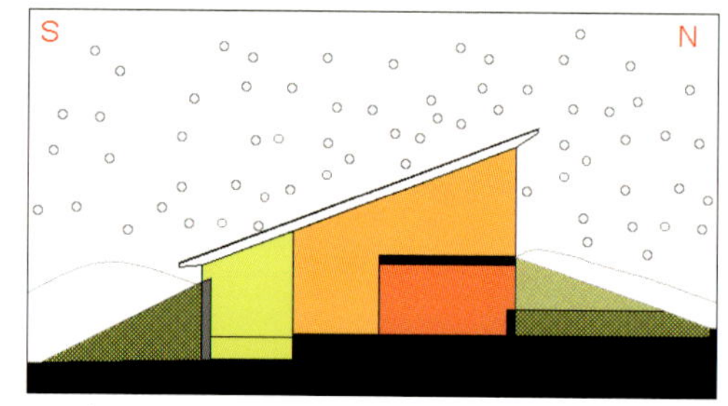

section

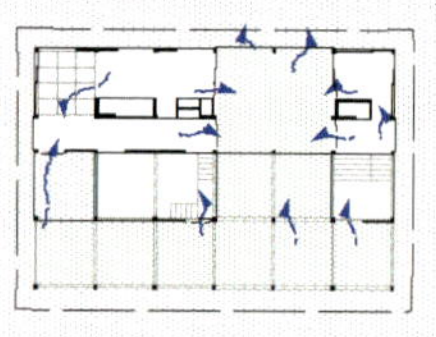
upper floor / guest house

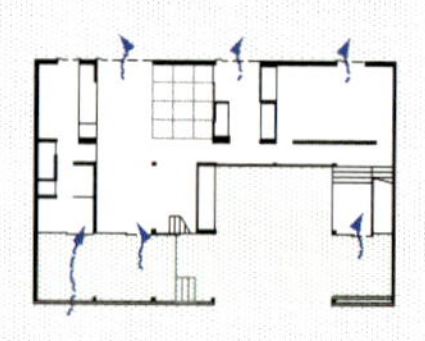
lower floor / main house

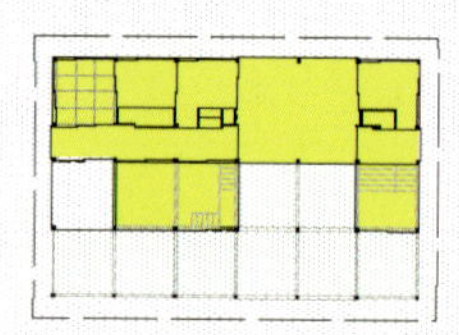
upper floor / guest house

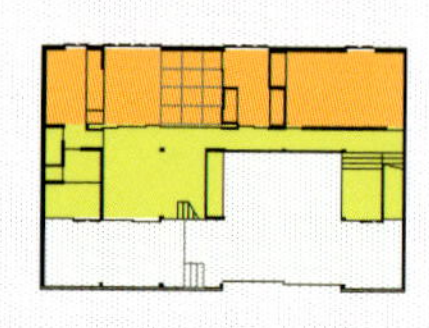
lower floor / main house

0414

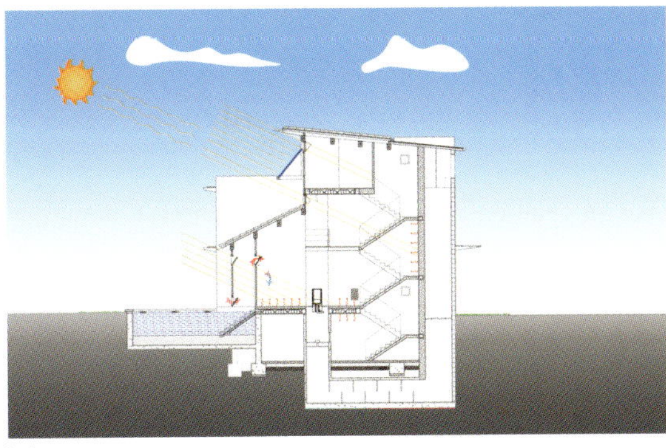

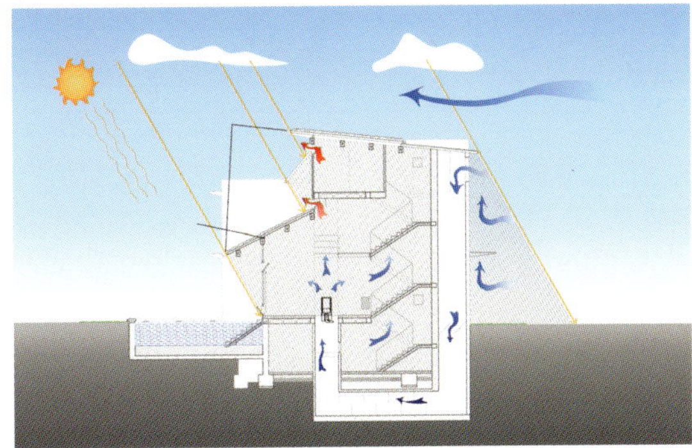

0415

The large metal girders slavaged from the Big Dig project can be seen in the interior. The slabs supporting the roof are pieces of precast concrete that were previouly a part of a demolished freeway ramp. The double height of the stairwell creates a solar chimney effect.

À l'intérieur, apparaissent les grandes poutres métalliques de la structure récupérée du projet Big Dig. Les dalles qui soutiennent le toit sont des morceaux de béton préfabriqué qui faisait auparavant partie de la rampe qui a été démolie. Dans la cage d'escalier, la double hauteur crée un effet de cheminée solaire.

Im Inneren sind die großen Metallträger der beim Projekt Big Dig genutzten Struktur zu sehen. Die Platten, die das Dach tragen, bestehen aus Betonfertigteilen, welche zuvor Bestandteil der abgerissenen Rampe waren. Im Treppenhaus erzeugt die doppelte Raumhöhe einen Kamineffekt.

In het interieur zijn de grote metalen balken van de gerecupereerde structuur van het project Big Dig zichtbaar. De tegels van het dak zijn stukken geprefabriceerd beton die vroeger deel uitmaakten van de vernietigde hellingbaan. In de traphal creëert de dubbele hoogte een zonnehaardeffect.

0416

0417

0418

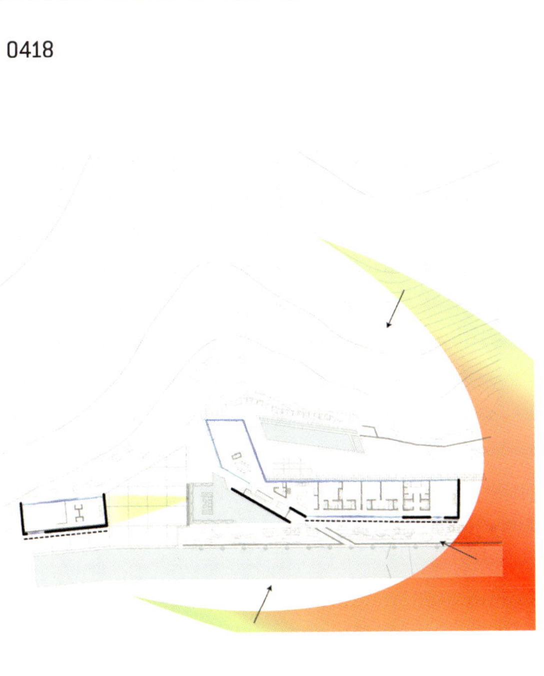

0419

0421

0422

0423

0424

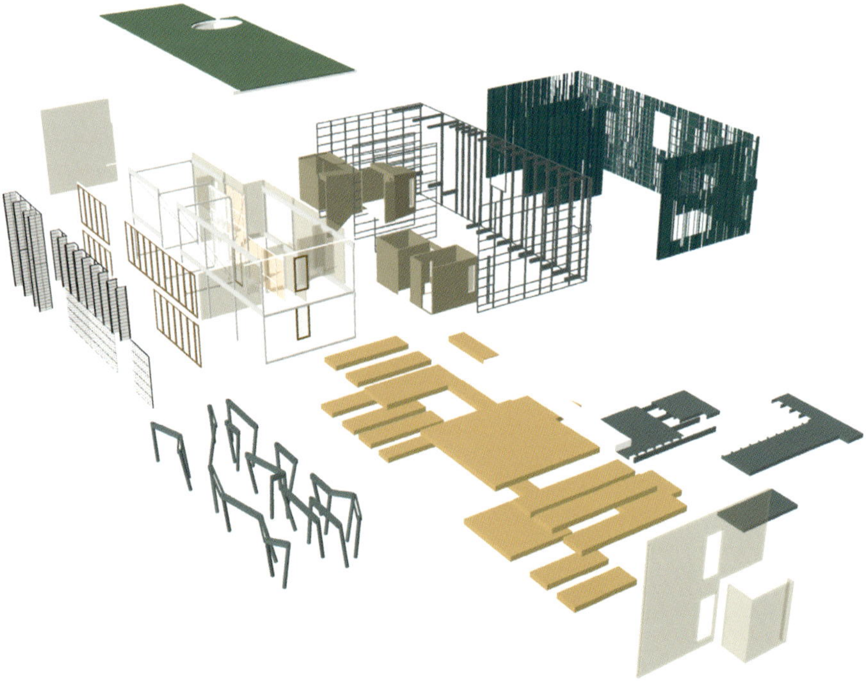

425

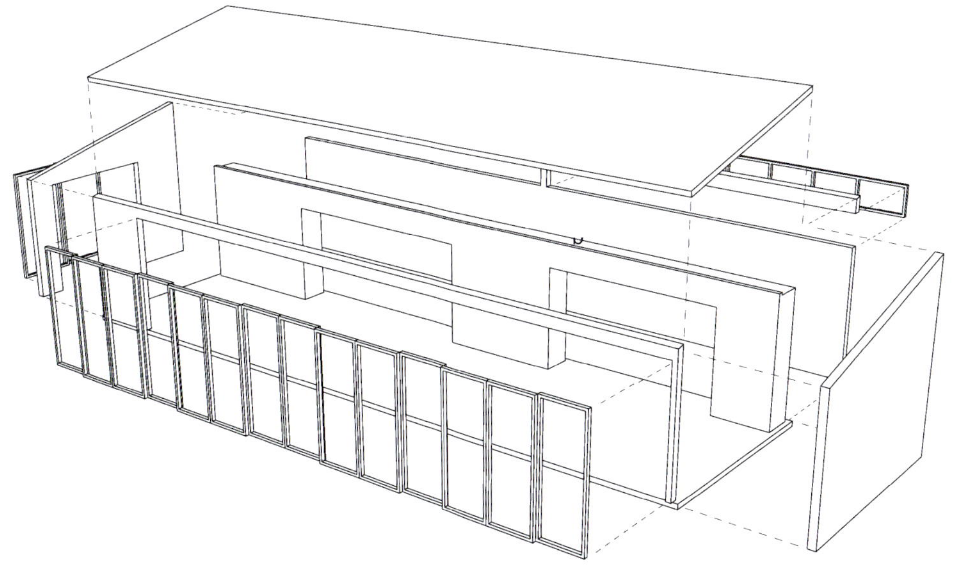

0426

The design for Rucksack House was materialized as a cube-shaped addition for a home that works like a parasite module. It was installed on two buildings in Leipzig and Cologne. It weighs 1,100 kg (2,425 lbs), and the plywood furniture inside is 100% foldable.

Les croquis de la maison-sac à dos ont été concrétisés avec l'agrandissement de l'habitation sous la forme d'un cube qui, en guise de module parasite, a été ajouté à deux bâtiments de Leipzig et de Cologne. Son poids final est de 1 100 kg et le mobilier intérieur en contreplaqué est entièrement pliable.

Die Skizzen des flexiblen Raums wurden als würfelförmige Erweiterung von Wohnraum umgesetzt, die wie ein Parasit als Modul an zwei Gebäude in Leipzig und Köln angebaut wurde. Das Endgewicht betrug 1.100 kg und das Mobiliar aus Sperrholz ist zu 100 % zusammenklappbar.

De ontwerpen van het rugzakhuis werden verwezenlijkt door middel van een kubusvormige uitbreiding van de woning die, zoals een parasietmodule, op twee gebouwen in Leipzig en Keulen geïnstalleerd werd. Het eindgewicht bedroeg 1.100 kg en het meubilair uit gelaagd hout binnenin is 100% opvouwbaar.

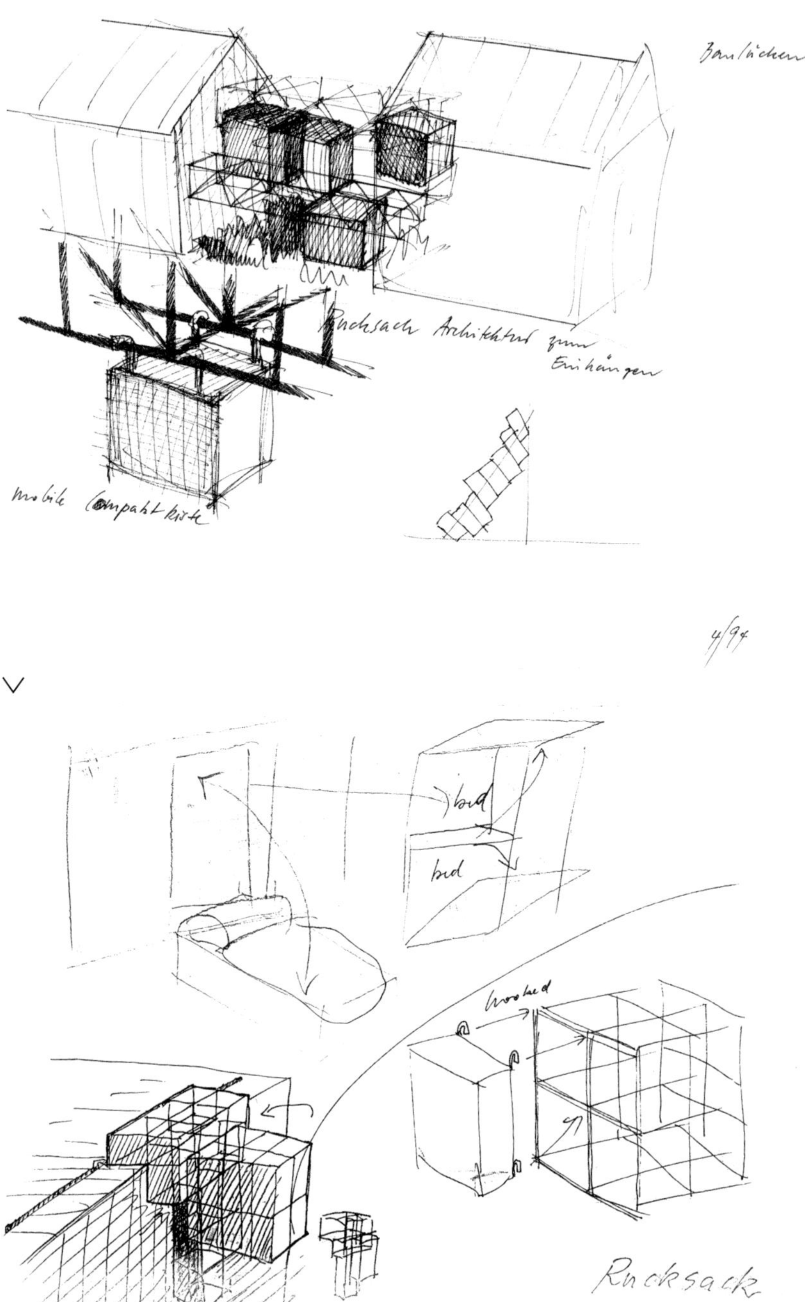

0427

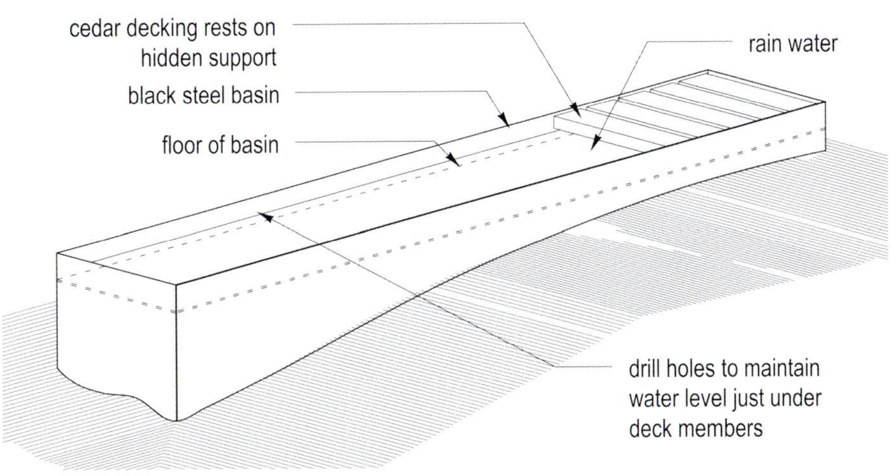

cedar decking rests on hidden support
black steel basin
floor of basin
rain water
drill holes to maintain water level just under deck members

0428

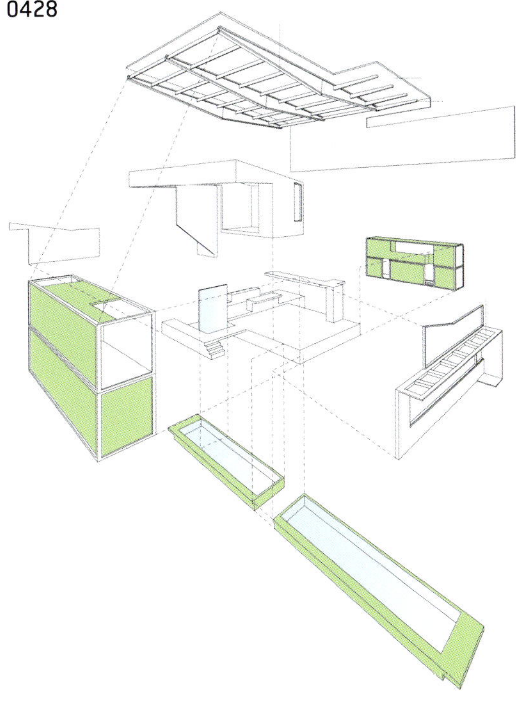

0429

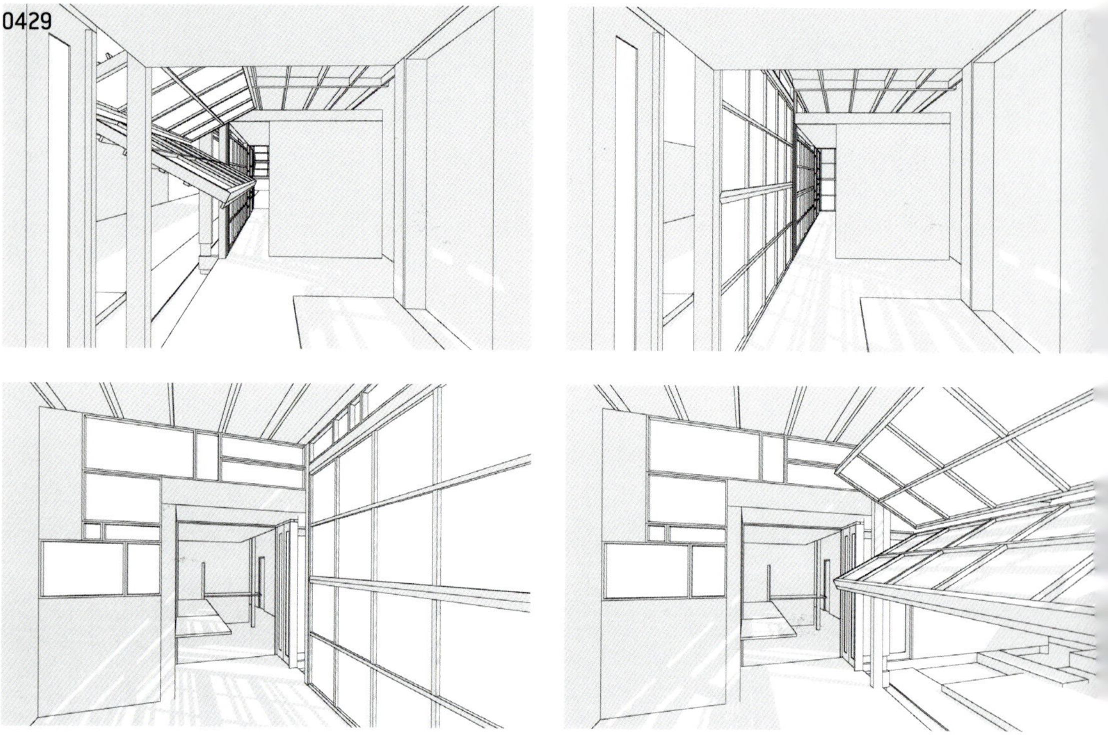

0430

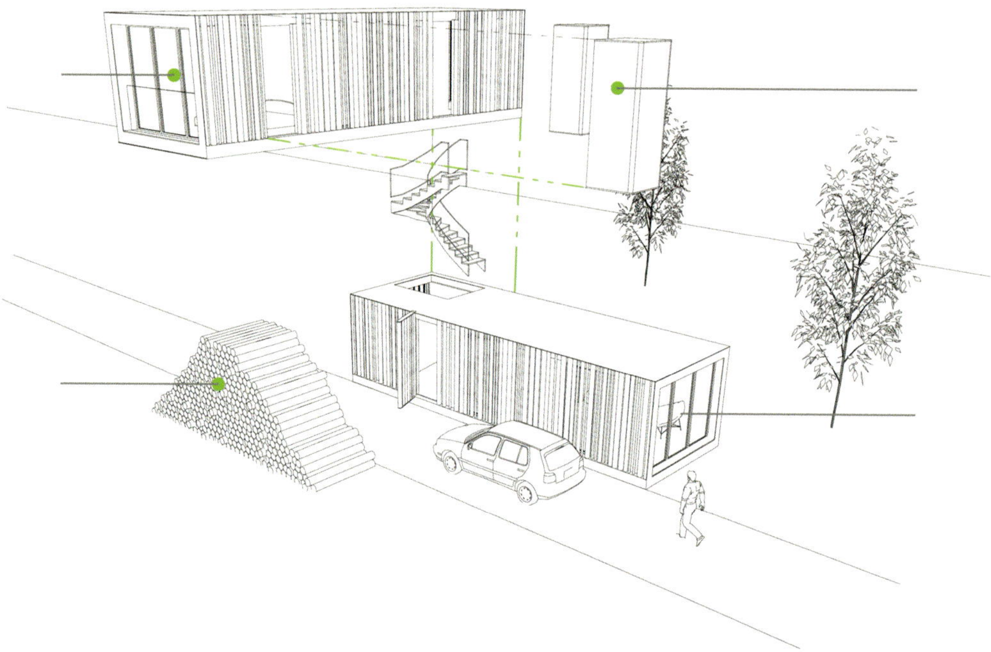

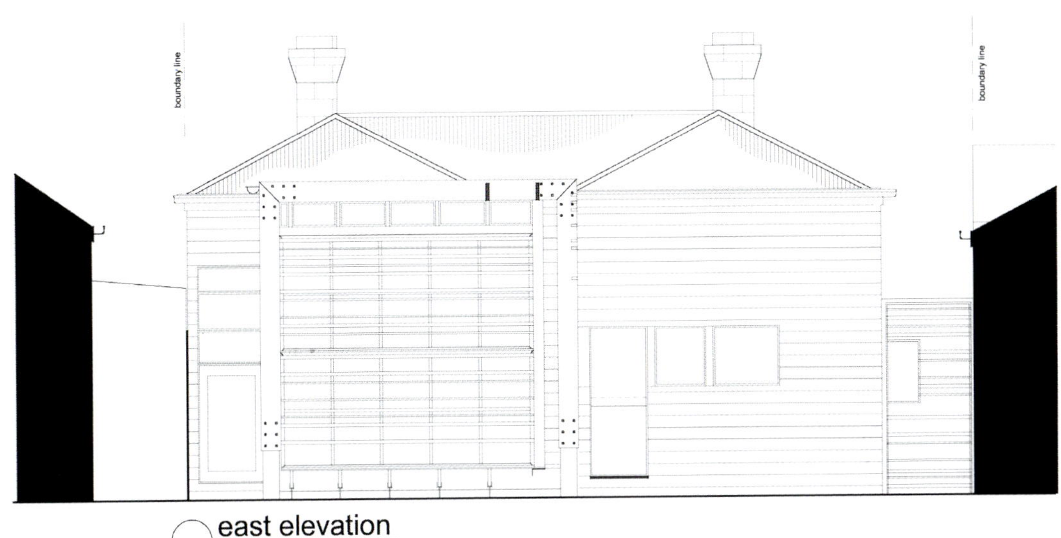
boundary line
boundary line
east elevation
1:50

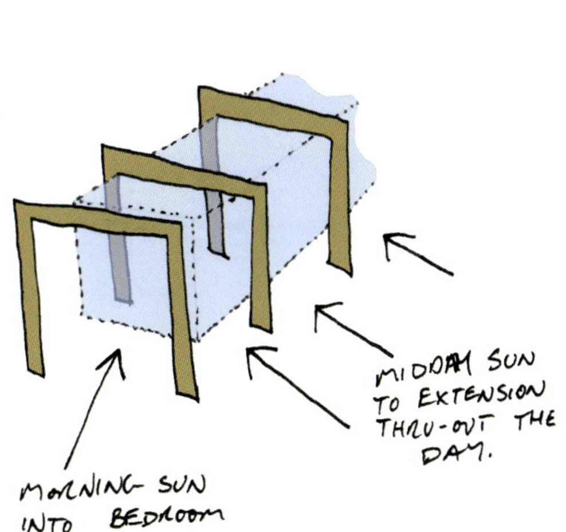
MIDDAY SUN
TO EXTENSION
THRU-OUT THE
DAY.
MORNING SUN
INTO BEDROOM

RECYCLED
IRON BARK
RECYCLED &
FARMED
TIMBERS
USED TO
MINUMISE
ENVIRONMENTAL
IMPACT.
ENVIRONMENT

0432

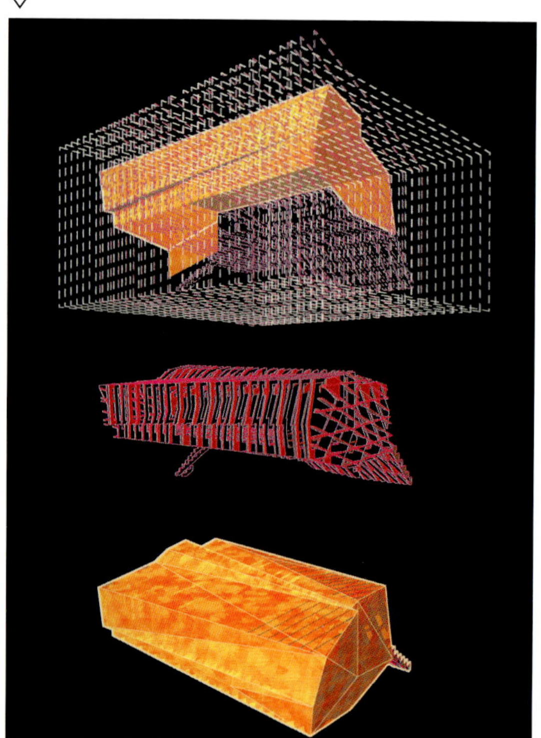

0433

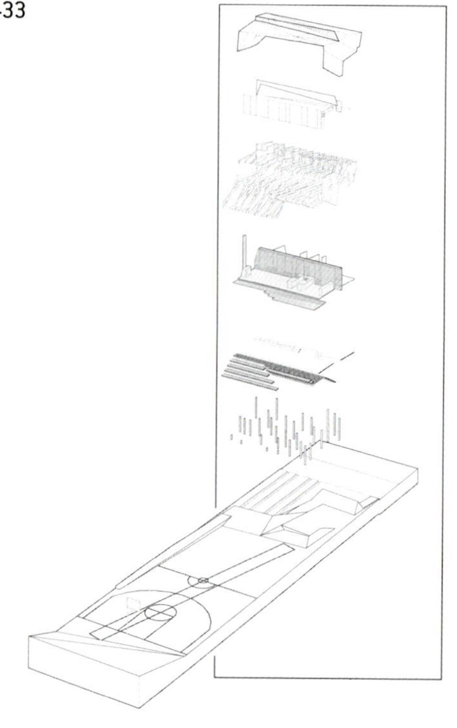

0434

Nomadhome is a patented system for flexible construction and involves joining 11 m² (118 sq ft) modules together. They can be used for commercial or residential purposes. The modules are interchangeable and expandable, and they can be disassembled at any time in just two or three days.

Nomadhome est un système breveté de construction flexible qui consiste dans l'assemblage de modules de 11 m². Son application peut être commerciale ou résidentielle. Les modules sont interchangeables entre eux, extensibles ou peuvent être démontés à tout moment en seulement trois jours.

Nomadhome ist ein patentiertes System für das flexible Bauen, bei dem 11 m² große Module miteinander verbunden werden. Das System kann für die Schaffung von gewerblichen Gebäuden oder Wohnhäusern eingesetzt werden. Die Module können jederzeit, innerhalb von nur zwei bis drei Tagen, untereinander ausgetauscht, erweitert oder abgebaut werden.

Nomadhome is een gepatenteerd flexibel bouwsysteem dat bestaat uit het samenstel van modules van 11 m². Het kan zowel commercieel als residentieel toegepast worden. De modules kunnen in twee of drie dagen tijd onderling verwisseld, uitgebreid of gedemonteerd worden.

0435

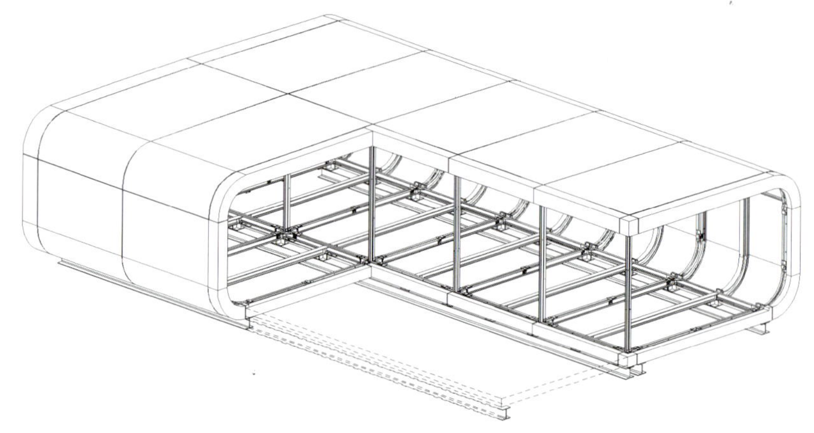

0436

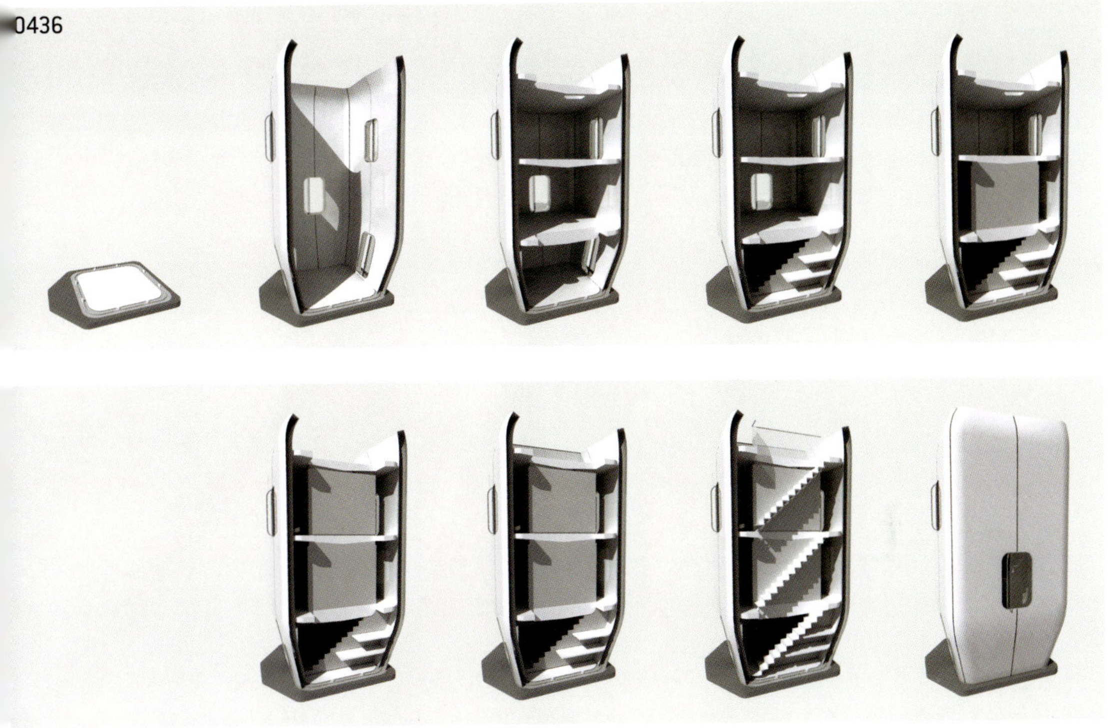

0437

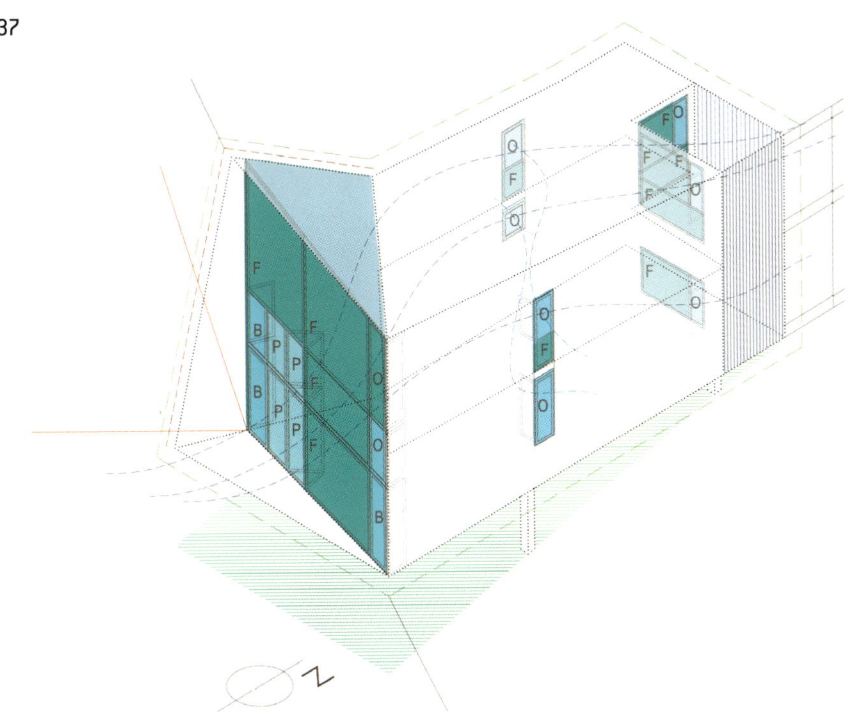

0438

0439

0440

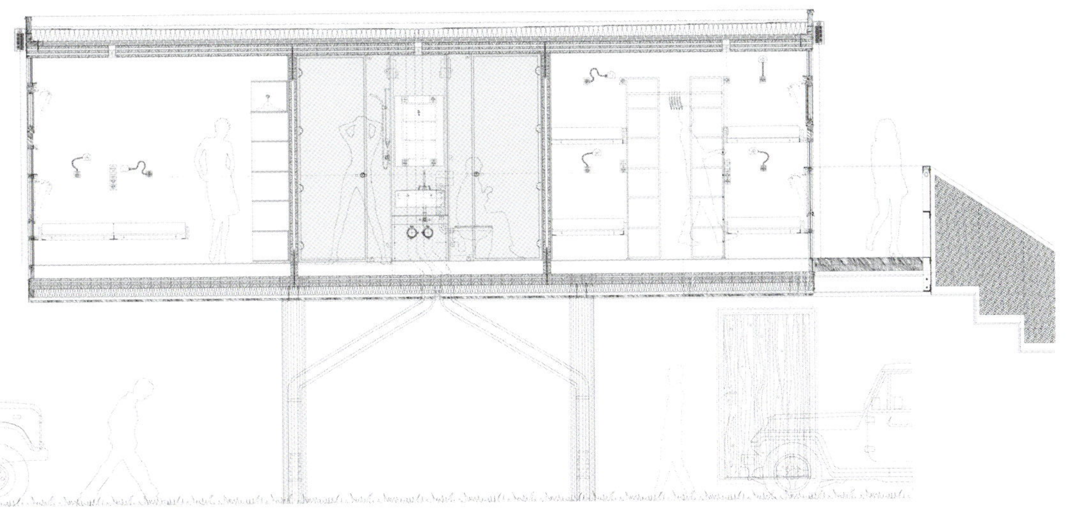

0441

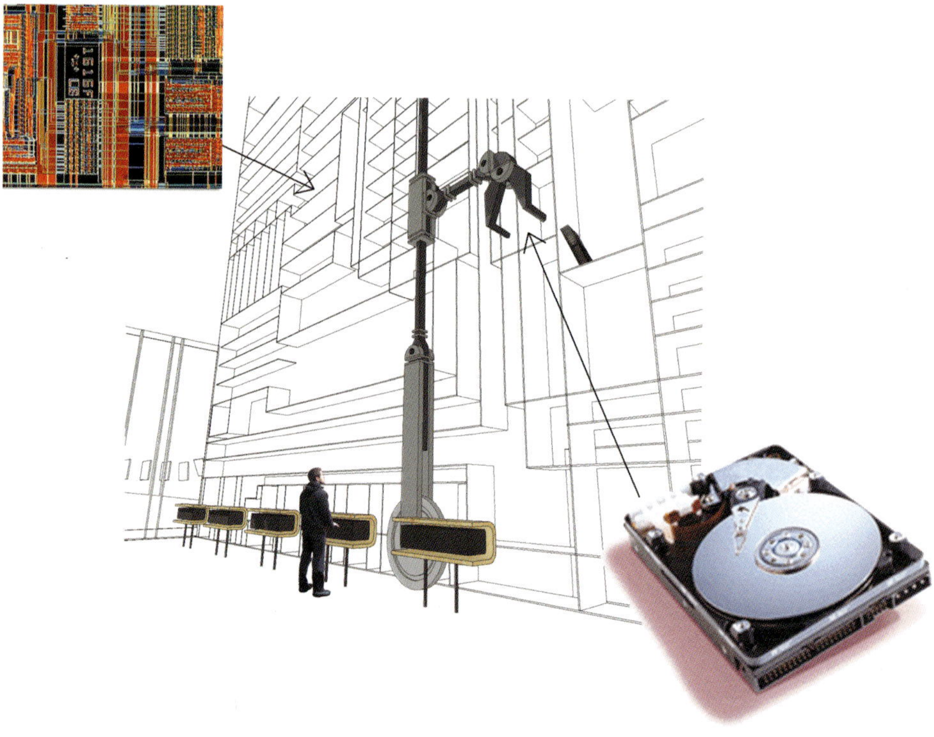

0442

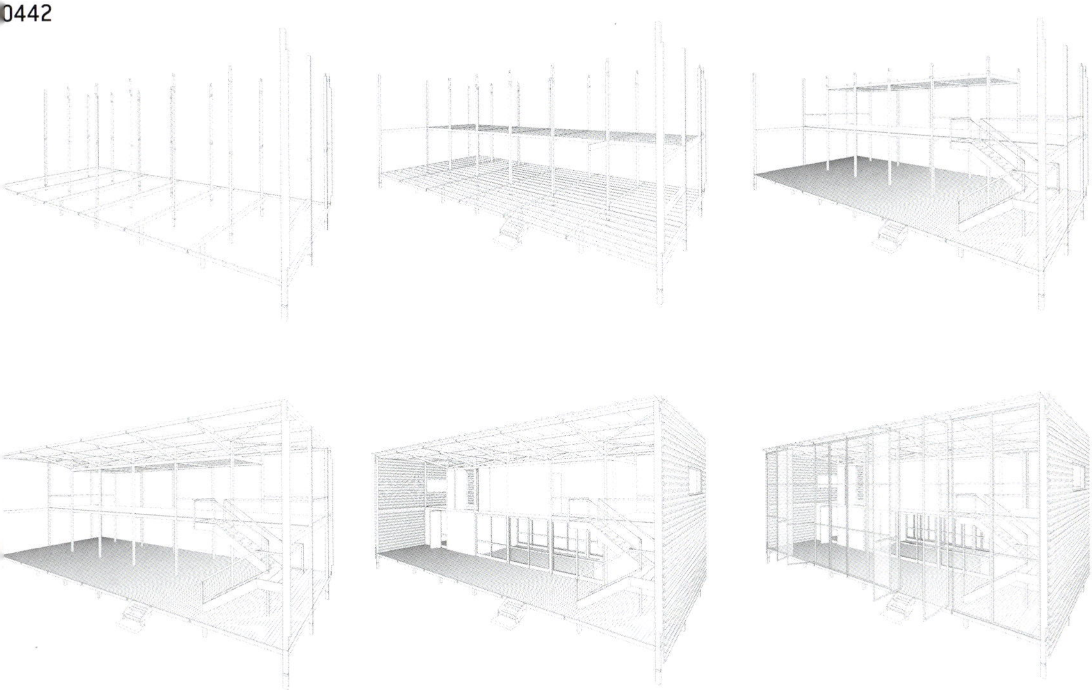

0443

0444

The edges of this indoor pool gradually flow upwards, to enable access to the hot tub. The great height of the glass pavilion allowed for this difference in levels, transforming the site into a complete home spa.

Le bord de cette piscine intérieure se prolonge en s'élevant progressivement afin de permettre l'accès au *jacuzzi*. La hauteur élevée du pavillon vitré permet d'avoir cette différence de niveaux, en transformant cet ouvrage en un véritable spa familial.

Der Rand dieses Hallenbads verläuft aufsteigend, um den Zugang zum Whirlpool zu ermöglichen. Die außergewöhnliche Höhe des Glaspavillons erlaubte diese unterschiedlichen Ebenen und machte das Projekt zu einem regelrechten Heim-Spa.

De rand van dit binnenzwembad loopt langzamerhand naar boven om de toegang tot de jacuzzi te vergemakkelijken. De grote hoogte van het paviljoen maakte dit niveauverschil mogelijk. Daardoor werd dit bouwwerk een echte huisspa.

0445

0446

0447

0448

0450

0451

0452

0453

0454

A low wall covered in the same blue mosaic tiles as on the bottom, divides this pool into a bathing area and an area which has Thalassotherapy water jets. This increases enjoyment of the pool, as it prevents excess movement in the water.

Le choix spécifique des carreaux et des tesselles donnent à cette piscine intérieure un aspect très élégant, entre le moderne et le classique. Leur association avec des éléments décoratifs traditionnels, tels que des amphores, est spectaculaire.

Eine mit den gleichen Mosaiksteinchen wie der Poolboden verkleidete Wand trennt hier den Badebereich von einem Becken mit Thalassotherapie-Massagestrahlen. Auf diese Weise wird das Schwimmen angenehmer, da ein übermäßiges Aufwühlen des Wassers vermieden wird.

Een muurtje dat bekleed werd met dezelfde blauwe mozaïeksteentjes scheidt dit zwembad in een badzone en een thalassotherapiezone met waterstralen. Deze maatregel zorgt ervoor dat men meer van het baden kan genieten omdat het water niet te veel beweegt.

0456

0457

0458

0459

0460

0461

Carefully chosen decorative glazed tiles and mosaic tiles give this indoor pool and extremely elegant look, somewhere between modern and classical. Combined with traditional decorative elements such as amphorae, they create a spectacular effect.

Le choix spécifique des carreaux et des tesselles donnent à cette piscine intérieure un aspect très élégant, entre le moderne et le classique. Leur association avec des éléments décoratifs traditionnels, tels que des amphores, est spectaculaire.

Die wohl überlegte Auswahl von Fliesen und Mosaiksteinchen verleiht diesem Hallenbad ein höchst elegantes Aussehen zwischen Moderne und Klassik. Die Kombination mit traditionellen Zierelementen wie Amphoren erzielt eine spektakuläre Wirkung.

Een verzorgde selectie tegels en mozaïeksteentjes verschaffen aan dit binnenzwembad een uiterst elegant uitzicht, zowel modern als klassiek. De combinatie met traditionele sierelementen, zoals de amforen, geeft een spectaculair resultaat.

0463

0464

0465

0466

0467

0468

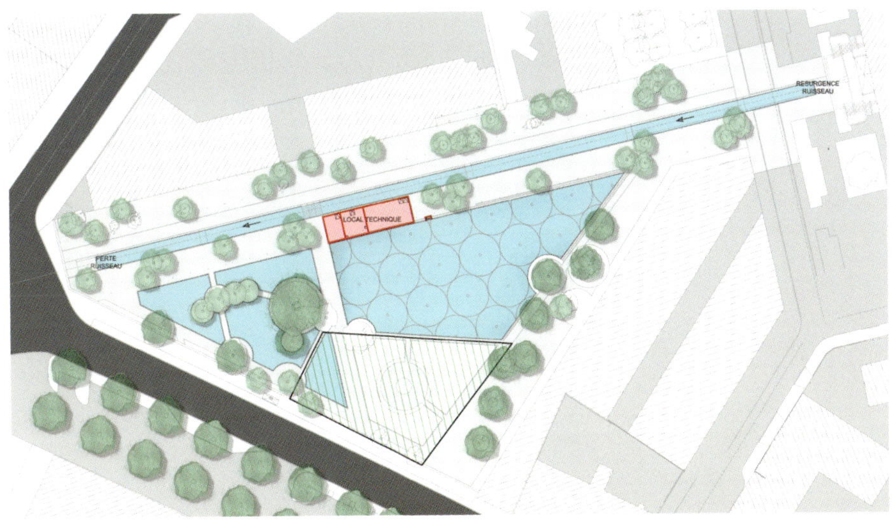

0469

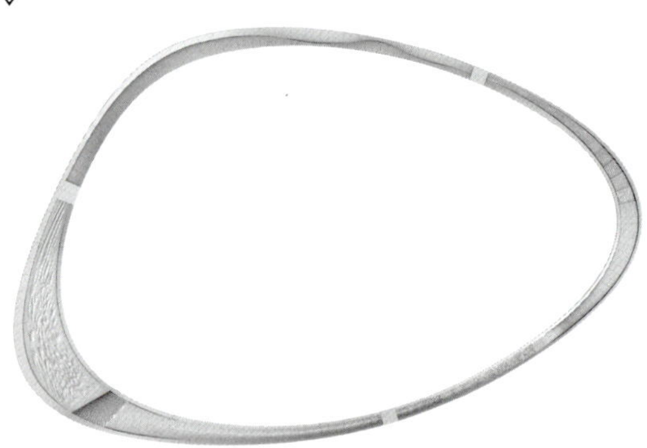

0470

0471

0472

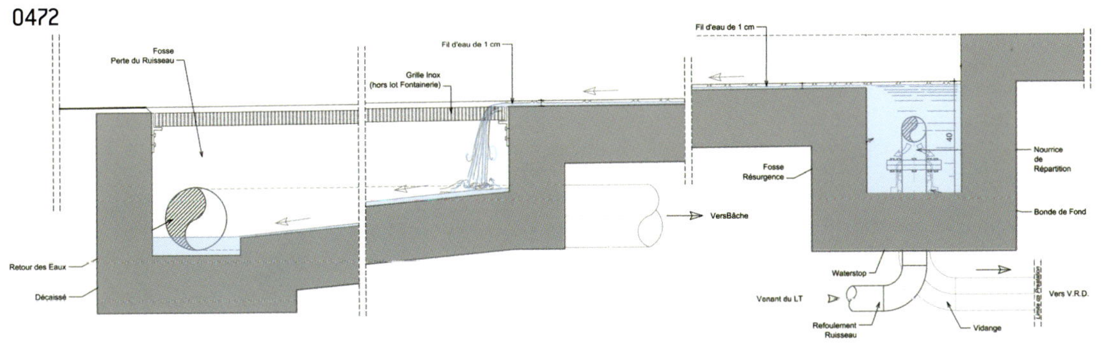

Fosse
Perte du Ruisseau
Grille Inox
(hors lot Fontainerie)
Fil d'eau de 1 cm
Fil d'eau de 1 cm
Retour des Eaux
Décaissé
VersBâche
Fosse
Résurgence
40
Nourrice
de
Répartition
Bonde de Fond
Waterstop
Venant du LT
Refoulement
Ruisseau
Vidange
Vers V.R.D.

Tanner Springs Park was designed as a space commemorating 200 years of the industrial past of this part of Portland. The site is characterized by the vegetation and the streams flowing into the pond. The detail shows a diagram of the water distribution system.

Pour le parc de Tanner Springs, Atelier Dreiseitl a pour projet de créer un espace mémorial des 200 ans de passé industriel de cette zone de Portland. Le site se caractérise par la végétation et les ruisseaux qui débouchent sur le bassin. Le détail présente un schéma du système de distribution de l'eau.

Für den Tanner Springs Park entwarf das Atelier Dreiseitl eine Fläche, die an die 200 Jahre der industriellen Vergangenheit dieser Gegend in Portland erinnern soll. Das Projekt zeichnet sich durch seine Vegetation und die Bäche, die zum Teich führen, aus. Die Detailansicht zeigt ein Schema des Systems zur Wasserumleitung.

Voor het park van Tanner Springs, projecteert het Atelier Dreiseitl een gedenkplaats voor het 200-jarig industrieel verleden van deze zone in Portland. De plaats wordt gekenmerkt door vegetatie en stroompjes die in de vijver uitkomen. Het detail toont een schema van het waterdistributiesysteem.

0473

>

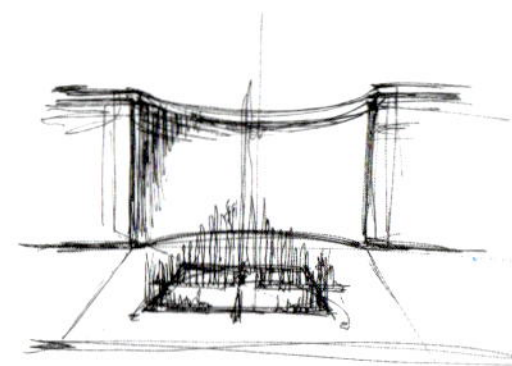

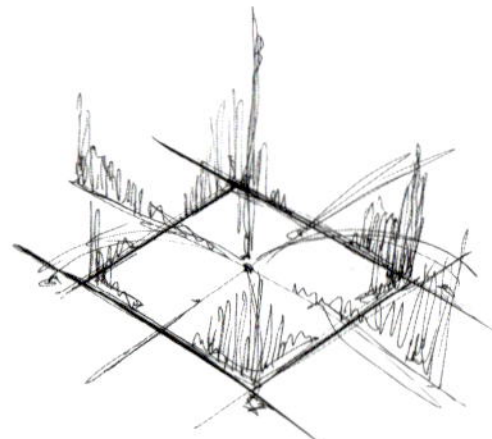

0475

0476

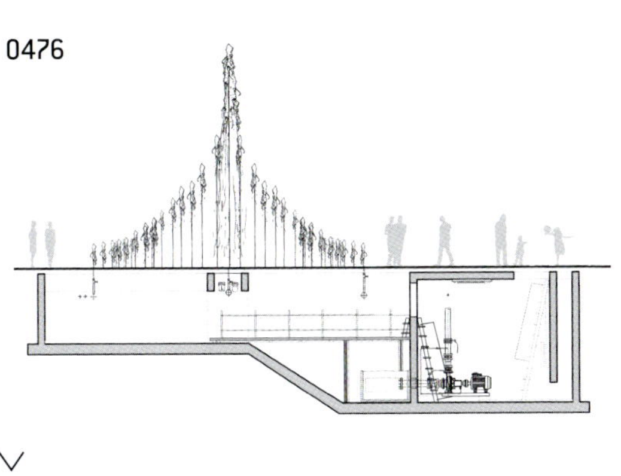

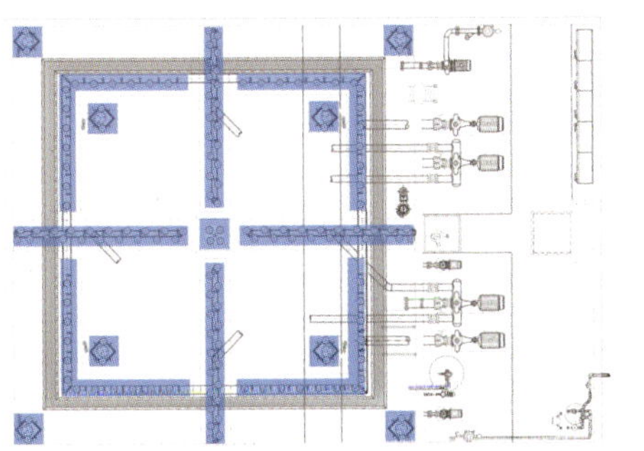

0477

0478

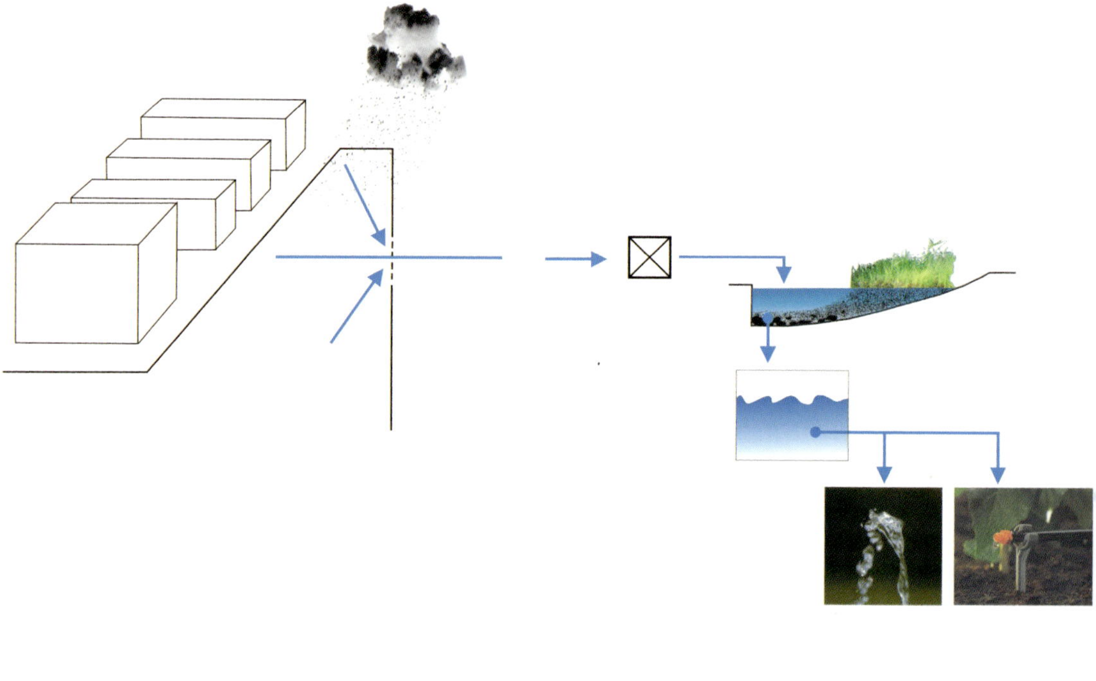

0479

0480

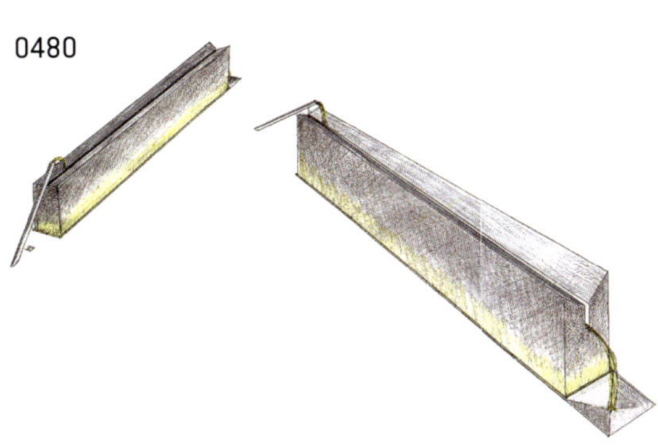

0481

0482

0483

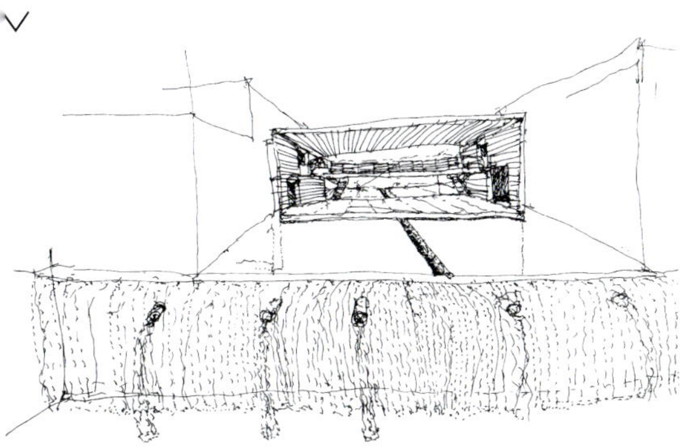

0484

0485

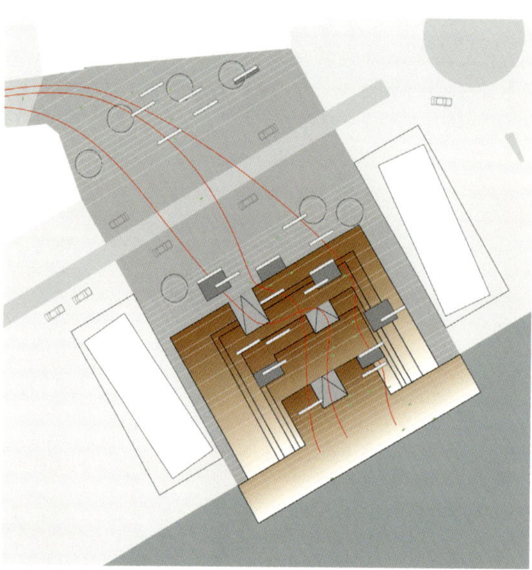

0486

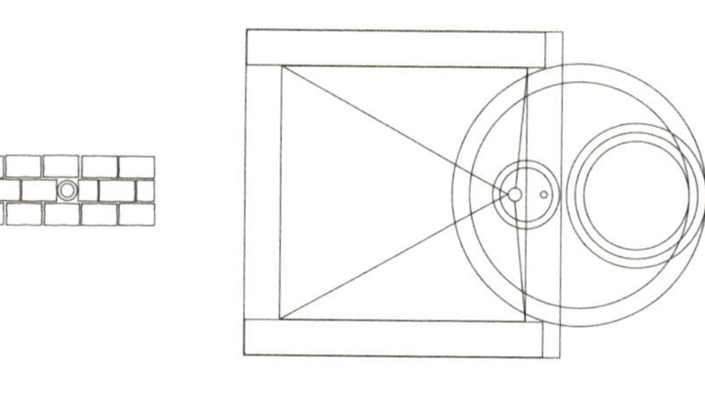

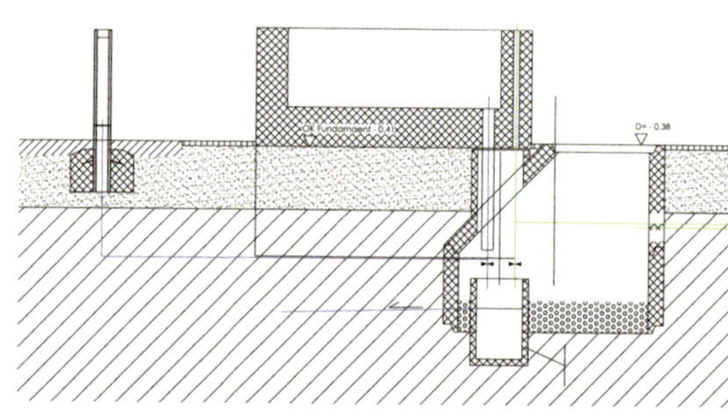

0487

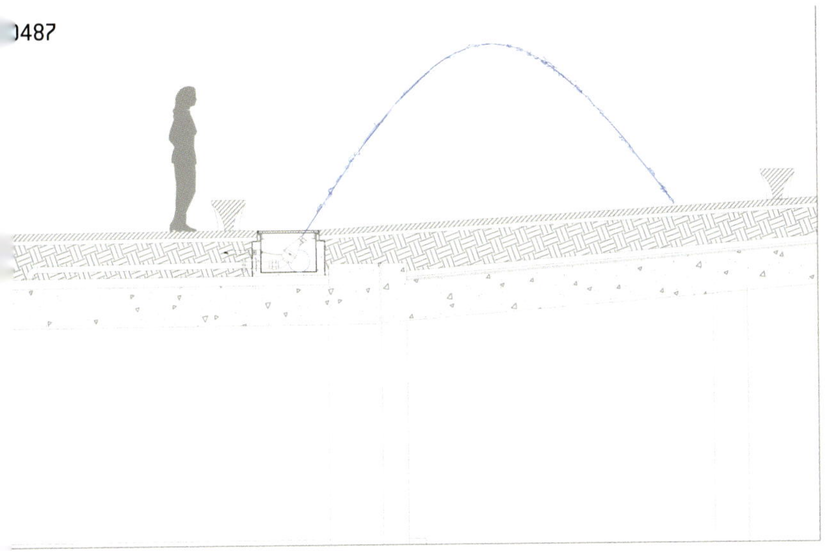

0488

This green area has gained space from a site previously occupied by homes in Enschede, Netherlands, which were destroyed by the explosion of a nearby fireworks factory. The design enhances the presence of water flowing through canals of differing widths (some over 7 m / 22 ft), where an asymmetric series of stone slabs allows easy movement from one side to the other.

Cet espace vert gagne de l'espace sur une zone auparavant occupée par des maisons à Enschede (Hollande), qui ont été Détruites par l'explosion d'une usine de pétards située à proximité. Le design favorise la présence d'eau conduite par des canaux à largeur variable (jusqu'à plus de 7 m), au sein desquels une série asymétrique de dalles en pierre permettent le passage de l'un à l'autre.

Diese Grünfläche gewinnt einem Bereich in Enschede (Niederlande) Raum ab, der ehemals von Wohnhäusern belegt war, welche bei einer Explosion in einer nahe gelegenen Feuerwerksfabrik zerstört wurden. Der Entwurf unterstreicht die Präsenz des Wassers, das durch Kanäle mit unterschiedlicher Breite (bis über 7 m) geleitet wird. Eine Reihe asymmetrisch angeordneter Steinplatten erlaubt das Überqueren der Kanäle.

Deze groenzone in Enschede (Nederland) wint terrein op een gebied dat voordien bebouwd was met huizen die vernietigd werden door de ontploffing van een nabijgelegen vuurwerkfabriek. Het ontwerp benadrukt de aanwezigheid van water door middel van kanalen van variabele breedten (tot maar dan 7 m), waarin een asymmetrische reeks stenen tegels de oversteek van de ene naar de andere kant mogelijk maakt.

0489

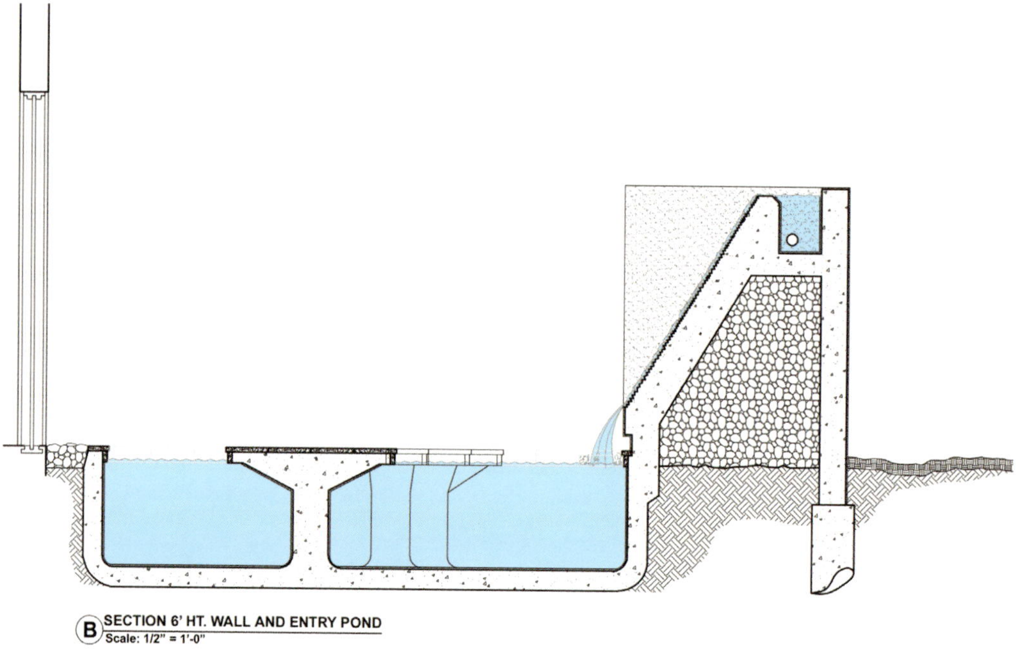

B SECTION 6' HT. WALL AND ENTRY POND
Scale: 1/2" = 1'-0"

0490

0491

0492

0493

0494

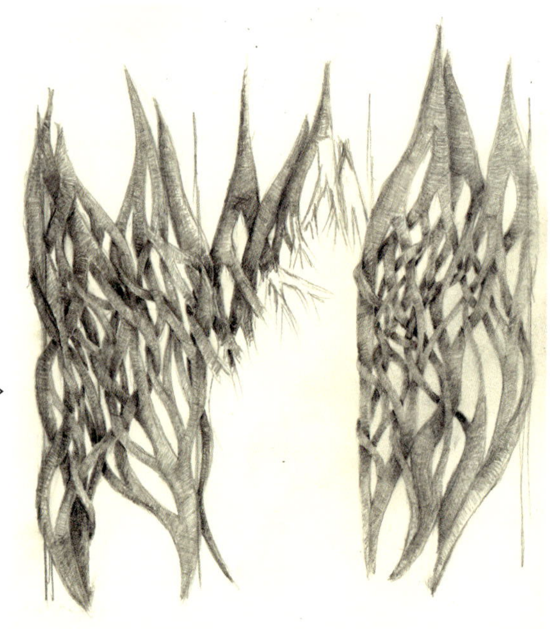

0495

0496

The pronounced slope on which the house is built incorporates the mountain as part of it while acting as a retaining wall. The rock appears in the lower-floor bathroom and in the living room, located in the entrance area on the upper floor.

Le dénivelé prononcé du terrain sur lequel est installée cette habitation permet à la montagne de pénétrer à l'intérieur de celle-ci pour devenir un mur de soutènement. La roche apparaît dans la salle de bains située au niveau inférieur, mais également dans le séjour, au niveau de la zone d'accès au niveau supérieur.

Aufgrund des deutlichen Gefälles des Grundstücks, auf dem das Wohngebäude errichtet wurde, tritt der Berg in das Haus ein und dient als Stützmauer. Der Fels dringt in das Badezimmer im Untergeschoss und in das Wohnzimmer im Obergeschoss ein.

Dankzij het uitgesproken niveauverschil van het terrein waarop de woning rust, dringt de berg de woning binnen en doet dienst als steunmuur. De rots is zichtbaar in de badkamer op de benedenverdieping evenals in de huiskamer, op het daarboven gelegen niveau.

0499

0500

0501

0502

0503

0505

0506

0507

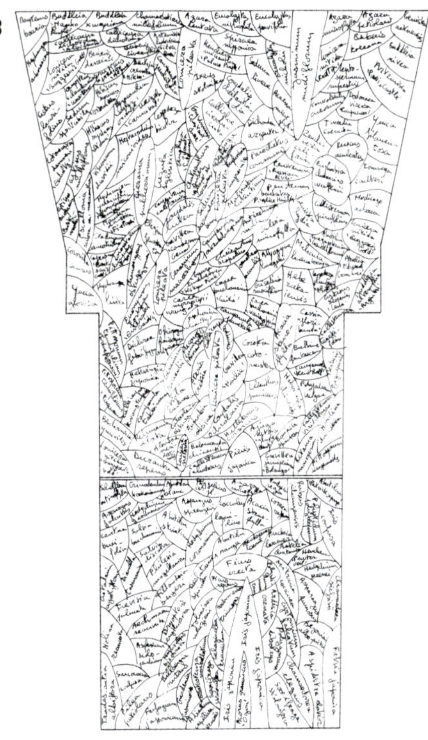
0508

For this small house located in Kobe, Japan, the architect's strategy was to highlight natural features to contrast with urban ones. This is a style that is typical of Japanese architecture, where natural features have a special presence on the inside and outside of the home.

Dans ce logement de taille réduite situé à Kobe, au Japon, l'architecte a misé sur le naturel plutôt que sur l'urbain. Une ressource, propre à l'architecture japonaise, où les éléments naturels à l'intérieur et à l'extérieur du logement sont d'une grande importance.

Bei diesem kleinen Wohnhaus in Kobe, Japan, setzte der Architekt auf die Betonung des Natürlichen im Gegensatz zum Urbanen. Dies ist ein besonderes Merkmal der japanischen Architektur, in der natürliche Elemente im Innen- und Außenbereich stets präsent sind.

Voor deze kleine woning in Kobe, Japan, koos de architect ervoor het natuurlijke tegenover het stedelijke te benadrukken. Dit is kenmerkend voor de Japanse architectuur, waarin natuurlijke elementen zowel in het interieur als aan de buitenkant van de woning duidelijk aanwezig zijn.

0509

0510

0511

0512

0513

0514

0515

0516

0517

0518

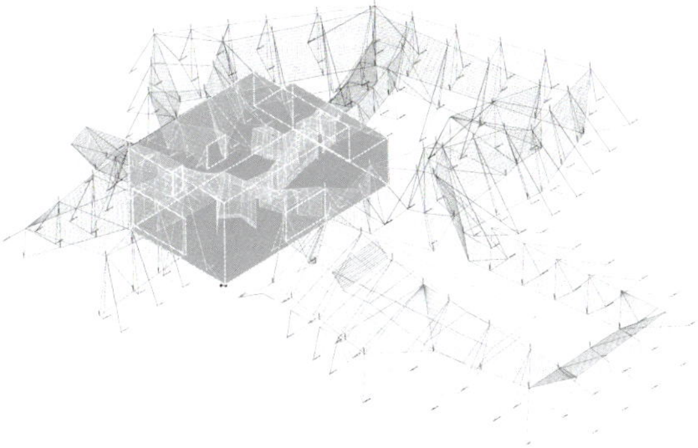

Water is the main feature of this garden located in the central courtyard of the new IBM offices in Amsterdam. A system of gradients on the landscaped slopes of the central courtyard transports the water to the lowest level, and there is a waterfall near to the pathway giving access to the site.

L'eau est l'élément clé de ce jardin situé dans le patio central du nouvel immeuble de bureaux d'IBM à Amsterdam. Sur le versant aménagé en jardin du patio central, un système de pentes transportant de l'eau jusqu'au niveau le plus bas a été mis en place, avec une chute d'eau à proximité de la passerelle d'entrée à l'enceinte.

Wasser ist das Hauptelement in diesem Garten im Innenhof des neuen IBM-Gebäudes in Amsterdam. Am begrünten Hang im Innenhof wurde ein System unterschiedlicher Gefälle angelegt, die das Wasser bis zur untersten Ebene leiten. In der Nähe des Stegs am Hofeingang befindet sich ein Wasserfall.

Water is het belangrijkste element in deze tuin in de binnenplaats van het nieuwe kantoorgebouw van IBM in Amsterdam. In de glooiende tuin van de binnenplaats werd gebruik gemaakt van een hellingssysteem dat het water naar het laagst gelegen deel voert, met een waterval aan de ingangspasserelle.

0519

0520

0521

0522

0523

0524

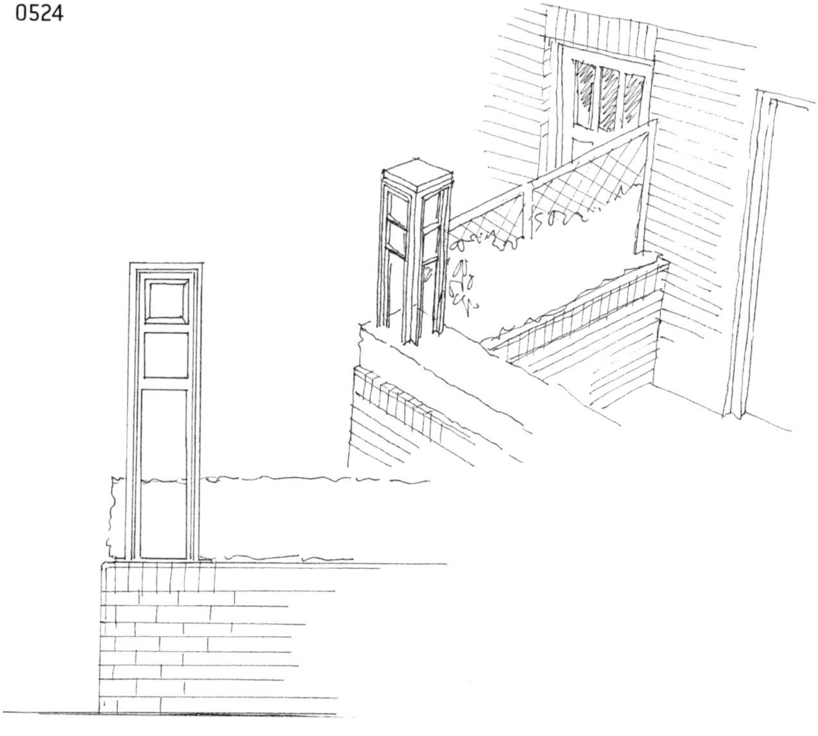

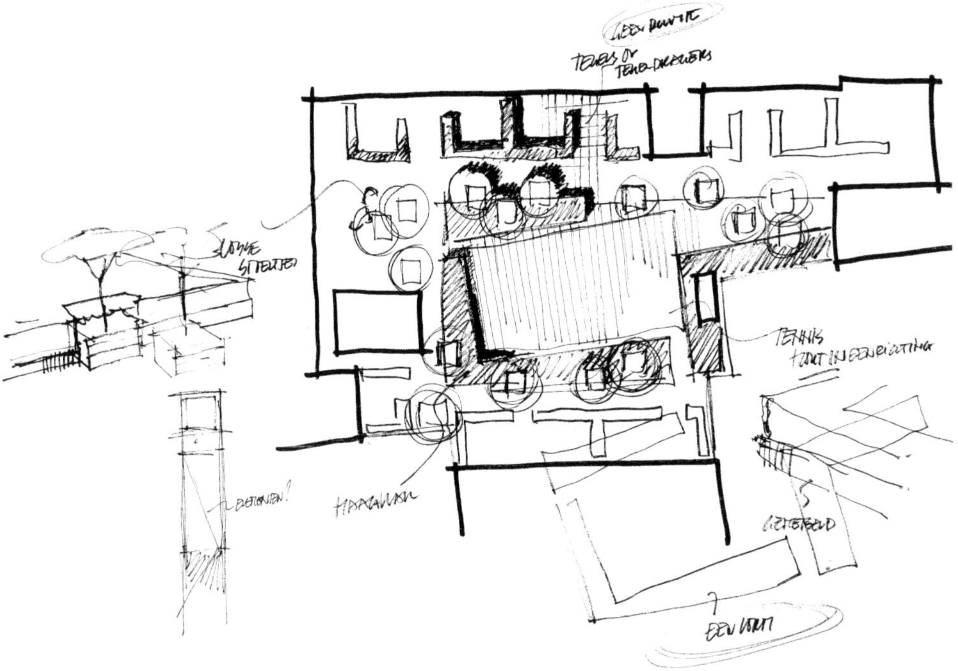

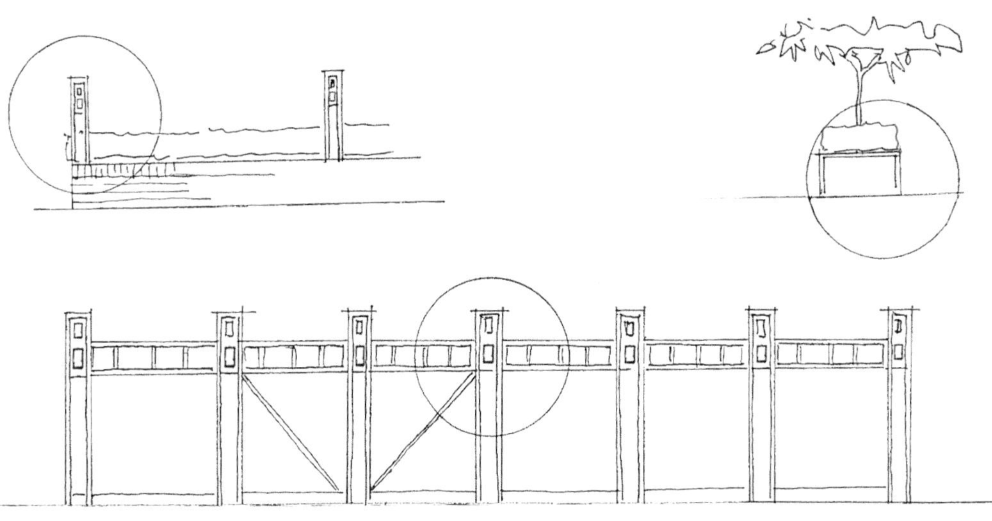

0525

0526

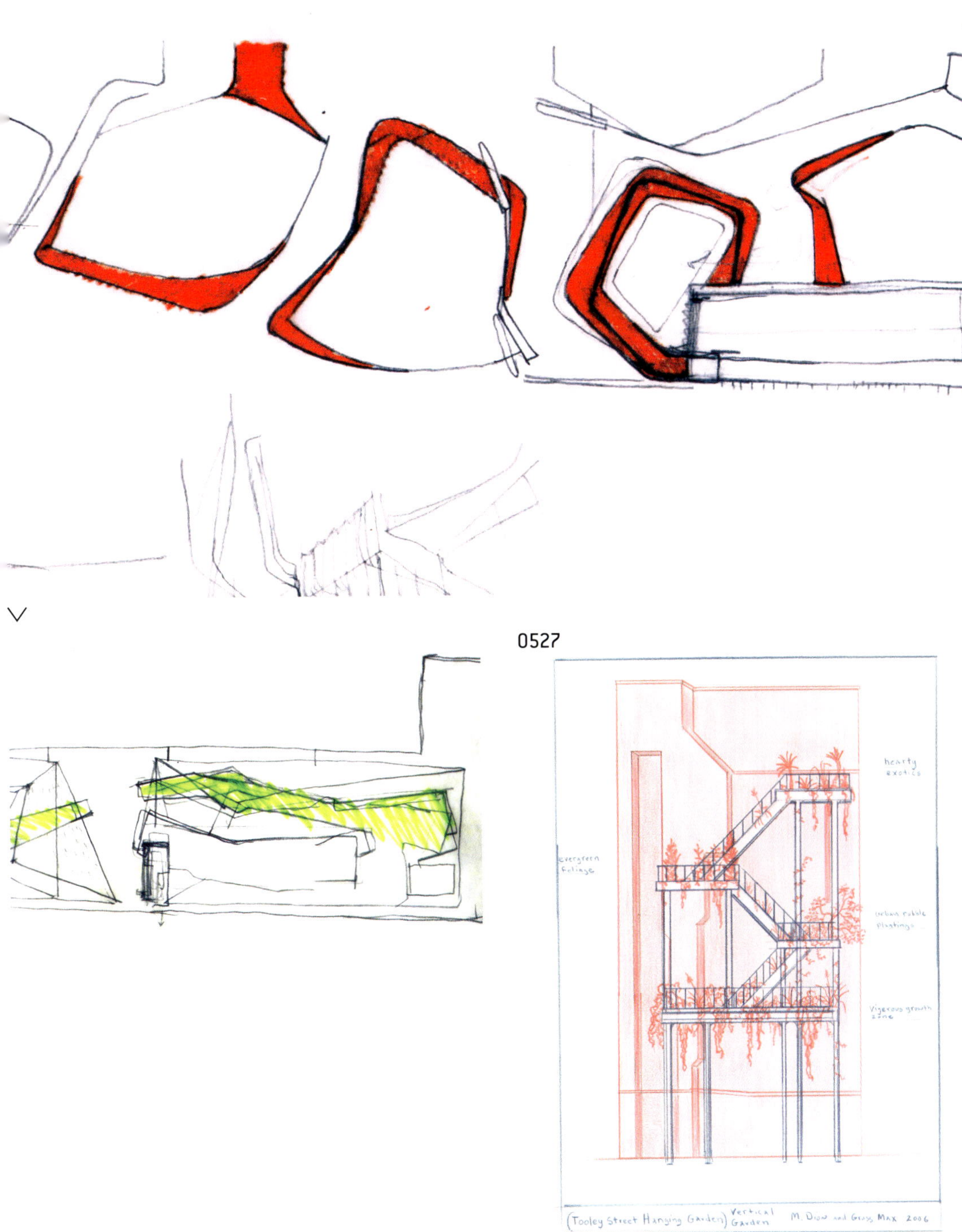
0527
hearty
exotics
evergreen
foliage
urban rubble
plantings
Vigerous growth
zone
(Tooley Street Hanging Garden) Vertical
Garden
M. Dion and Gross Max 2006

The materials used in this small garden in Brazil are granite, gravel, pebbles, and wood, as well as plant species such as *Ophiopogon japonicus* and *Phyllostachys heteroclytaforma*. The result is a space with geometric shapes where textures and colors alternate.

Les matériaux employés dans ce petit jardin au Brésil sont le granit, les gravillons, les galets et des espèces végétales comme l'*Ophiopogon japonicus* et le *Phyllostachys heteroclytaforma*. Le résultat offre un espace aux formes géométriques où les différentes textures et couleurs se marient.

Die in diesem kleinen Garten in Brasilien verwendeten Materialien sind Granit, Schotter, Kies, Holz und Pflanzen wie *Ophiopogon japonicus* und *Phyllostachys heteroclytaforma*. Das Ergebnis ist ein Raum mit geometrischen Formen, in dem sich unterschiedliche Texturen und Farben abwechseln.

De materialen die in deze kleine tuin in Brazilië gebruikt werden zijn graniet, grind, rolstenen, hout, en plantsoorten zoals *Ophiopogon japonicus* en *Phyllostachys heteroclytaforma*. Het resultaat is een ruimte met geometrische vormen waarin verschillende texturen en kleuren elkaar afwisselen.

0530

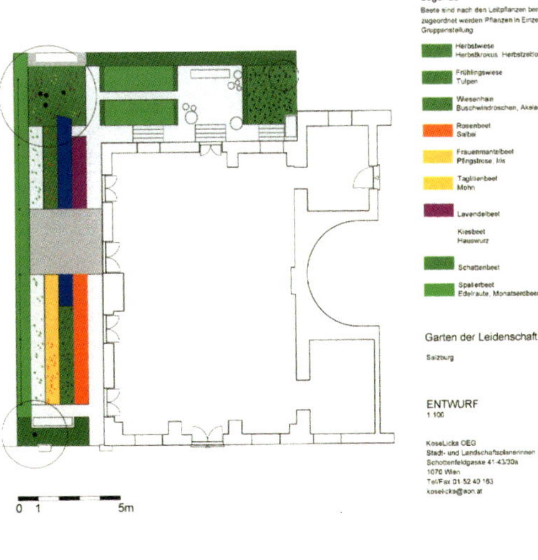
Legende
Beete sind nach den Leitpflanzen benannt, zugeordnet werden Pflanzen in Einzel- bzw Gruppenstellung
Herbstwiese
Herbstkrokus, Herbstzeitlose
Frühlingswiese
Tulpen
Wiesenhain
Buschwindröschen, Akelei, Veilchen
Rosenbeet
Salbei
Frauenmantelbeet
Pfingstrose, Iris
Taglilienbeet
Mohn
Lavendelbeet
Kiesbeet
Hauswurz
Schattenbeet
Spalierbeet
Edelraute, Monatserdbeere
Garten der Leidenschaft
Salzburg
ENTWURF
1:100
KoseLicka OEG
Stadt- und Landschaftsplanerinnen
Schottenfeldgasse 41-43/30a
1070 Wien
Tel/Fax 01 52 40 183
koselicka@aon.at
0 1 5m

0531

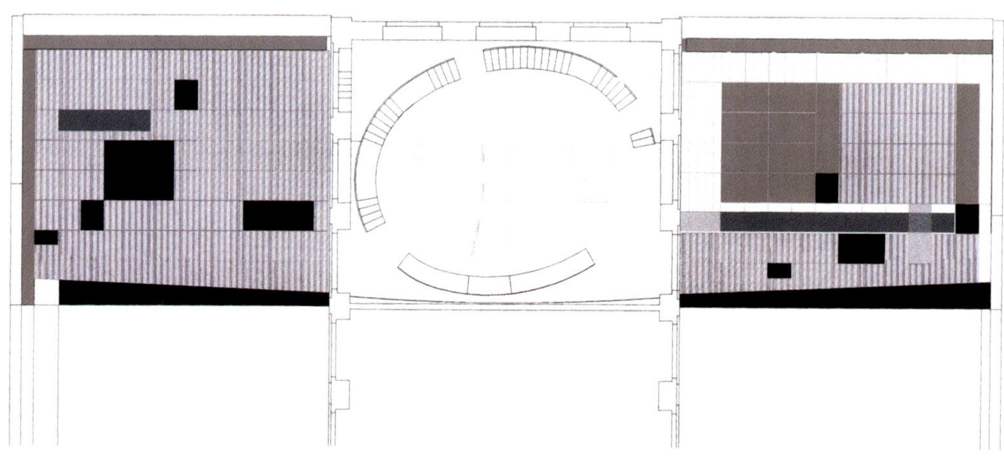

0532

0533

0534

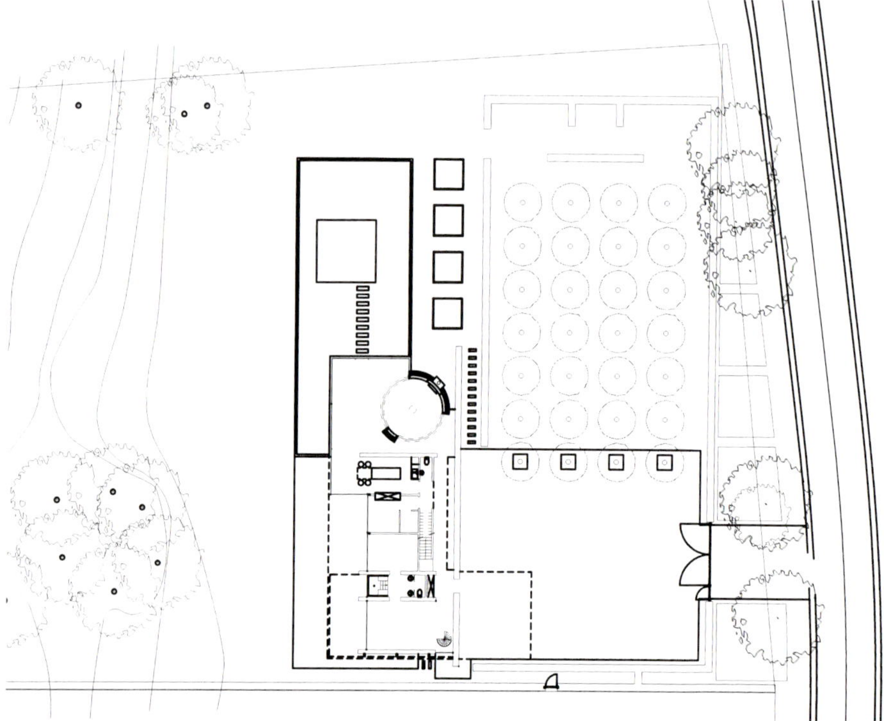

0535

0536

>

The structure of metal pillars providing shade to this area of a public square is practically a substitute for vegetation. In fact, its color scheme and the tree shapes formed by the slats are indicative of this function.

La structure en piliers métalliques qui fournit de l'ombre à cette zone d'une place publique devient presque un substitut à la végétation. D'ailleurs, son apparence chromatique et la forme arborescente de ses lames soulignent cette fonction.

Die Struktur aus Metallpfeilern, die diesem Bereich eines öffentlichen Platzes Schatten spendet, wirkt beinahe wie eine Ersatz-Vegetation. Die Farbwirkung und die verzweigten Lamellen unterstreichen diese Funktion.

De structuur van metalen zuilen die aan deze zone van een openbaar plein schaduw verschaft, lijkt bijna een substituut voor de vegetatie. Het chromatische uitzicht en de boomvorm van de platen benadrukken deze functie trouwens duidelijk.

0538

0539

0540 >

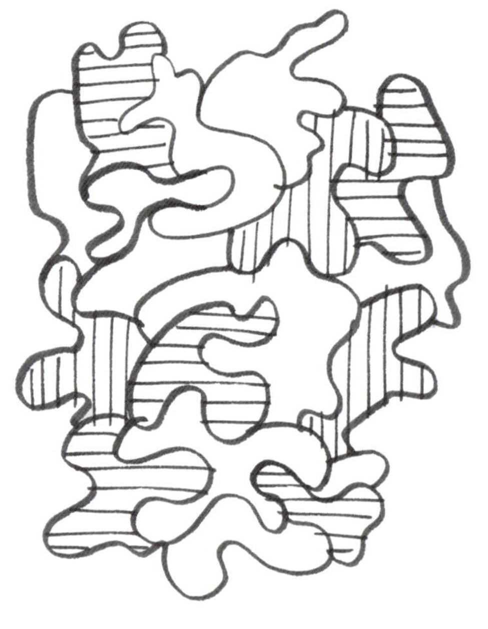

0541 >

0542

0543

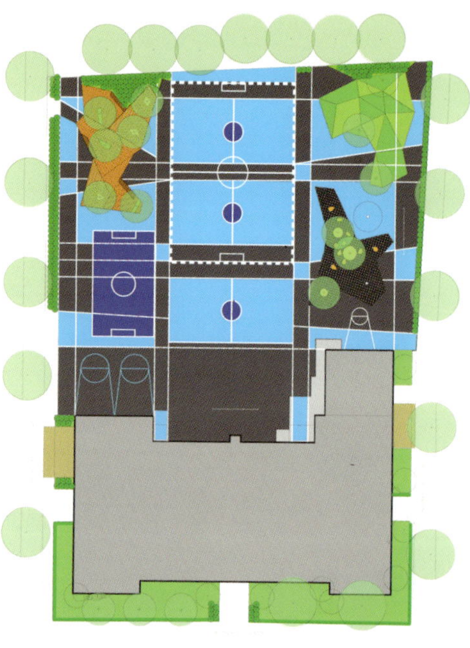

0544

0545

>

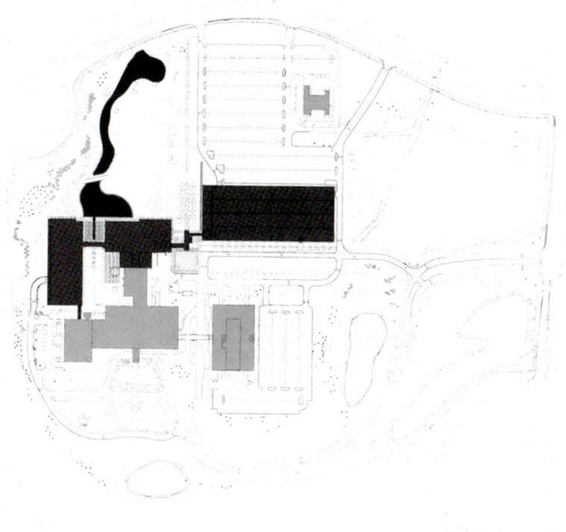

The illuminated walls and overhangs create and demarcate meeting areas and spaces for different activites. In this square, various architectural resources were used, such as roof structures, illuminated walls and built-in furniture, circular benches, and green hedges as dividers.

Les murs illuminés et les structures en porte-à-faux créent et délimitent des zones destinées aux regroupements de personnes ou à la pratique de diverses activités. Différents recours architecturaux ont été utilisés sur cette place, tels que des auvents, des murs avec éclairage et mobilier encastré, des bancs circulaires et des haies.

Die beleuchteten Mauern und die Vorsprünge erzeugen und begrenzen Bereiche für Zusammentreffen und die Ausübung diverser Aktivitäten. An diesem Platz wurden verschiedene architektonische Mittel eingesetzt, wie z. B. Markisen, Mauern mit Lichtelementen und eingebautem Mobiliar, runde Sitzbänke und grüne Hecken.

De verlichte muren en de uitsteeksels genereren en begrenzen zones voor samenkomsten of diverse activiteiten. Op dit plein werden diverse architectonische middelen gebruikt zoals luifels, muren met verlichting en ingebouwd meubilair, ronde banken en groene hagen.

0546

0547

0548

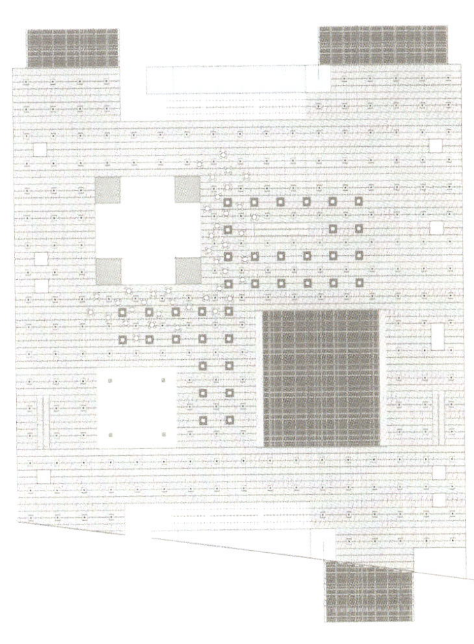

0549

0550

0551

0552

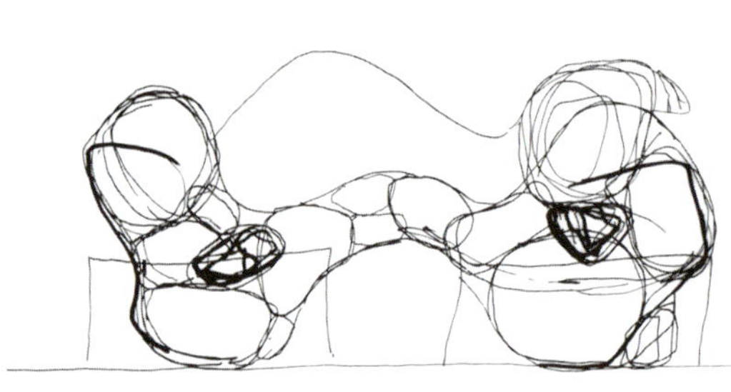

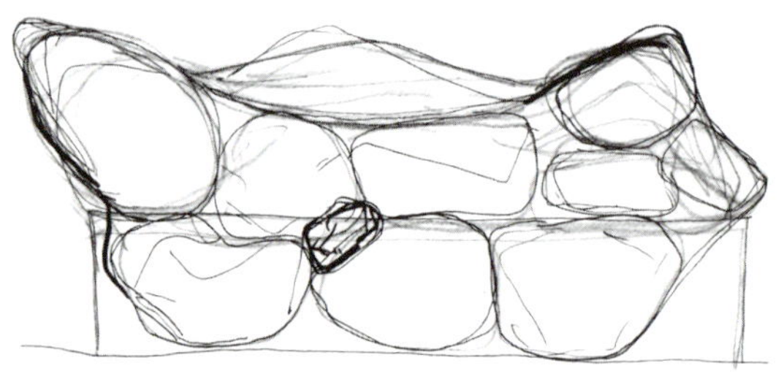

0553

0554

>

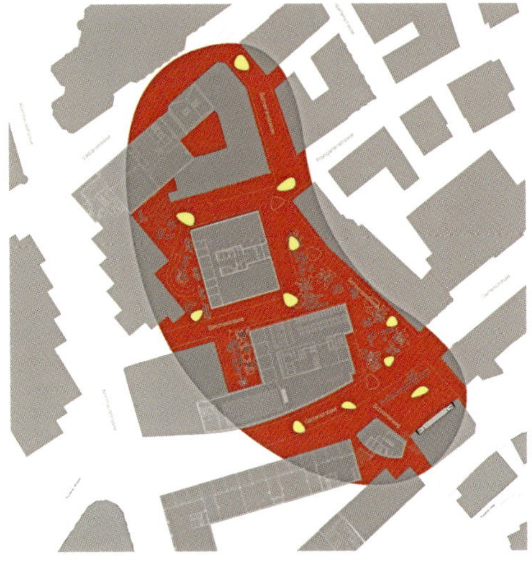

Water is an ever-present feature in the design of this space; the water jets were laid out to reflect the geometry of the architecture. These create controlled volumes of water and are inserted between the benches, the lines of which soften the forms.

L'eau est un élément omniprésent dans la conception de cet espace et les jets ont été pensés pour refléter la géométrie de l'ensemble architectural. Ceux-ci forment des volumes d'eau étudiés qui passent entre les bancs, dont les lignes atténuent les formes.

Das Element Wasser ist im Entwurf dieses öffentlichen Raums allgegenwärtig. Die Wasserstrahlen sollen die Geometrie des Bauensembles widerspiegeln. Sie bilden genau kalkulierte Wassermengen und wurden zwischen den Sitzbänken platziert, deren Linienführung die Formen nuanciert.

Water is een alomtegenwoordig element in het ontwerp van deze ruimte; de stralen werden zodanig bedacht dat ze de geometrie van het architectonisch geheel weerspiegelen. Deze vormen bestudeerde watervolumes die tussen de banken, die de vormen nuanceren, doorlopen.

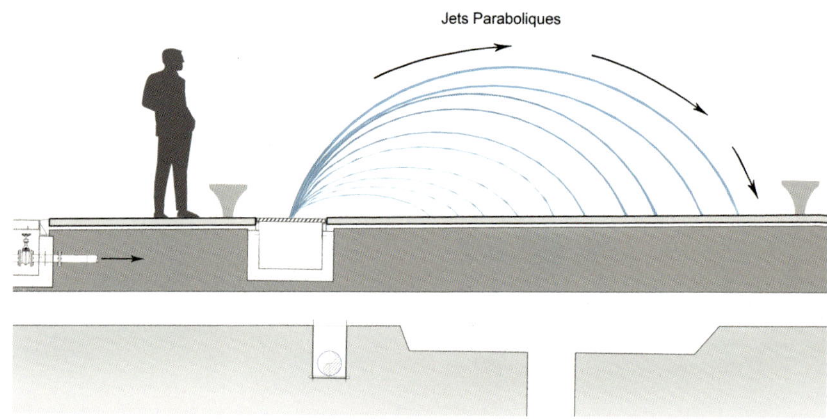

556

✓

0557

HORIZONTAL AND VERTICAL CONNECTIONS

COMMUNICATION HORIZONTALE ET VERTICALE
HORIZONTALE UND VERTIKALE VERBINDUNGEN
HORIZONTALE EN VERTICALE COMMUNICATIE

0558

0559

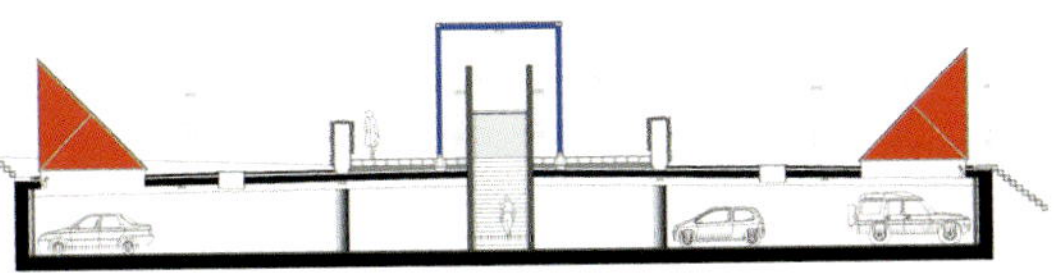

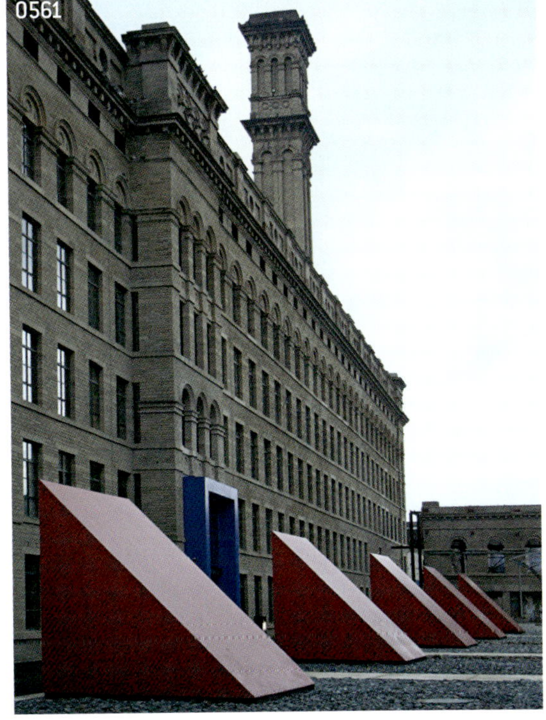

0562

0563

>

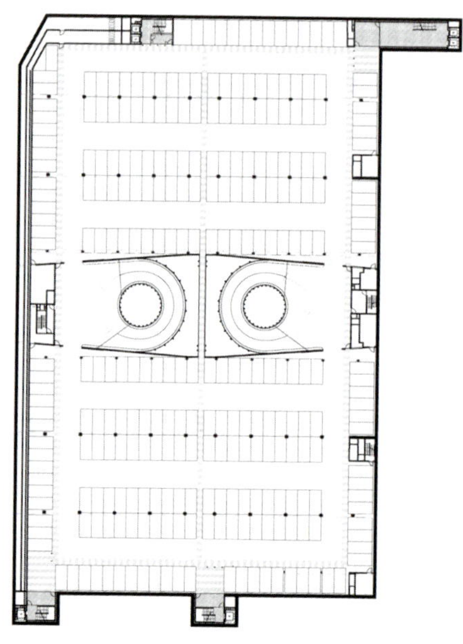

0564

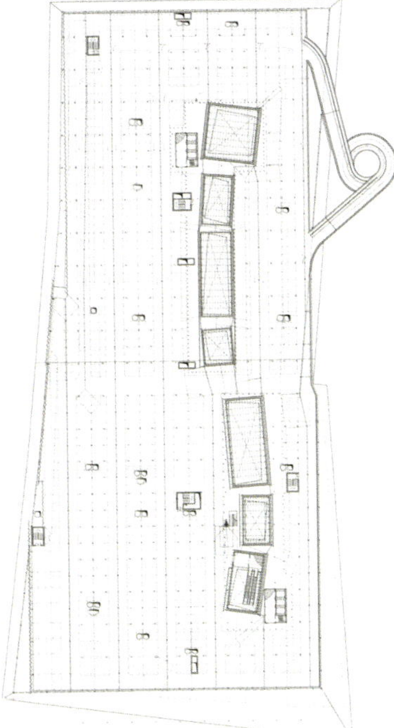

0565

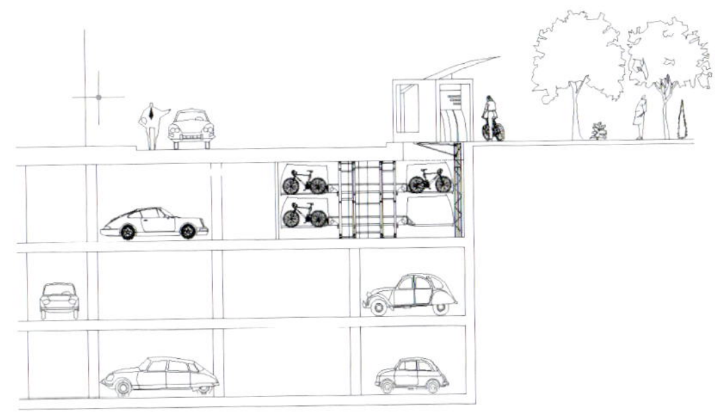

The car park has a central courtyard with two emergency staircases on the ends. This central void permits ventilation and the entry of daylight. The concrete framework has an oval-shaped surface, allowing circulation in the center as well as parking spaces at both sides.

L'envie de grimper aux arbres fait de cette maison-arbre un endroit idéal pour les enfants et une zone de détente pour les adultes. Dans la salle de repos, deux des arbres soutenant cette structure apparaissent entre des coussins, comme un invité qui se souviendrait à chaque instant de la raison qui a motivé cette construction.

Das Parkhaus verfügt über einen Innenhof, an dessen Enden sich zwei Nottreppen befinden. Dieser Innenhof ermöglicht die Belüftung und den Einfall von Tageslicht. Das Betongerüst beschreibt eine ovale Fläche und erlaubt den Fußgängerverkehr im Zentrum und die Nutzung von Parkplätzen auf beiden Seiten.

De parkeergarage beschikt over een binnenplaats die aan de uiteinden begrensd wordt door de twee noodtrappen. Deze centrale opening zorgt voor ventilatie en de inval van natuurlijk licht. Dit betonnen geraamte heeft een ovale oppervlakte en zorgt voor circulatie in het midden met parkeerplaatsen aan beide kanten.

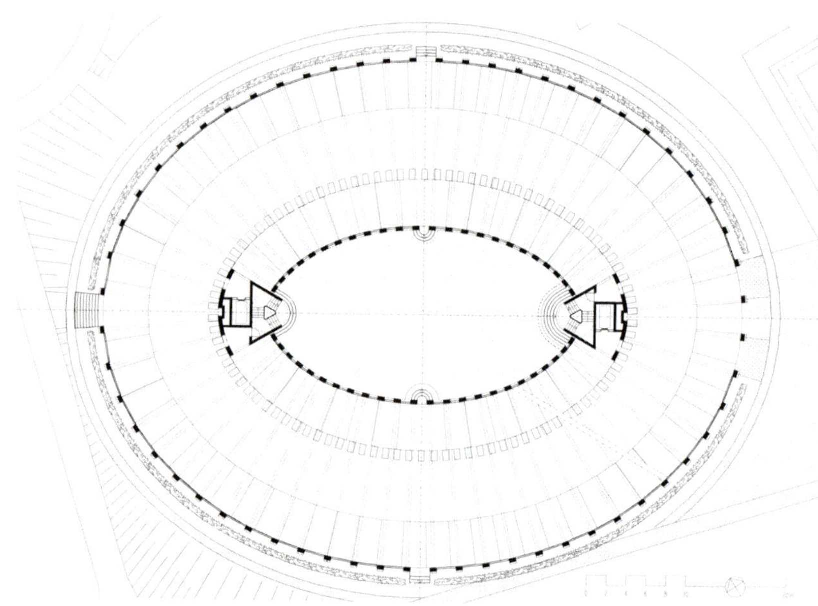

0567

0568

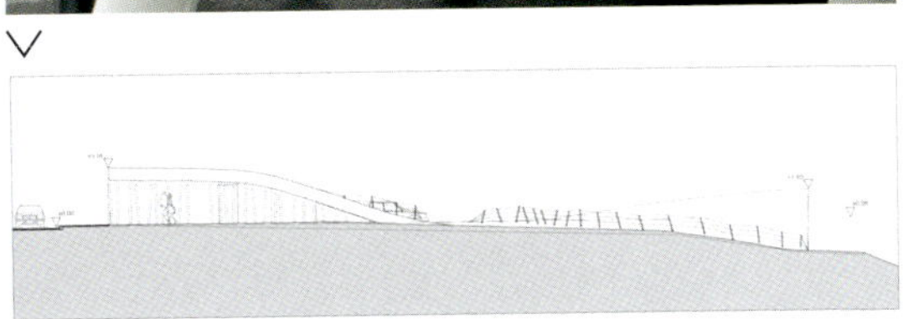

0569

0570

0571

0572

0573

0574

0575

0576

0577

0578

0579

0580

0581

0582

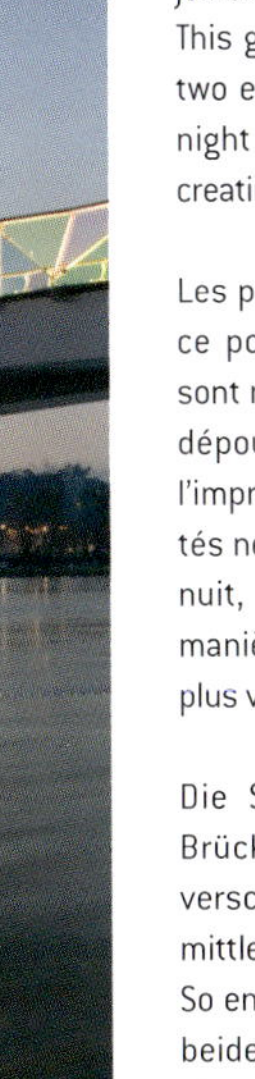

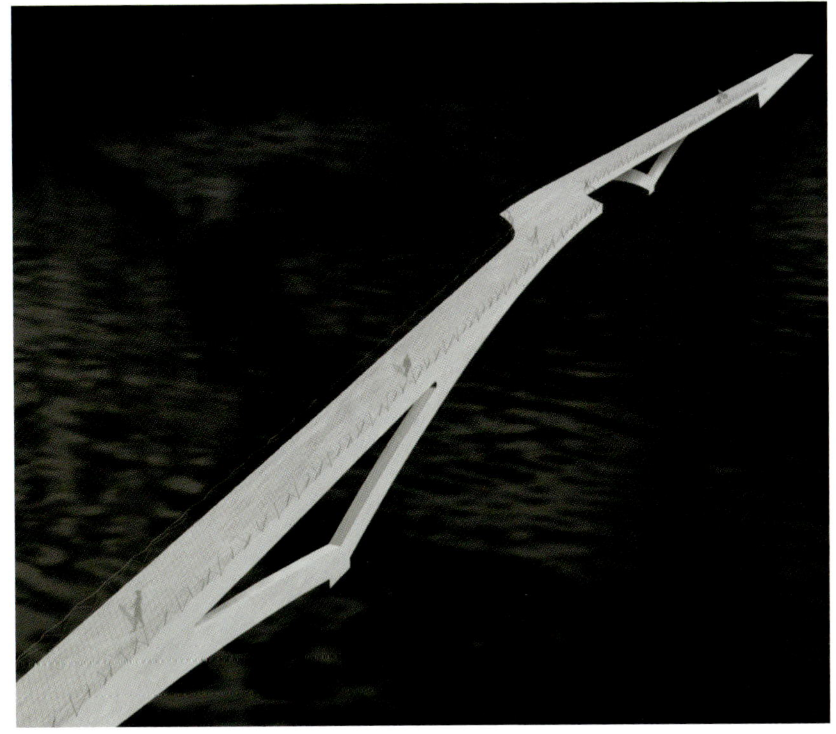

The walkways of this bridge structure appear to be dislocated and are joined in a pillar-free central span. This gives the impression that the two ends do not meet. During the night the railings are illuminated, creating a rainbow of colors.

Les passerelles de la structure de ce pont semblent disloquées et sont reliées à une section centrale dépourvue de piliers. Ceci donne l'impression que les deux extrémités ne se touchent pas. Pendant la nuit, la rambarde est éclairée de manière à produire les couleurs les plus variées.

Die Stege der Struktur dieser Brücke scheinen gegeneinander verschoben und vereinen sich im mittleren Bereich ohne Stützpfeiler. So entsteht der Eindruck, dass die beiden Brückenenden nicht aufeinander treffen. Nachts wird das Geländer beleuchtet und lockt mit einem heiteren Farbenspiel.

De passerelles van deze brugstructuur lijken van elkaar losgekoppeld te zijn en komen samen op een middendeel zonder zuilen. Dit feit geeft de indruk dat de twee uiteinden elkaar niet raken. 's Nachts wordt de leuning verlicht waardoor een uitgebreid gamma verschillende kleuren gegenereerd wordt.

0583

0584

0585

0586

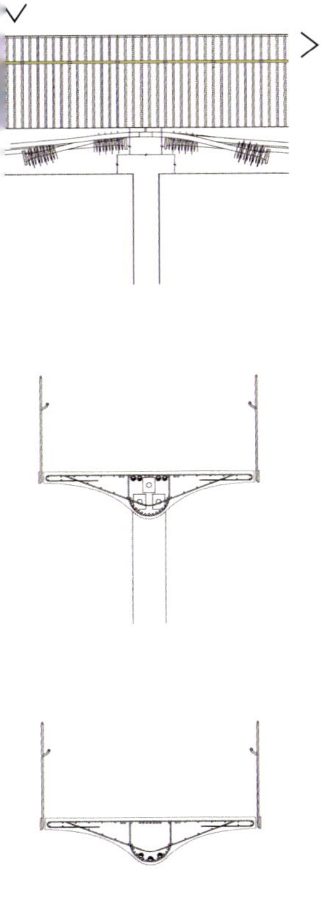

0587

0588

0589

0590

The lake in Parque de Beja, Portugal, features a number of walkways, pavilions and terraces, which protect from the sun and invite visitors to relax. Concrete is the predominant material of the structures.

Des passerelles, des pavillons et des terrasses se trouvent au-dessus du lac du Parque de Beja (Portugal) en protégeant du soleil et en invitant au repos. Le matériau utilisé est le béton qui domine la plupart des constructions.

Über den See im Park von Beja (Portugal) erstrecken sich mehrere Stege, Pavillons und Terrassen, die die Besucher vor der Sonne schützen und zum Ausruhen einladen. Beim verwendeten Material handelt es sich um Beton, der bei den meisten Strukturen vorherrscht.

Over het meer in het Park van Beja (Portugal) lopen enkele passerelles, paviljoenen en terrassen die tegen de zon beschermen en uitnodigen tot rust. Het gebruikte materiaal is beton, dat in de meeste constructies overheerst.

0591

0592

0593

0594

0595

0596

0597

0598

0599

0600

0601

>

0602

This house located in Colonia Roma in Mexico City and dating from 1916 features central wrought-iron staircase in Art Nouveau-style. This vertical access leads to 6 apartments laid out over 2 floors.

Dans cette ancienne maison de 1916, située dans le quartier de Colonia Roma à Mexico D.F., un escalier a été construit en fer forgé dans le style Art Nouveau. Cet escalier vertical permet d'accéder aux 6 appartements répartis sur 2 étages.

Diese im Bezirk Colonia Roma in Mexiko-City gelegene alte Villa wurde 1916 unter Verwendung einer zentralen schmiedeeisernen Treppe im Stil des Art Nouveau erbaut. Dieser vertikale Zugang führt zu den 6 Wohnungen, die sich auf 2 Etagen verteilen.

In dit oude herenhuis van 1916, gelegen in het district Colonia Roma in Mexico D.F., werd een centrale smeedijzeren trap gebouwd in Art-nouveaustijl. Deze verticale toegangsweg geeft uit op de 6 appartementen, verdeeld over 2 verdiepingen.

0603

0604

0605

0606

>

0607

0608

0609

0610

0611

0612

0613

0614

>

0615

0616

The originality of the staircase in this duplex lies not only in the way the steps are anchored to the wall, but also in the way it turns on a 90-degree angle, forming a small landing with a slightly wider platform, made of the same material.

L'escalier de ce duplex possède non seulement des marches fixées directement au mur, mais tourne également de manière très originale en angle de 90 degrés, en formant un petit palier avec une plateforme un peu plus large faite dans le même matériau.

Der besondere Reiz der Treppe in dieser Maisonettewohnung liegt neben der Befestigung der Stufen an der Wand in der 90-Grad-Drehung, in deren Verlauf ein kleines Podest aus dem Stufenmaterial eingebaut wurde.

Bij de trap van deze duplex is, naast de bevestiging van de trappen in de muur, ook de wending van 90 graden zeer origineel omdat zo een klein trapportaal gevormd wordt met een iets breder platform uit hetzelfde materiaal.

>

0619

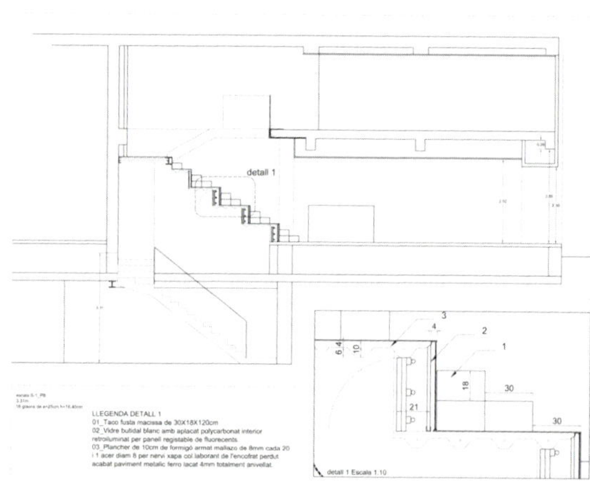

detall 1
LLEGENDA DETALL 1
01_Taco fusta macissa de 30X18X120cm
02_Vidre butidal blanc amb aplacat polycarbonat interior retroiluminat per panell registable de fluorecents
03_Plancher de 10cm de formigó armat mallazo de 8mm cada 20 i 1 acer diam 8 per nervi xapa col laborant de l'encofrat perdut acabat paviment metalic ferro lacat 4mm totalment anivellat.
detall 1 Escala 1.10

0620

0621

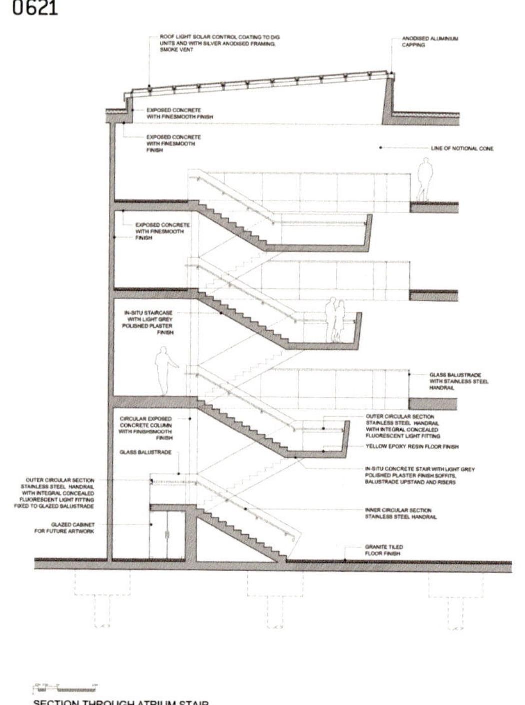

SECTION THROUGH ATRIUM STAIR

0622

0623

0624

0625

0626

The stairwell of this penthouse is protected by simple metal banisters on three sides. To make this feature less of a focal point, the wall side has no protection.

Dans cet appartement sous les toits, la cage d'escalier est protégée sur trois côtés par de simples rampes métalliques. Pour alléger le poids visuel de cette structure, le côté donnant sur le mur a été laissé sans protection.

In dieser Dachwohnung ist der Treppenaufgang an drei Seiten durch ein einfaches Metallgeländer geschützt. Um die optische Wirkung dieser Struktur etwas zu reduzieren, wurde an der Wandseite kein Geländer installiert.

In deze penthouse wordt het trapgat aan drie kanten afgeschermd door enkele eenvoudige metalen balustrades. Om de visuele impact van deze structuur te beperken, werd de kant die op de muur uitgeeft onbeschermd gelaten.

0627

0628

0629

0630

0631

0632

0633

0634

0635

0636

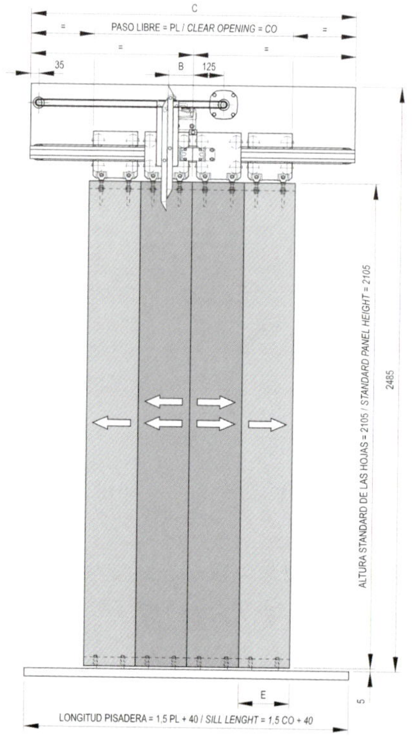
C
=
PASO LIBRE = PL / CLEAR OPENING = CO
=
=
=
35
B
125
ALTURA STANDARD DE LAS HOJAS = 2105 / STANDARD PANEL HEIGHT = 2105
2485
E
5
LONGITUD PISADERA = 1,5 PL + 40 / SILL LENGHT = 1,5 CO + 40

0637

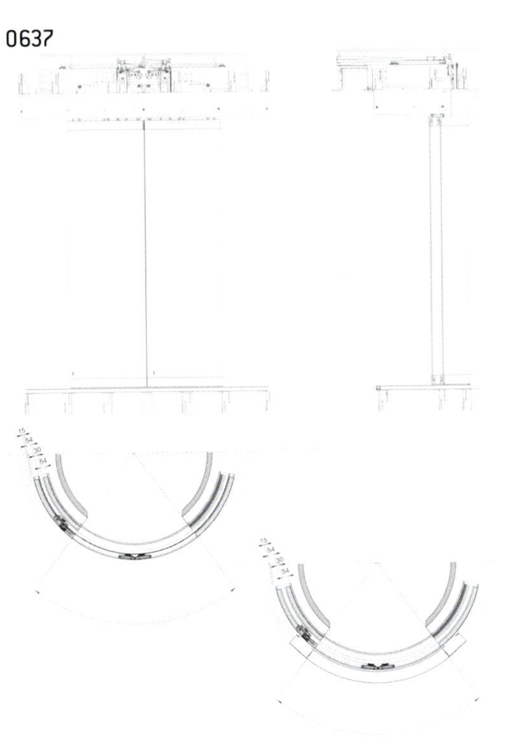

0638

0639

Fermator is a world leader in the manufacture of elevator doors. In this case, an elevator was installed in the National Art Museum of Catalonia (MNAC) with its main feature being a 2-panel telescopic glass door.

La compagnie Fermator est l'un des leaders mondiaux dans la fabrication de portes pour ascenseur. Dans cet exemple, elle a installé, dans le Musée National d'Art de Catalogne (MNAC), un ascenseur dont la principale caractéristique est la porte télescopique à 2 battants entièrement vitrée.

Fermator ist ein weltweit führendes Unternehmen im Bereich der Fertigung von Aufzugtüren. Hier wurde im Katalanischen Museum für Kunst (MNAC) ein Aufzug installiert, dessen Hauptmerkmal in der vollverglasten Teleskoptür mit 2 Blättern besteht.

Fermator is wereldwijd een toonaangevend bedrijf in de fabricage van liftdeuren. In dit geval, voor het Nationaal Kunstmuseum van Catalonië (MNAC), werd een lift geinstalleerd met als hoofdkenmerk de telescopische volledig glazen tweevleugelige deur.

0640

0641

0642

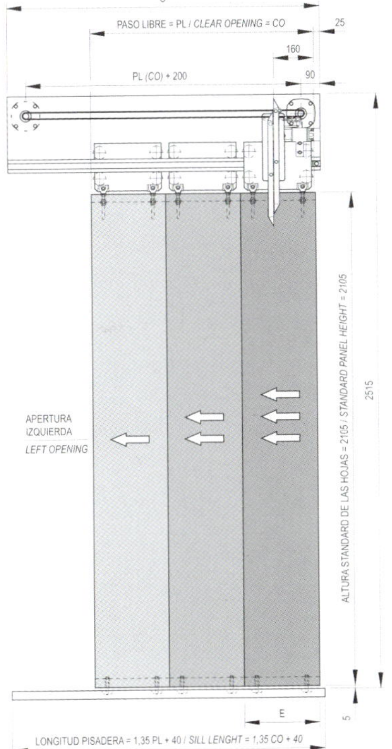

PASO LIBRE = PL / *CLEAR OPENING = CO*
25
160
PL (CO) + 200
90
APERTURA IZQUIERDA
LEFT OPENING
ALTURA STANDARD DE LAS HOJAS = 2105 / *STANDARD PANEL HEIGHT = 2105*
2515
E
5
LONGITUD PISADERA = 1,35 PL + 40 / *SILL LENGHT = 1,35 CO + 40*

0643

0644

0645

0646

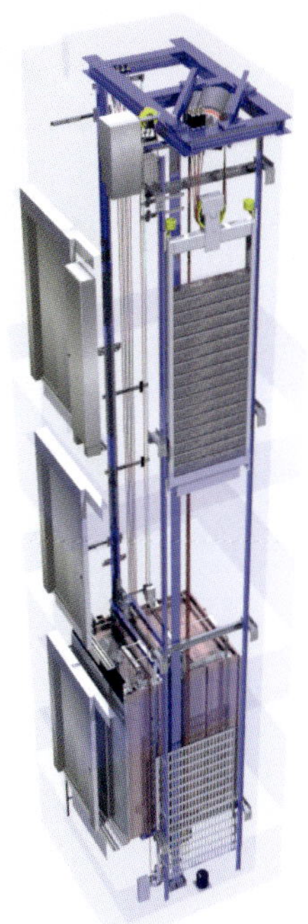

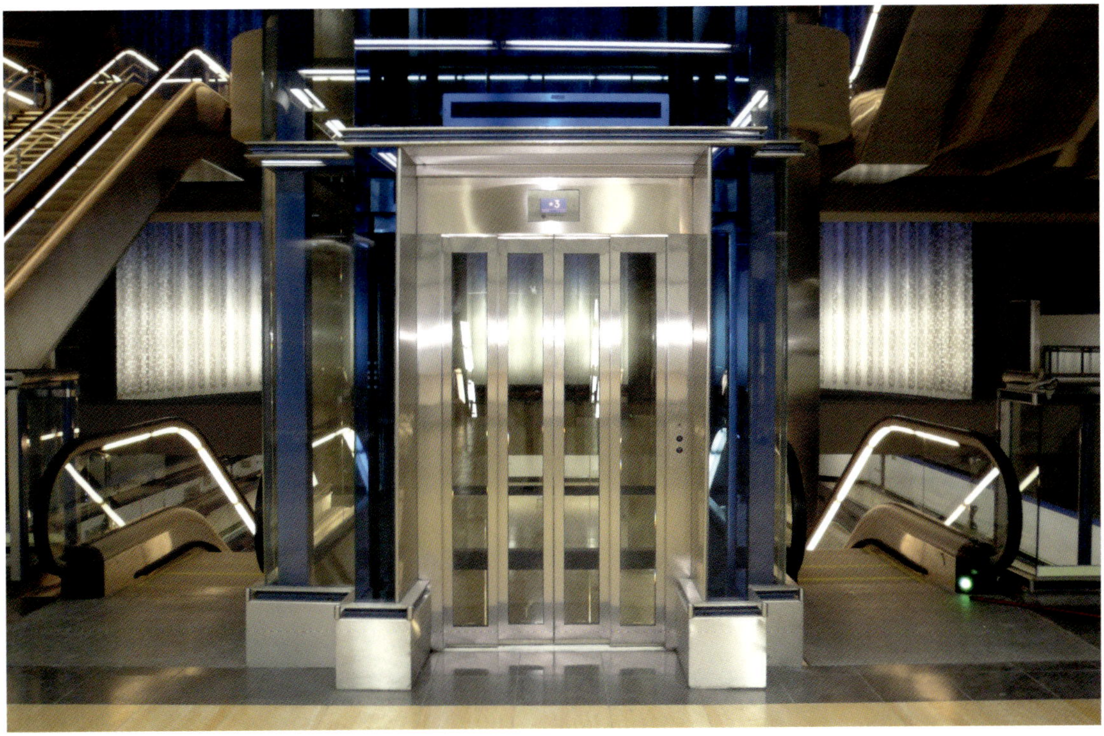

STRUCTURE AND ENCLOSURES

STRUCTURE ET CLOISONS

STRUKTUR, WÄNDE UND DECKEN

STRUCTUUR EN KAPPEN

0647

0648

0649

0650

With ventilated façades clad in travertine marble, this house is the striking combination of basically traditional materials like stone and glass arranged over a cutting-edge structural frame. With a simple rectangle as a starting point, the design was developed into numerous spaces with very pronounced angles.

Cette maison, dont les façades ventilées sont recouvertes de travertin, présente une combinaison attrayante de matériaux classiques par essence, comme la pierre et le verre, disposés sur une structure formidablement moderne. Le plan se projette hors de sa forme rectangulaire de base pour former de nombreux espaces aux angles très prononcés.

Dieses Wohnhaus, dessen querbelüftete Fassaden allesamt mit Travertin verkleidet wurden, zeigt eine ansprechende Kombination von klassischen Materialien wie Stein und Glas, die ein höchst modernes Gebäude bilden. Ausgehend von einer rechteckigen Basis erstreckt sich der Grundriss über zahlreiche Räume mit spitzen Winkeln.

Dit huis, waarvan de doorgeventileerde gevels met travertijns marmer bekleed zijn, toont een aantrekkelijke combinatie van voornamelijk klassieke materialen, zoals steen en glas, in een uiterst moderne structuur. Vertrekkende van een rechthoekige basis, projecteert de etage zich in talrijke ruimten met zeer uitgesproken hoeken.

0651

0652

0653

0654

0655

0656

>

0657

0658

0659

0660

0661

0662

0663

Four steel beams tilted to an angle of 50 degrees hold up this impressive roof, modeled on a typical gabled roof but made with panels of armored glass. The views are guaranteed.

Quatre poutres en acier inclinées formant un angle à 50 degrés supportent cette impressionnante toiture, qui reproduit le toit à deux pentes typique à partir de lames de verre blindées. Les possibilités d'un point de vue panoramique sont plus qu'évidentes.

Vier in einem Winkel von 50 Grad geneigte Stahlträger stützen dieses beeindruckende Dach, eine Nachahmung des typischen Satteldachs, in diesem Fall aus Panzerglas. Die Wirkung des Panoramablicks aus den Fenstern ist eindeutig.

Vier stalen balken met een hellingshoek van 50 graden ondersteunen dit indrukwekkende dak, een nabootsing van het typische puntdak, vervaardigd uit platen van gewapend glas. De panoramische mogelijkheden zijn overduidelijk.

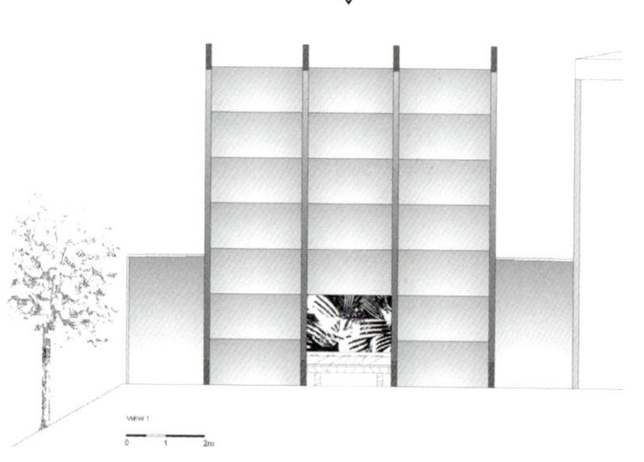

0664

0665

0666

0667

0668

0669

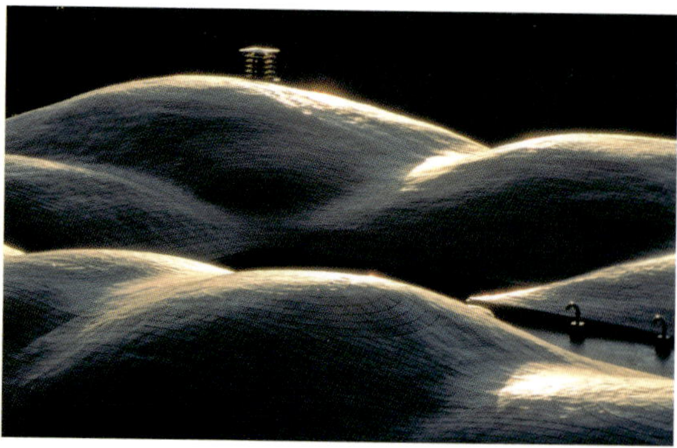

0670

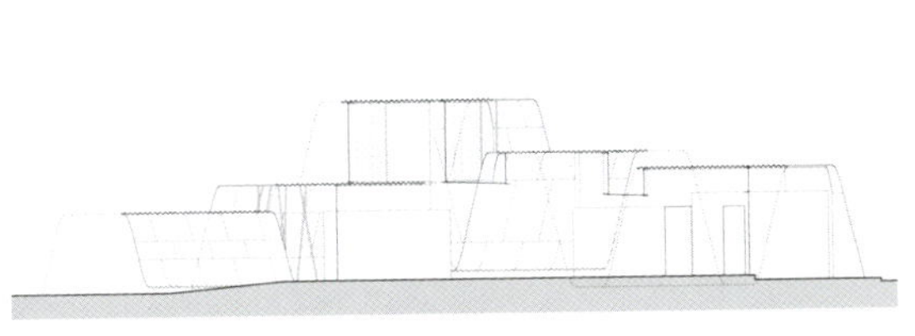

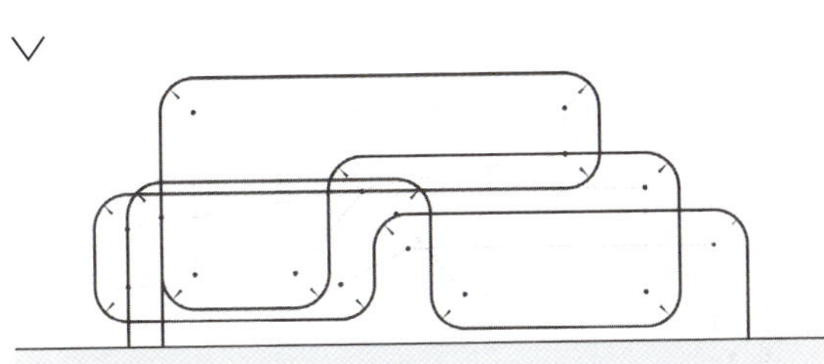

0671

0672

0673

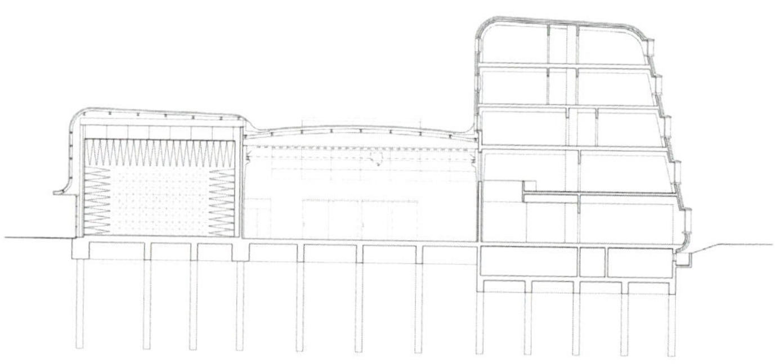

0674

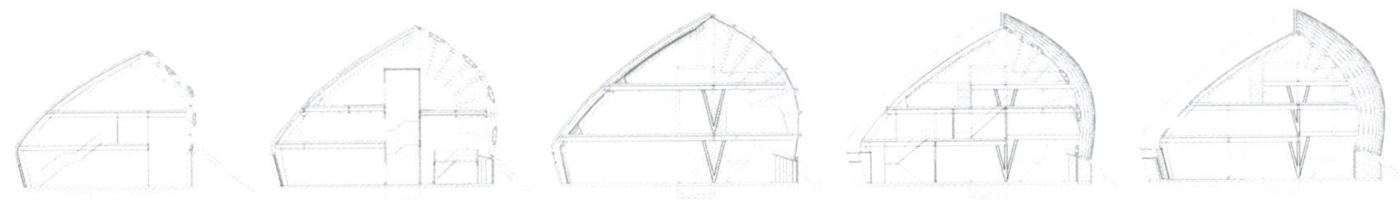

0675

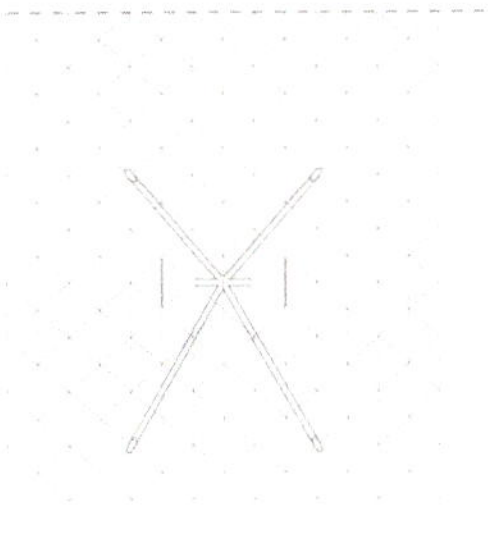

The three metal arches passing through the roof transversally also the stress it produces. The rest is a wave-like mantle covered with hexagonal mosaic tiles in a wide range of colors, reminiscent of the work of Antoni Gaudí.

Les trois arcs métalliques qui traversent le toit transversalement supportent également sa tension. Le reste est un manteau ondulant recouvert de mosaïques hexagonales d'une grande variété chromatique, qui rappellent l'œuvre de Gaudí.

Die drei Metallbögen, die das Dach quer durchlaufen, tragen die Spannung. Die wellenförmige Verkleidung ist mit vielfarbigen sechseckigen Mosaiken versehen, die an Werke von Antoni Gaudí erinnern.

De drie metalen bogen die het dak transversaal doorboren, ondersteunen eveneens de overspanning. De rest is een golvende mantel bedekt met hexagonale mozaïeken in een grote kleurenvariëteit, die doet denken aan het werk van Antoni Gaudí.

0676

0677

0678

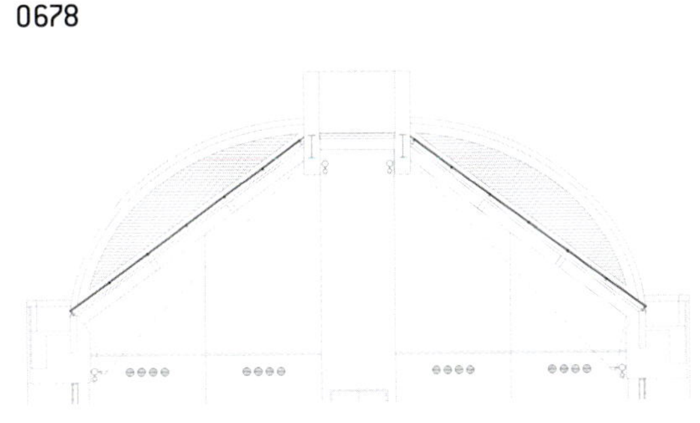

0679

0680

0681

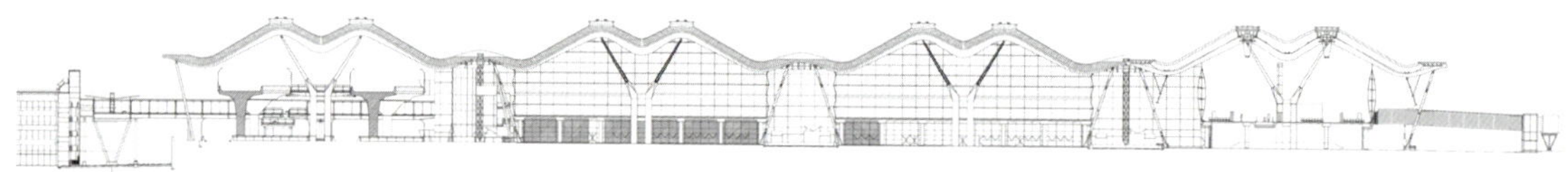

0682

0683

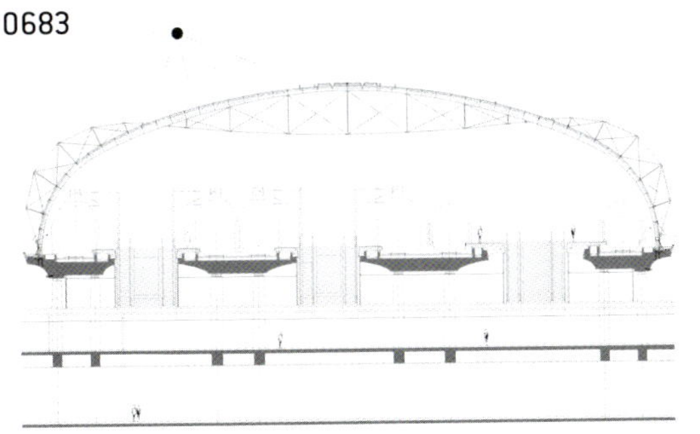

>

0684

0685

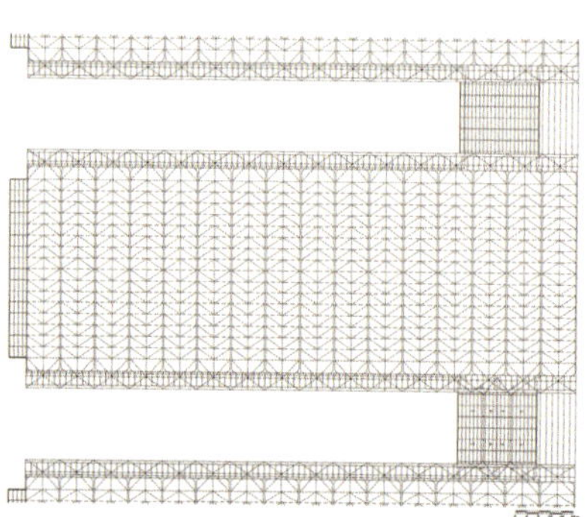

0686

0687

The detail in this image shows a tensioner hub, for both the general frame and the cables supporting the roof of this arena. The cables also help to keep the canvas cover taut over the frame, which consists of triangular forms.

L'image détaillée montre un ensemble de tendeurs, aussi bien de la structure générale que de câbles, qui supportent la toiture d'une enceinte. Les câbles permettent également de maintenir tendue la toile qui recouvre la structure aux formes triangulaires.

Die Detailansicht zeigt die Verbindung der Spannelemente der Grundstruktur wie auch der Stahlseile, die das Dach stützen. Die Seile tragen außerdem dazu bei, die Plane, welche die Struktur aus Dreiecken bedeckt, straff zu halten.

Het detail op de afbeelding toont een verbinding van spanners, zowel van de algemene structuur als van de kabels, die het dak van een arena ondersteunt. De kabels helpen ook het doek dat de structuur van driehoekige vormen bedekt strak gespannen te houden.

0688

0689

0690

0691

0692

0693

0694

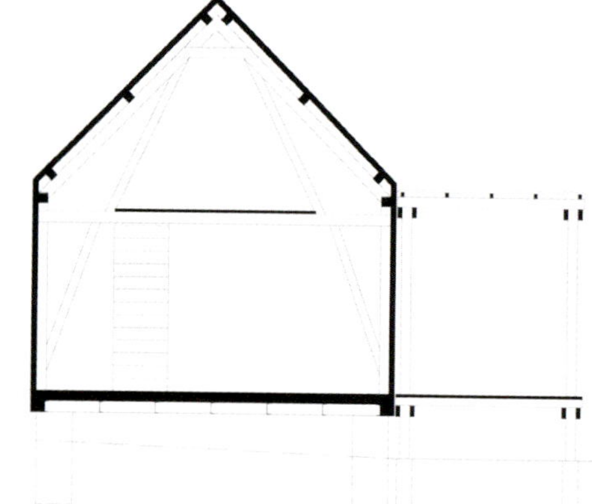

0695

0696

∨

0697 >

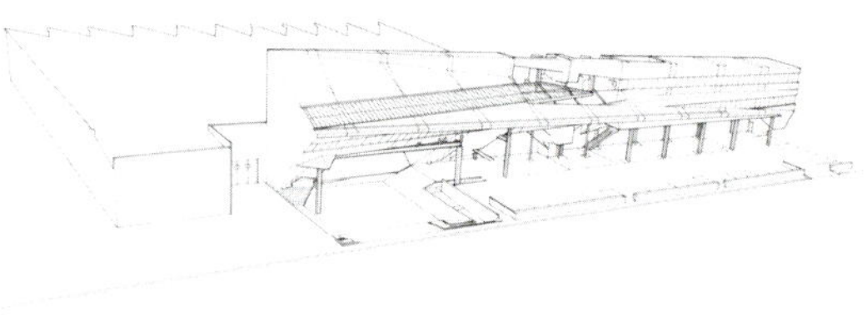

0698

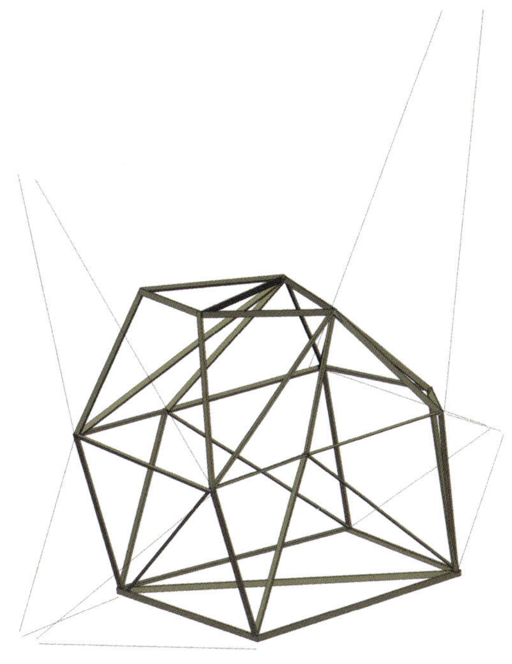

0699

0700

0701

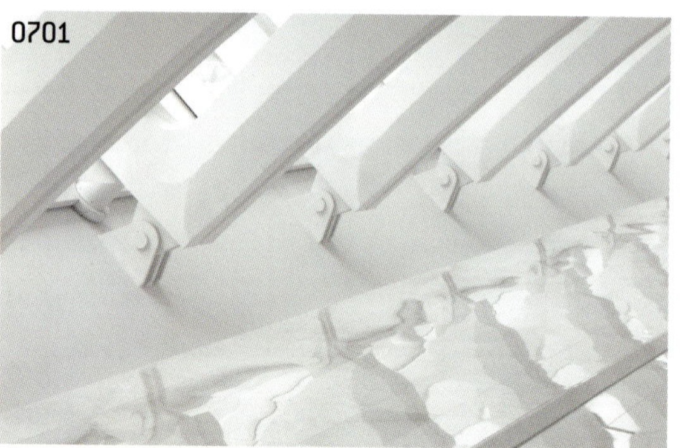

0702

0703

A structure of timber and steel beams was designed to statically stabilize the addition built to this house dating from the turn of the 20th century. In this way, a new 8 x 8 x 8-m (26 x 26 x 26-ft) cube was erected, giving the building more space and allowing more daylight in.

Une structure de poutres en bois et en acier a été ajoutée pour consolider la stabilité de l'annexe d'une habitation construite au début du XXème siècle. Un nouveau cube de 8 x 8 x 8 m a donc été érigé et a permis au bâtiment de bénéficier de plus d'espace et de lumière naturelle.

Es wurde eine Struktur aus Holzträgern und Stahl geschaffen, um den Anbau eines Wohnhauses aus der Zeit Anfang des 20. Jahrhunderts statisch zu stabilisieren. Man errichtete einen neuen Würfel mit 8 Kantenlänge, der dem Gebäude mehr Raum und mehr Tageslicht schenkt.

Er werd een structuur van houten balken en staal gecreëerd om de aanbouw van een woning die gebouwd werd in het begin van de XXe eeuw statisch te stabiliseren. Op die manier werd een nieuwe kubus van 8 x 8 x 8 m opgetrokken, die aan het gebouw meer ruimte en natuurlijk licht verschaft.

0704

0705

0706

0707

0708

0709

0710

0711

The cylindrical columns supporting the overhang of this office block are lined with a molded aluminum sheet to protect them from the weather and possible acts of vandalism.

Les colonnes cylindriques, qui supportent l'élément saillant de ce bâtiment de bureaux, sont recouvertes d'une plaque moulée en aluminium qui les protège des phénomènes météorologiques et d'éventuels actes de vandalisme.

Die zylindrischen Säulen, welche den Vorsprung an diesem Bürogebäude stützen, sind mit geformten Aluminiumblech umhüllt, das sie vor Witterungseinflüssen und Vandalismus schützt.

De cilindrische zuilen die de saillie van dit kantoorgebouw ondersteunen zijn bekleed met platen van gegoten aluminium die ze beschermen tegen meteorologische fenomenen en mogelijk vandalisme.

0712

0713

0714

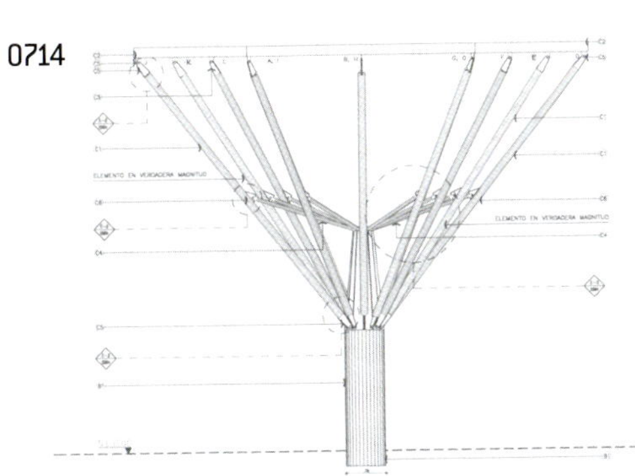

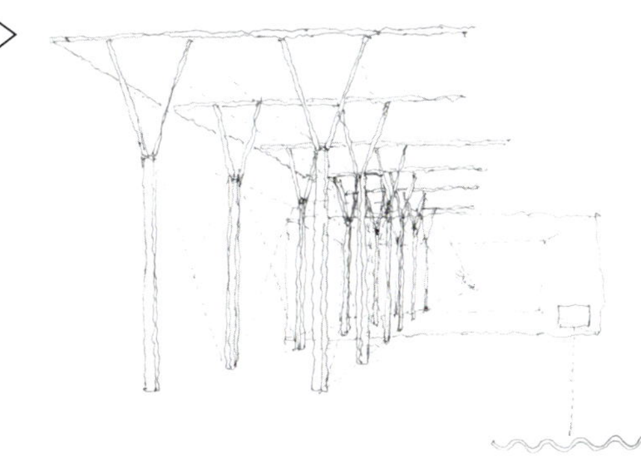

0715

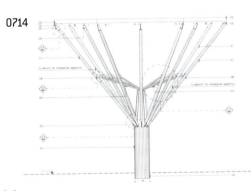

0716

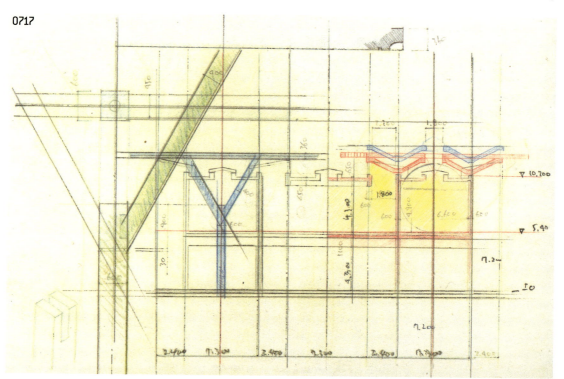

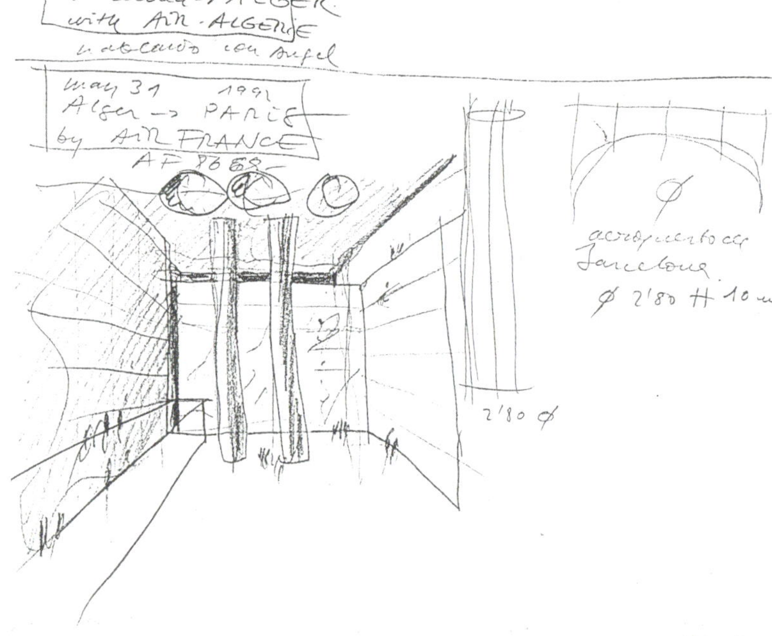

may 31. 1992

0717

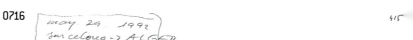

0718

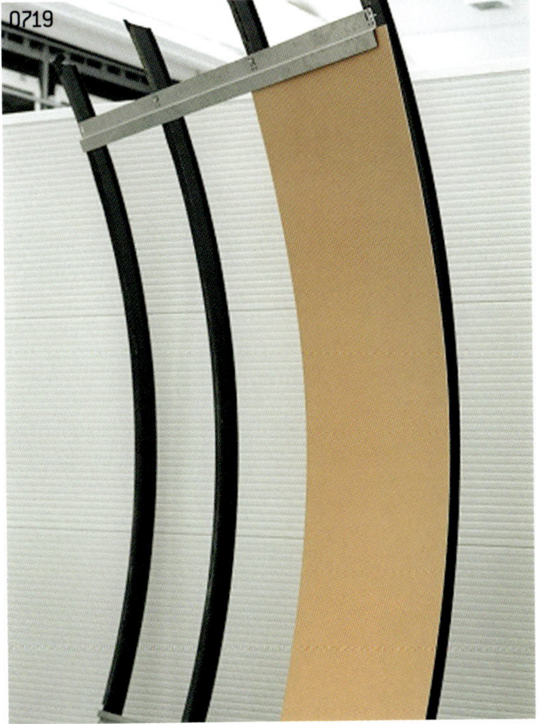

0719

0720

721

0722

0723

>

This unusual alternative was designed by the architects at Arteks to separate the fitting room area in a clothes store. The timber trunks are anchored to the floor and ceiling with metal fasteners and there is an inner curtain to cover gaps and protect the privacy of the space.

Cette curieuse alternative a été conçue par les architectes d'Arteks pour isoler la zone des cabines d'essayage dans une boutique de vêtements. Les troncs en bois sont incrustés à l'aide de fixations métalliques dans le sol et au plafond, un rideau intérieur dissimule les espaces vides pour donner de l'intimité à l'endroit.

Diese außergewöhnliche Alternative wurde von den Architekten von Arteks entworfen, um den Bereich der Umkleidekabinen in einem Bekleidungsgeschäft räumlich abzutrennen. Die Holzstämme wurden mithilfe von Metallverankerungen an Boden und Decke befestigt, ein Vorhang verdeckt die Kabinen, um dem Bereich ausreichend Intimsphäre zu verleihen.

Dit merkwaardig alternatief werd bedacht door de architecten van Arteks om de zone van de kleedkamers in een kledingzaak te isoleren. De houten stammen zijn met metalen bevestigingen zowel aan de grond als aan het dak verankerd en een binnengordijn dekt de openingen af om aan de ruimte privacy te verschaffen.

0724

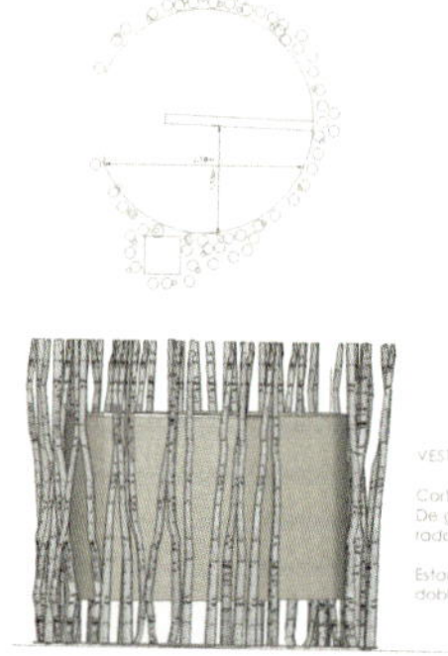

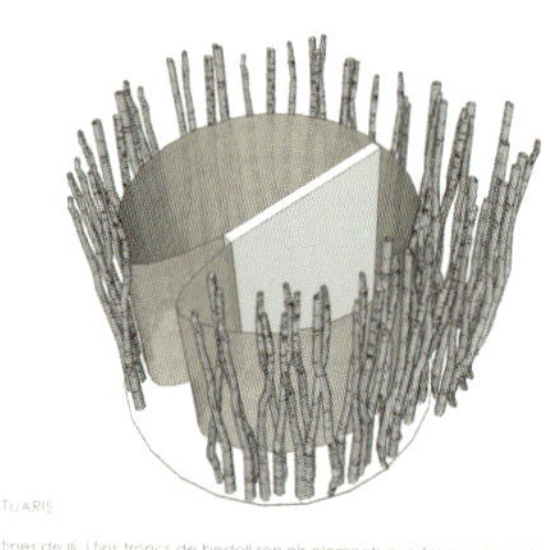

VESTUARIS
Cortines de lli, i fins troncs de bedoll son els elements que formen aquests vestuaris. De generoses dimensions, faciliten els moviments a l'interior. Un gran element separador conte penjadors i mirall.
Estan posicionats de manera a crear un ambient d'intimitat, tot i que el fet de esser dobles permet intercanviar impressions en aquest espai comu.

0725

0726

0727

0728

0729

0730

0731

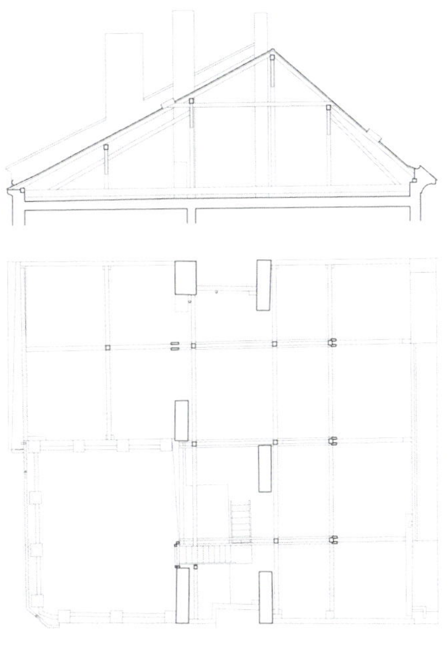

0732

0733

0734

0735

The continuously curved façade of this spa is clad in thin pine wood strips, letting the building blend seamlessly with its natural setting and giving it the appearance of a large sauna.

La façade de ce centre thermal, dont la volumétrie ondule constamment, est recouverte de fines bandes de bois de pin qui font le lien avec l'environnement naturel et le font ressembler à un grand sauna.

Die Fassade dieses wellenförmig gestalteten Thermalbads wurde mit schmalen Kiefernholzlamellen verkleidet, die das Gebäude mit seiner natürlichen Umgebung verbinden und es wie große Sauna wirken lassen.

De gevel van dit kuuroord, met een golvende volumetrie, is bekleed met fijne dennenhouten stroken, die het gebouw in verband brengen met de natuurlijke omgeving en ervoor zorgen dat het een grote sauna lijkt.

0736

0737

0738

0739

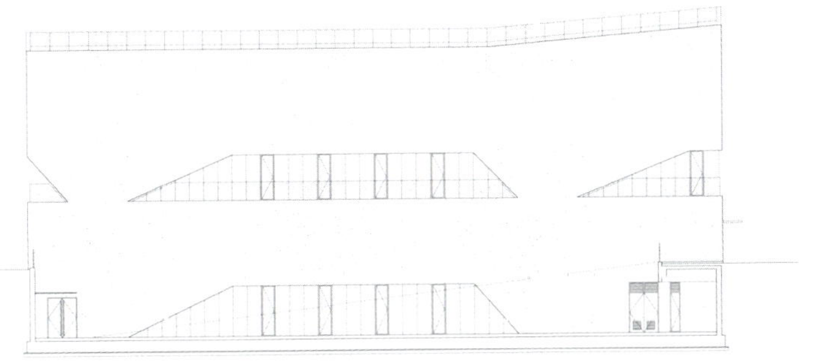

0740

0741

0742

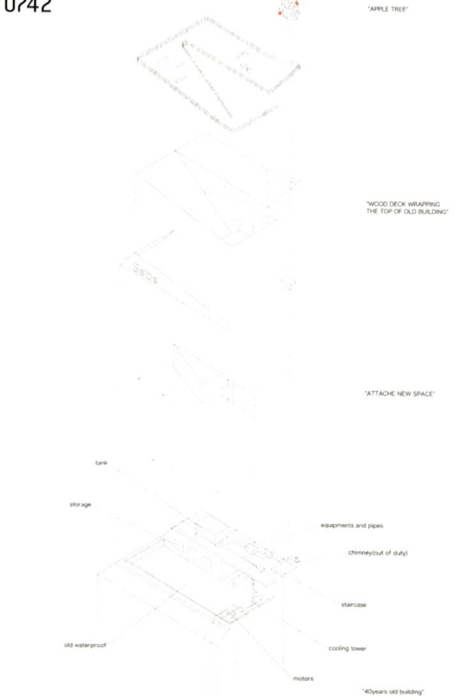

0743

0744

0745

0746

0747

0748

The cladding of this metal structure is predominantly timber. The positioning of strips vertically, horizontally and crosswise creates an original and iconic façade. The house is also crowned by a timber roof.

La couverture de cette construction métallique a essentiellement été réalisée à l'aide de bois. La disposition des différentes plaques, horizontalement, verticalement et transversalement dessine une façade caractéristique et originale. La maison est couronnée par une couverture également construite en bois.

Die Verkleidung dieses Metallgebäudes erfolgte im Wesentlichen mit Holz. Die Anordnung der einzelnen Lamellen – waagerecht, senkrecht und diagonal – verleiht der Fassade ihr originelles Aussehen. Gekrönt wird das Haus von einem Holzdach.

De bekleding van dit metalen bouwsel werd hoofdzakelijk uit hout gerealiseerd. De horizontale, verticale en transversale schikking van de diverse platen vormt een typerende en originele gevel. Het huis wordt bekroond met een dak dat eveneens uit hout vervaardigd werd.

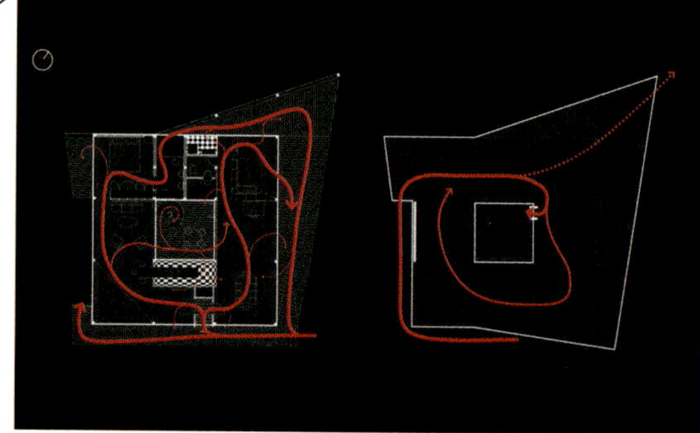

0749

0750

>

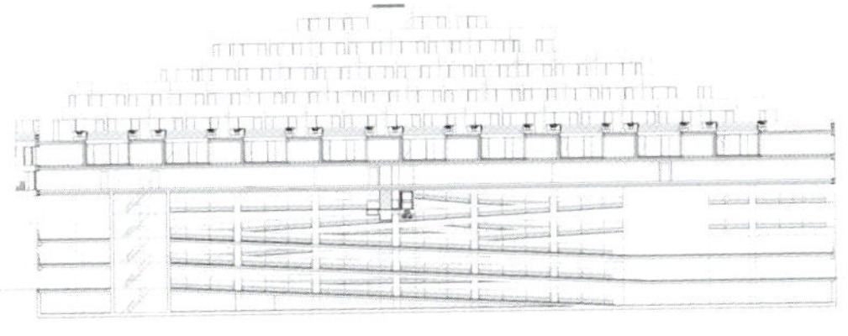

0751

0752

0753

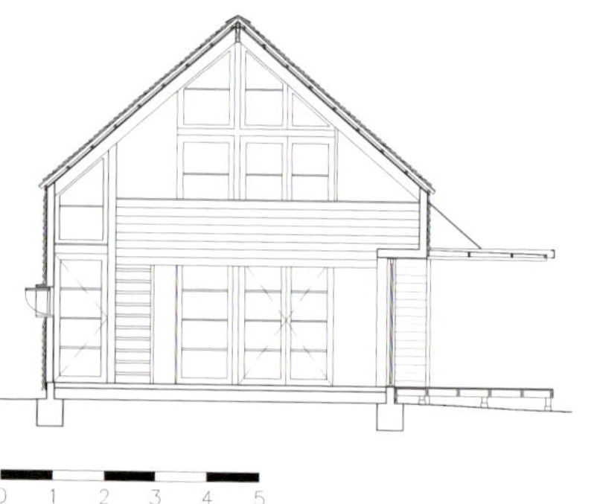

0754

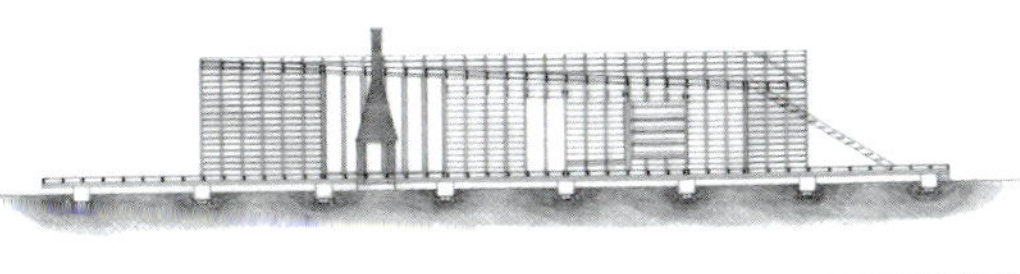

0755

0756

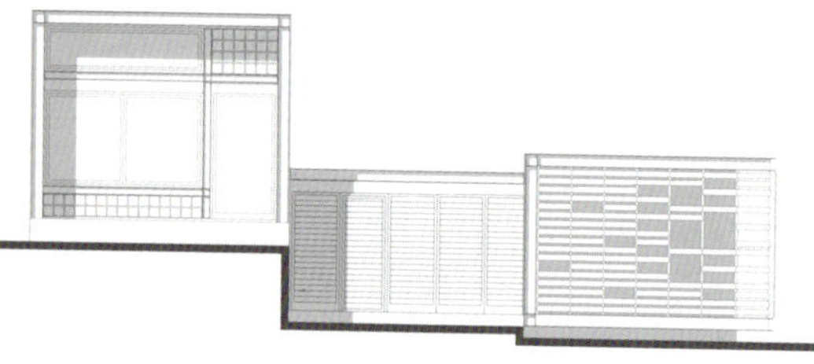

0757

0758

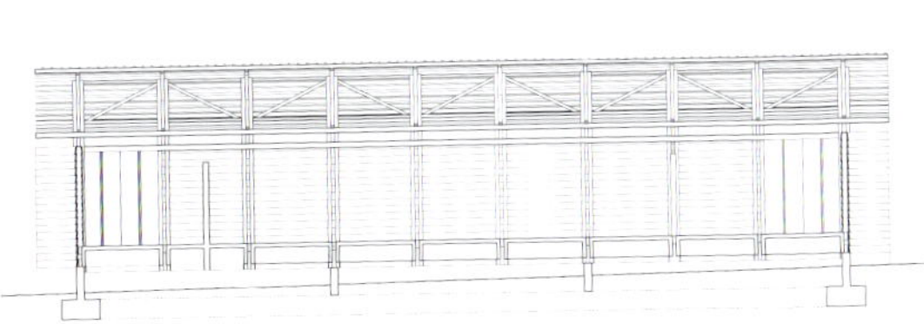

0759

The thick unrendered concrete exterior walls of this house have a metal border at the top. This band marks the start of the roof and acts as a parapet.

Les murs extérieurs épais de cette maison sont en béton brut avec une bordure métallique sur la partie supérieure. Cette frange indique le début du toit et lui sert de barre d'appui.

Die dicken Außenmauern dieses Hauses aus allseitig unverkleidetem Beton sind auf der Oberseite mit einem Metallstreifen versehen. Dieser Streifen kennzeichnet den Beginn des Dachs und dient als Geländer dafür.

De dikke, onbeklede, betonnen buitenmuren van dit huis zijn bovenaan met een metalen boord omzoomd. Deze strook geeft het begin van het dak aan en dient tevens als dakbalustrade.

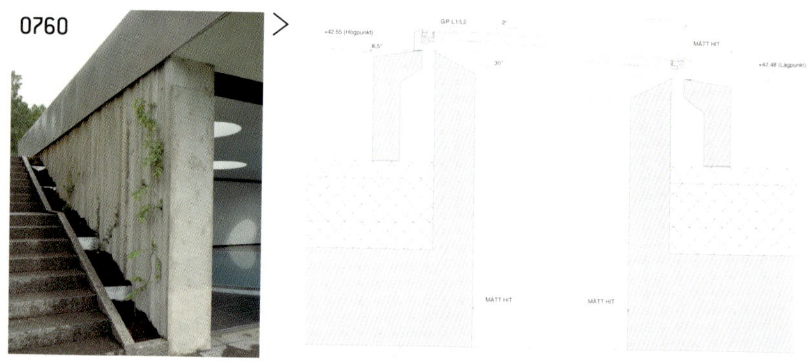

0761

0762

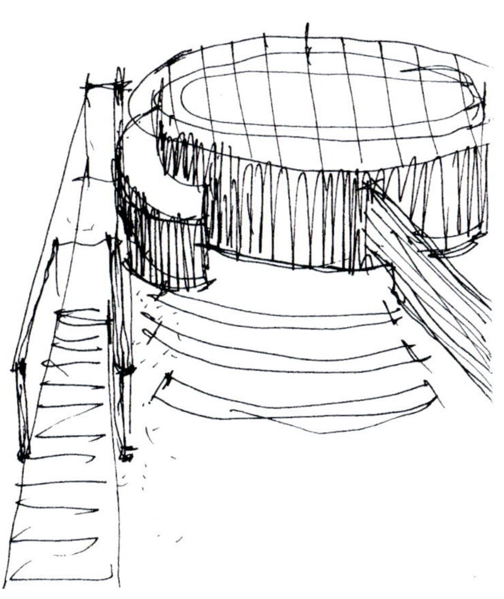

0763

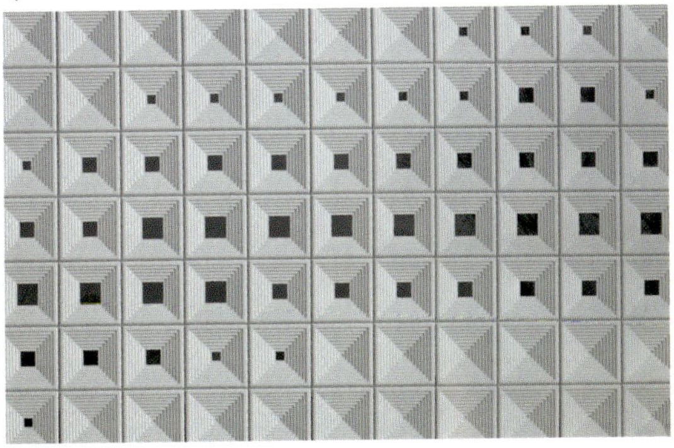

0764

0765

0766

>

0767

>

0768

0769

0770

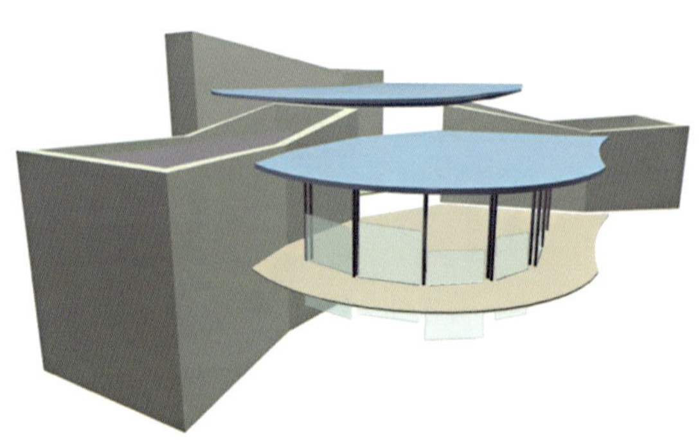

0771

0772

0773

0774

The architects chose concrete for this complex project, as it was the material that best resembles the art of sculptor Jorge Yazpik. Concrete is a malleable, modifiable, versatile material and it perfectly blends with other materials such as stone and wood.

Afin de réaliser ce projet complexe, les architectes ont choisi le béton car il s'agit du matériau qui ressemble le plus à l'art du sculpteur Jorge Yazpik. Le béton est un matériau malléable, versatile, modifiable qui se combine à la perfection avec d'autres matériaux tels que la pierre et le bois.

Bei diesem komplexen Projekt entschieden sich die Architekten für Beton, da er das Baumaterial darstellte, welches der Kunst des Bildhauers Jorge Yazpik am ähnlichsten war. Beton ist ein verformbarer, vielseitiger und veränderlicher Werkstoff, der ausgezeichnet mit anderen Baumaterialien wie Stein oder Holz kombiniert werden kann.

Om dit complexe project te realiseren, kozen de architecten voor beton omdat dat het materiaal is dat het best overeenstemt met de kunst van de beeldhouwer Jorge Yazpik. Beton is een kneedbaar, veelzijdig, aanpasbaar materiaal dat perfect combineert met andere materialen zoals steen en hout.

0775

0776

0777

0778

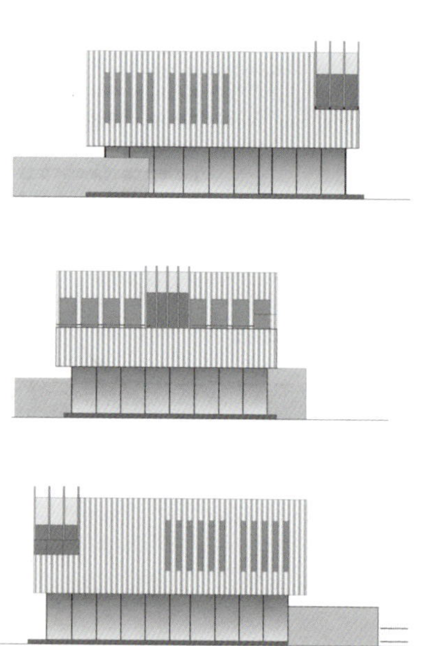

>

0779

0780

0781

0782

0783

The skeleton of this theater is wrapped in a circular skin made with a PVC membrane. Tinted electric red, this material bathes the interiors in an extraordinary orange light.

La structure de ce théâtre est entourée d'une enveloppe circulaire composée d'une membrane en PVC. Ce matériau, teint en rouge électrique, plonge l'intérieur dans une lumière orangée qui attire réellement l'attention.

Die Struktur dieses Theaters ist von einer kreisförmigen Hülle aus einer PVC-Membrane umgeben. Dieses elektrisch rot gefärbte Baumaterial umspielt die Innenbereiche mit einem in der Tat grellen orangefarbenen Licht.

De structuur van dit theater wordt omhuld door een circulaire mantel die bestaat uit een pvc-membraan. Dit materiaal, dat hier rood gekleurd is, baadt de interieurs in een heel opvallend oranje licht.

0784

0785

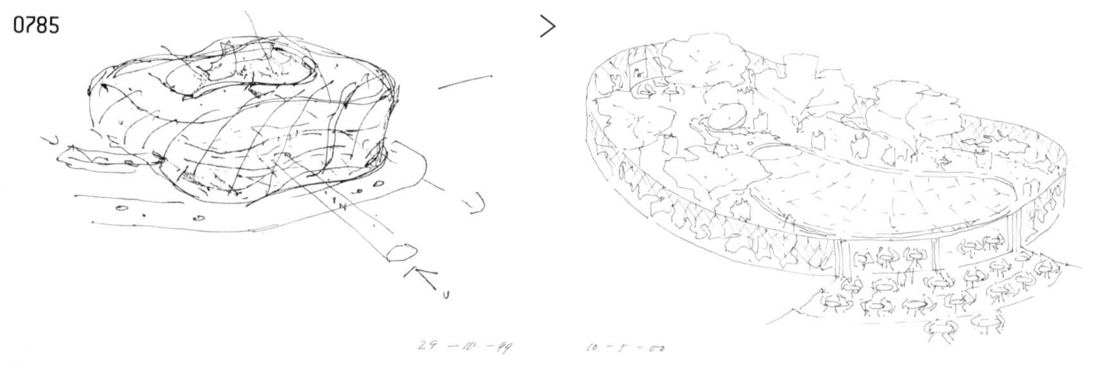

0786

0787

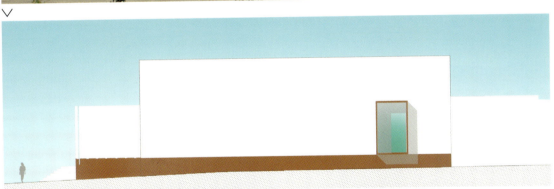

0788

0789

0790

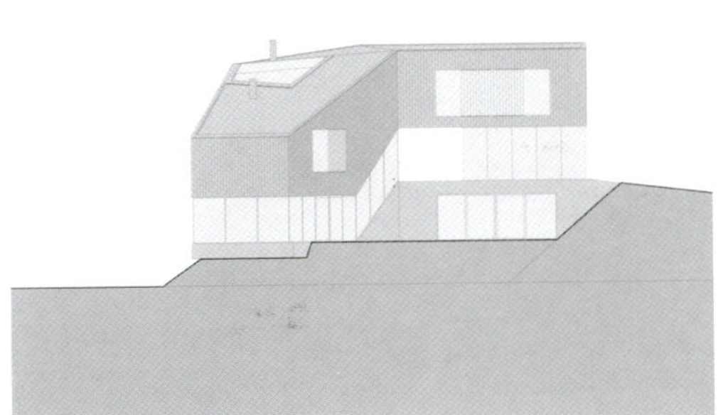

0791

0792

0793

0794

0795

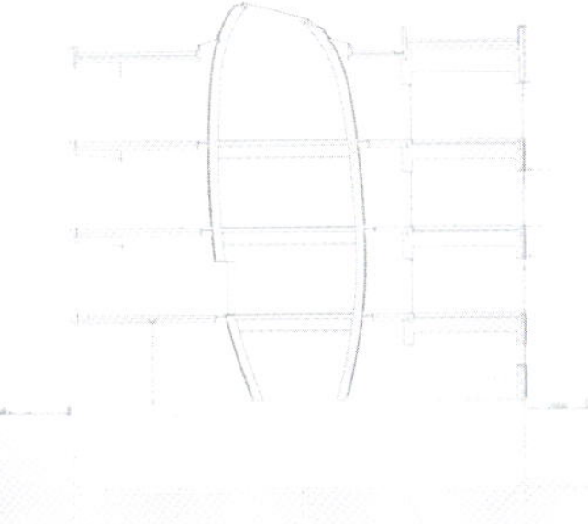

A fine translucent mesh of stainless steel covers the glass façade of this Camenzind Evolution building. This "skin" elegantly unfurls as it ascends, adapting to the spiral shaped building.

Une fine grille translucide en acier inoxydable recouvre la façade en verre de ce bâtiment de Camenzind Evolution. Cette enveloppe s'enroule progressivement avec élégance au fur et à mesure qu'elle descend, en s'adaptant à la spirale que dessine la structure.

Ein dünnes, durchscheinendes Edelstahlnetz verkleidet die Glasfassade dieses Gebäudes von Camenzind Evolution. Diese „Haut" wickelt sich auf elegante Art in Aufwärtsrichtung auf, indem sie sich an die Spirale anpasst, die das Volumen zeichnet.

De glazen gevel van dit gebouw van Camenzind Evolution wordt bedekt door een fijn doorschijnend netwerk van roestvrij staal. Naarmate men stijgt, rolt deze «huid» elegant omhoog terwijl ze zich aan de door het volume afgetekende spiraal aanpast.

0796

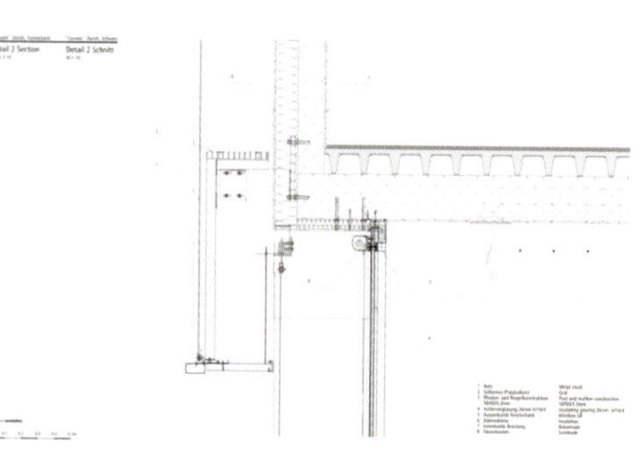

0797

0798

0799

0800

0801

0802

0803

0806

0807

In this Australian restaurant located in Sydney Harbour, a façade has been voluntarily created to install a double glazed elongated terrace. The narrow, covered terrace serves as a vantage point and at times as outdoor dining area.

Dans ce restaurant australien situé dans la baie de Sydney, une façade avec une double baie vitrée a volontairement été créée afin de pouvoir installer une terrasse allongée. La terrasse couverte, aux dimensions étroites, fait office de mirador et parfois de salle à manger extérieure.

Für dieses australische Restaurant in der Bucht von Sydney wurde absichtlich eine Doppelglasfassade geschaffen, um eine längliche Terrasse einrichten zu können. Die schmale aber überdachte Terrasse dient als Aussichtspunkt und manchmal als Speisesaal im Freien.

In dit Australische restaurant aan de baai van Sydney werd opzettelijk een dubbel beglaasde gevel gecreeerd om er een langwerpig terras te kunnen installeren. Het smalle, overdekte terras doet dienst als beglaasd balkon en wordt soms als eetterras gebruikt.

0808

0809

0810

0811

0812

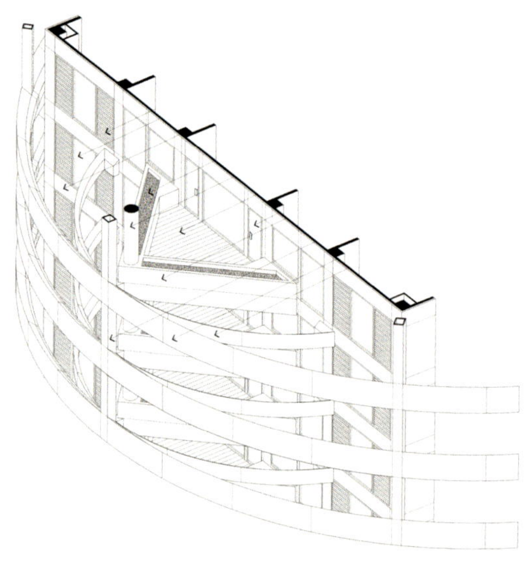

0813

0814

0815

0816

0817

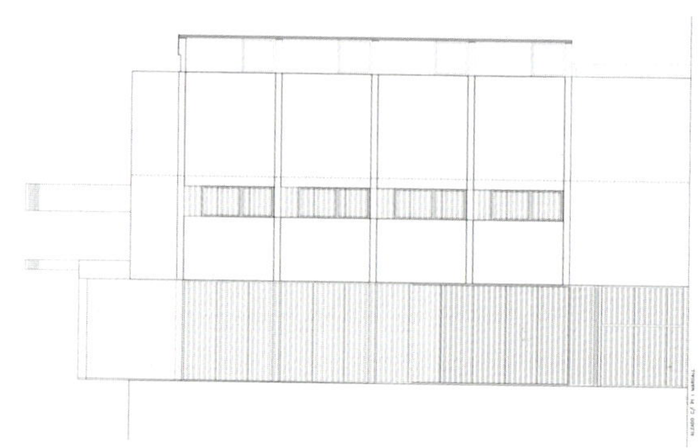

0818

0819

>

0820

0821

0822

The land around this residence is intelligently fenced off by a broken succession of vertical panels of 150-millimeter thick weathering steel that form wedges in different directions and allow a certain amount of light to pass from one side to the other.

Le terrain qui entoure cette habitation est délimité de façon astucieuse par une succession discontinue de plaques verticales en acier Corten, de 150 mm d'épaisseur. Elles sont en forme de coin et implantées dans différentes directions, ce qui permet le passage de la lumière d'un côté à l'autre.

Das Grundstück, das dieses Haus umgibt, ist auf intelligente Art mit einer unterbrochenen Reihenfolge an senkrechten, 150 mm dicken Corten-Stahlplatten umgeben, die Keile in abwechselnde Richtungen bilden und einen gewissen Lichtdurchgang von einer Seite zur anderen ermöglichen.

Het perceel dat deze woning omringt werd op intelligente wijze afgebakend door een onderbroken opeenvolging van verticale cortenstalen platen, met een dikte van 150 mm. Ze vormen afwisselende wigvormige scheidingswanden die een zekere hoeveelheid licht doorlaten.

0823

0824

0825

>

0826

∨

0827

0828

0829

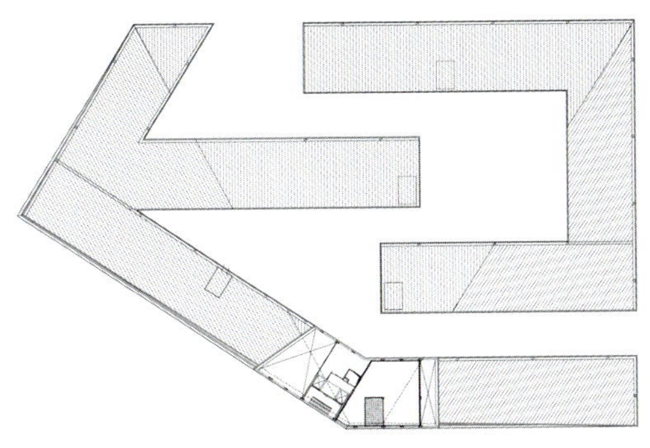

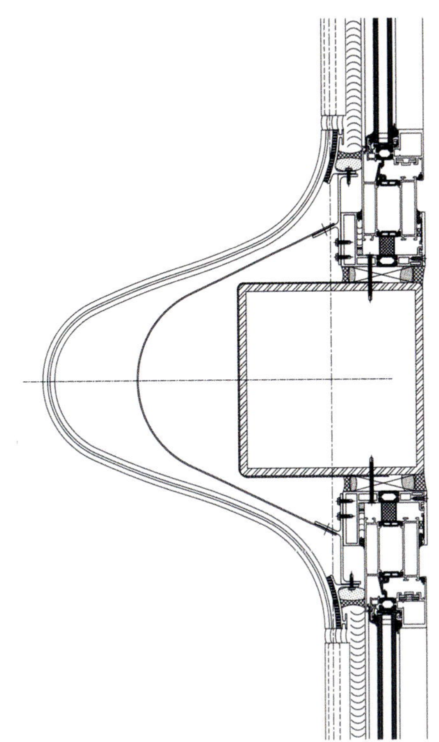

0830

0831

This museum located in the US city of Ohio is divided into three bodies, one of which is called The Glass Pavilion. The large façade is glazed and, because of its volume, the interior temperature can be controlled using very little artificial energy.

« Le pavillon de verre » est l'un de trois ailes de ce musée situé dans l'état américain de l'Ohio. Les grandes baies vitrées qui constituent la façade permettent grâce à leur volume une la climatisation à l'intérieur avec très peu d'énergie artificielle.

„El Cristal" ist eins der drei Teile, in die dieses Museum in der nordamerikanischen Stadt Ohio aufgeteilt ist. Die groÀlächige Fassade ist verglast und ermöglicht aufgrund ihres Volumens eine Klimatisierung im Inneren, die wenig zusätzliche Energie benötigt.

Het «Crystal» is een van de drie delen waaruit dit museum in de Noord-Amerikaanse stad Ohio samengesteld is. De grote gevel bestaat uit glas en kan binnenin dankzij zijn volume met zeer weinig artificiële energie geklimatiseerd worden.

0832

0833

0834

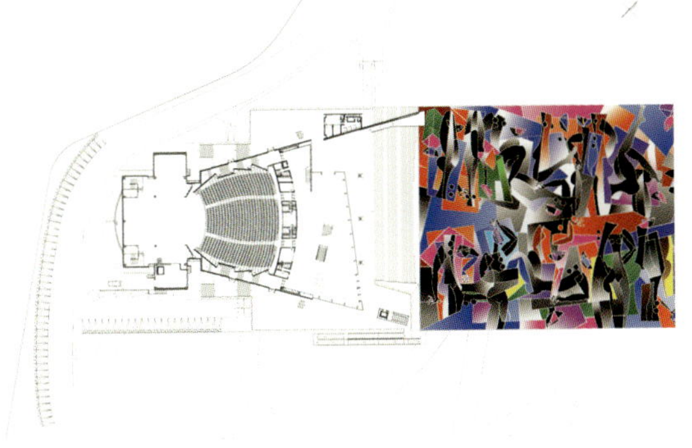

0835

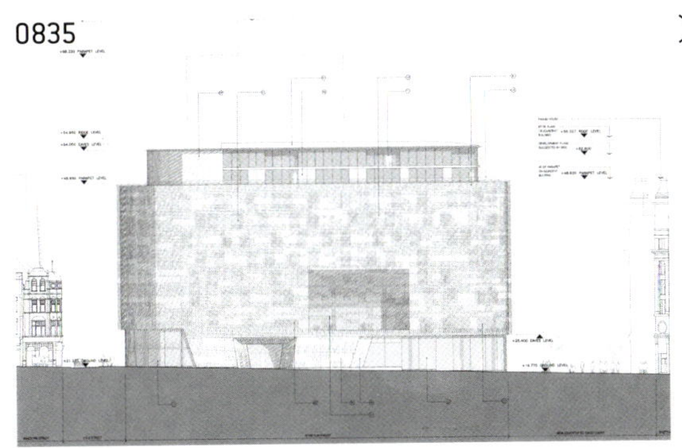

0836

0837

0838

0839

0840

0841

0842

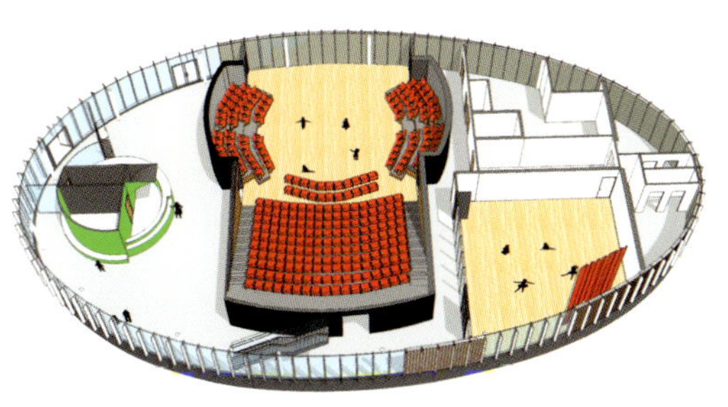

0843

Transparent and open, the outer layer features a series of aluminum panels that give a rippled effect reminiscent of spirals. An LED lighting system illuminates the facade at night with different patterns.

L'enveloppe extérieure, transparente et ouverte, dispose d'une série de plaques en aluminium qui forment un motif en forme de spirale. La nuit, l'éclairage de cette structure crée différents dessins grâce à un système de lampes LED.

Die transparente und offene Außenhülle besitzt eine Reihe an Aluminiumlamellen, die das Modell der Spiraleffekte bilden. In der Nacht wird diese Struktur anhand eines Systems aus LED – Leuchten mit verschiedenen Mustern beleuchtet.

De doorzichtige, open buitenlaag bestaat uit een reeks aluminiumplaten die een patroon met spiraaleffecten vormt. 's Nachts wordt deze structuur dankzij een ledlampensysteem met diverse tekeningen verlicht.

0844

0845

0846

0847

0848

0849

0850

0851

0852
UNI
QLO

0853
area 机房
bar 酒吧
office 办公室
office 办公室
conference 商务研讨室
exhibition 展览大厅
studio 舞台
shop 商场
shop 商场
storage 库房
parking 车位
parking 车位
机房 technical area
east-west se

0854

GIORGIO ARMANI

GIORGIO ARMANI
ECC
ECC
ECC
ECC
英会話
0120-086-144
Matsumoto KiYoshi
マツモトキヨシ

0855

0856

0857

0858

This gigantic residential and leisure development designed by Steven Holl features different buildings connected by a series of walkways positioned at different levels on each volume, with no supports other than at the ends and clad in practically unbroken glazed surfaces.

Dans ce gigantesque projet de résidence et de loisir conçu par Steven Holl, les différents bâtiments du complexe sont connectés au moyen de passerelles situées à différentes hauteurs sur chaque volume. Elles sont suspendues et ne sont rattachées qu'aux extrémités. Elles se composent de verrières sur presque toute la longueur.

Bei diesem riesigen, von Steven Holl entworfenen Wohn-und Freizeitprojekt sind die einzelnen Gebäude des Komplexes anhand einer Reihe von Laufstegen verbunden. Diese befinden sich bei jedem Volumen auf unterschiedlicher Höhe und sind nur an den Enden befestigt. Ihre Verkleidung wird von praktisch ununterbrochenen Glasflächen gebildet.

In dit gigantische woning- en vrijetijdsproject dat ontworpen werd door Steven Holl, worden de verschillende gebouwen van het complex op verschillende hoogten met elkaar verbonden door passerelles. Deze zijn uitsluitend aan de uiteinden opgehangen en bekleed met grote, bijna ononderbroken, glazen wanden.

0859

>

0860

0861

0862

0863

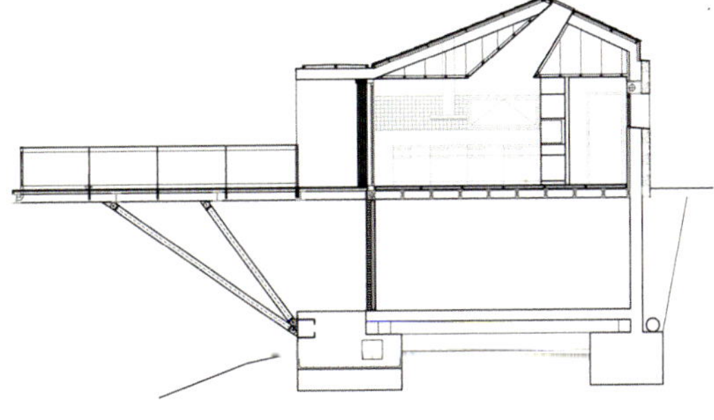

0864

0865

0866

0867

0868

0869

0870

0871

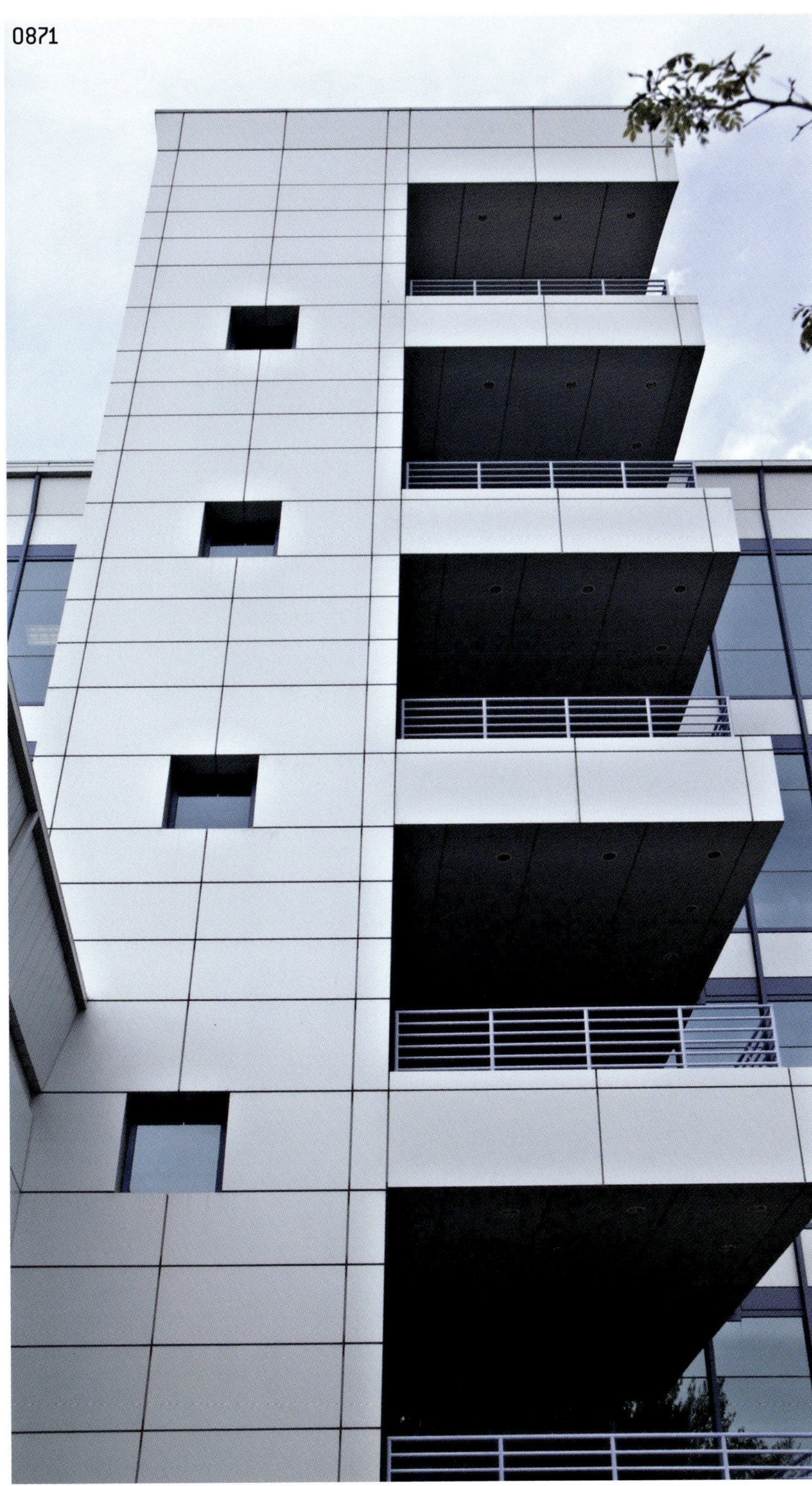

The volume cantilevered out from this large office building is divided into two: one part is totally covered with barely any windows breaking its façade. This is made possible because the other half is taken up by wide balconies that bathe the interior with light.

Le volume qui ressort de ce grand immeuble de bureaux est divisé en deux : une partie est totalement couverte et n'a presque aucune fenêtre sur la façade. Cela est rendu possible car l'autre partie se compose de vastes balcons qui inondent de lumière l'intérieur.

Das Volumen, das dieses große Bürogebäude überragt, ist zweigeteilt: ein Teil ist komplett abgedeckt und besitzt fast keine Fenster auf seiner Fassade. Das ist möglich, weil die andere Hälfte mit breiten Balkons belegt ist, die den Innenraum in Licht tauchen.

Het volume dat boven dit grote kantoorgebouw uitsteekt is in twee verdeeld: het ene deel is volledig overdekt met een bijna vensterloze gevel. Dit is mogelijk omdat de andere helft uit ruime balkons bestaat die het interieur van licht voorzien.

0872

0873

0874

0875

0876

0877

0878

0879

FINISHES

FINITIONS
FINISHS
AFWERKINGEN

The attractive tiger print effect flooring, present throughout the residence, is the main decorative element of these interiors, as it covers the floor, upper ramp, benches, table and the breakfast bar.

Ce chaleureux parquet d'aspect tigré est omniprésent et constitue le principal élément décoratif de cet espace intérieur, puisqu'il recouvre le plancher, la rampe supérieure, les bancs, la table ainsi que le comptoir du meuble bar.

Die Allgegenwärtigkeit dieses attraktiven Holzbodens mit Tigeroptik stellt das Hauptdekorationselement bei diesen Innenräumen dar, da es Boden, obere Rampe, Bänke, Tisch und Theke der eingebauten Bar verkleidet.

De mooie, getijgerde houten bekleding is het belangrijkste decoratieve element van deze interieurs. Ze wordt zowel gebruikt voor de vloer als voor de bovenste hellingbaan, de banken, de tafel en de toog van het barmeubel.

0880

0881

0882

0883

0884

0885

0886

0887

0888

0889

0890

0891

This Schotten & Hansen parquet flooring has the advantage of being extremely flexible and can be made to adjust to different layouts. Furthermore, it can be cut on a curve without splintering.

Ce parquet de Schotten & Hansen a l'avantage d'être particulièrement flexible et de pouvoir être assemblé de différentes manières. De plus, il peut être coupé en courbe sans se fendre.

Dieses Parkett von Schotten & Hansen bietet den Vorteil, enorm flexibel zu sein und mit verschiedenen Ausführungen eingebaut werden zu können. AuÀerdem ermöglicht es Kurvenschnitte ohne zu splittern.

Deze parketvloer van Schotten & Hansen biedt het voordeel dat hij heel flexibel is en volgens verschillende configuraties geassembleerd kan worden. Bovendien is het mogelijk zonder splinteren rondingen te snijden.

0892

0893

0894

0895

0896

0897

0898

0899

0900

0901

0902

0903

Corten steel, combined with concrete, has been used for the main façade. These materials were already present in the construction of the Botanical Garden. The architect wanted to reuse them to create this botanical institute and maintain a conceptual continuity.

La façade principale se compose d'acier Corten, combiné avec du béton apparent. Ces matériaux étaient déjà présents dans la construction du Jardin botanique. L'architecte a souhaité les récupérer pour créer cet institut botanique et maintenir ainsi une continuité conceptuelle.

Auf der Hauptfassade wurde Corten-Stahl mit Sichtbeton kombiniert eingesetzt. Diese Baumaterialien wurden schon beim Bau des botanischen Gartens verwendet. Der Architekt wollte sie beim Bau dieses botanischen Instituts wieder einsetzen, um auf diese Art eine konzeptuelle Kontinuität beizubehalten.

In de hoofdgevel werd cortenstaal gebruikt, in combinatie met zichtbeton. Deze materialen waren reeds aanwezig in de bouw van de Botanische Tuin. De architect wilde deze voor de creatie van dit botanische instituut recupereren om zo een conceptuele continuïteit te behouden.

0904

0905

0906

0907

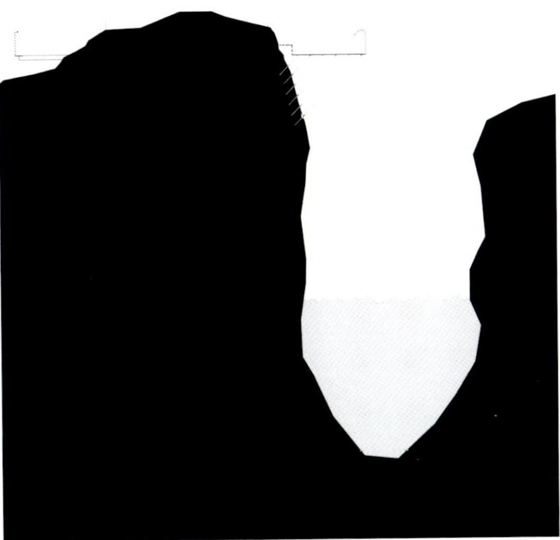

0908

0909

0910

>

0911

0912

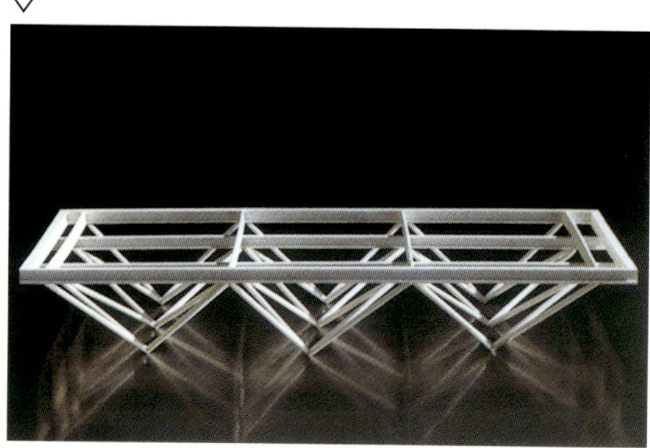

0913

0914

0915

>

0916

The building consists of 24 cubic cells 3 meters long, aligned and stacked on each other. The structure is constructed by using materials such as stainless steel and concrete. The concrete walls with a classic unfinished look are a central feature.

La construction se compose de 24 cellules cubiques de 3 m de côté, alignées et empilées les unes sur les autres. La structure est construite en combinant des matériaux comme l'acier inoxydable et le béton. Les murs en béton apparent avec leur aspect classique inachevé se distinguent.

Das Bauwerk besteht aus 24 würfelförmigen Zellen mit 3 m langen Seiten, die übereinander ausgerichtet und gestapelt sind. Die Struktur wurde anhand der Kombination von Baumaterialien wie Edelstahl und Beton erbaut. Dabei heben sich die Wände aus Sichtbeton mit ihrer klassischen unvollendeten Optik hervor.

Het gebouw is samengesteld uit 24 opeengestapelde kubusvormige cellen met een zijvlak van 3 m. De structuur bestaat uit een combinatie van materialen zoals roestvrij staal en beton. Vanwege hun onafgewerkte aanblik, vallen vooral de muren in zichtbeton op.

0917

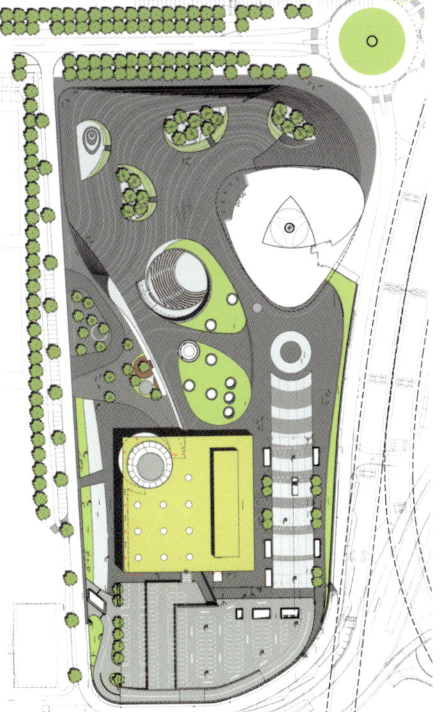

0918

0919

0920

0921

>

0922

0923

0924

Im Namen Gottes,
des Allerbarmers,
des Barmherzigen.
Lob sei Gott dem Herrn
der Welten.
Dem Allerbarmer,
dem Barmherzigen.
Dem Herrscher am Tage
des Gerichtes.
Dir dienen wir und Dich
bitten wir um Hilfe
Führe uns auf den rechten
Weg, den Weg derer,
denen Du gnädig bist,
nicht derer, denen Du
zürnst und nicht der
Irregehenden.
Im Namen Gottes,
des Allerbarmers,
des Barmherzigen.
Ihr Menschen!
Wir haben euch aus
Mann und Frau erschaffen
und haben euch zu
Völkern und Stämmen
werden lassen, damit ihr
euch kennenlernt.
Der Edelste vor Gott ist
der Gerechteste
unter euch
Gott hat das wahre
Wort gesprochen.

0925

0926

0927

0928

0929

0930

Usually there are no divisions inside this home in Peru. The only exception is the concrete kitchen, where there is an opening used as a bar counter. The concrete perfectly matches the terrazzo that paves most of the spaces.

D'une façon générale, il n'y a pas de cloisons à l'intérieur de ce logement péruvien. La seule exception est la cuisine, construite en béton apparent, avec une ouverture imitant le comptoir d'un bar. Le béton est en harmonie avec le granito qui recouvre presque tout le sol de ces espaces.

Generell gibt es in diesem peruanischen Haus keine Aufteilungen im Innenraum. Die einzige Ausnahme ist die aus Sichtbeton gebaute Küche, wo eine Öffnung in Form einer Theke entsteht. Der Beton harmonisiert mit dem Steinboden, der den gröÀen Teil der Räume belegt.

In het interieur van dit Peruaanse huis komen hoegenaamd geen scheidingen voor. De enige uitzondering is de keuken, opgetrokken in zichtbeton, waarin een opening gemaakt werd voor een bartoog. Het beton is in harmonie met de terrazzo waarmee de meeste ruimten bevloerd zijn.

0931

0932

0933

0934

0935

0936

kitchen island
This is a new project to take into account a new dimension of l itchen.
It is a new way of conceiving the worktops deriving from the modular progetto1 and expanding in a vertical and horizontal direction.
Kitchen Island also provides the possibility to create your own kitchen in a "tailor-made" way.
In fact, you can combine the modular and functional worktops and towers and create the most effective and efficient solutions.

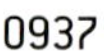

0937

1
2
3
4
5
6

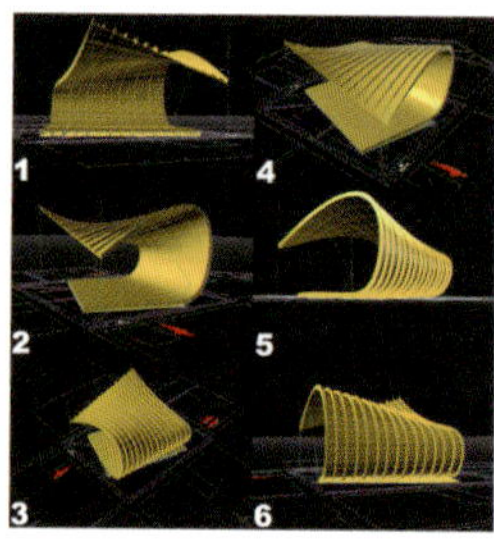
1
2
3
4
5
6

0938

0939

0940

White Life, measuring 80 x 80 cm, was the material chosen to pave Helsinki airport. These are full body technical porcelain tiles. This type of porcelain tile is the most common for use in public spaces, both for its extraordinary resistance and for its large size.

Le matériau utilisé pour le revêtement du sol de l'aéroport d'Helsinki est le Life blanc, dont les dimensions sont de 80 x 80 cm. Il s'agit d'un grès cérame pleine masse. C'est le type de grès cérame le plus souvent utilisé dans les espaces publics, en raison de son extraordinaire résistance et de son grand format.

Das für den Bodenbelag des Flughafens in Helsinki verwendete Material ist 80 x 80 cm großes weißes Life Feinsteinzeug, und zwar durchgefärbtes Feinsteinzeug. Dieses Feinsteinzeug wird aufgrund seiner außerordentlichen Festigkeit, wie auch aufgrund seines großen Formats am häufigsten für den Einbau in öffentlichen Bereichen eingesetzt.

Het materiaal dat gebruikt werd voor de bevloering van de vliegahaven van Helsinki is wit Life, van 80 x 80 cm. Het gaat om een technische, massieve porseleinsoort. Dit soort porselein is heel gebruikelijk voor de inrichting van openbare ruimten, vanwege de buitengewone degelijkheid ervan en het grote formaat.

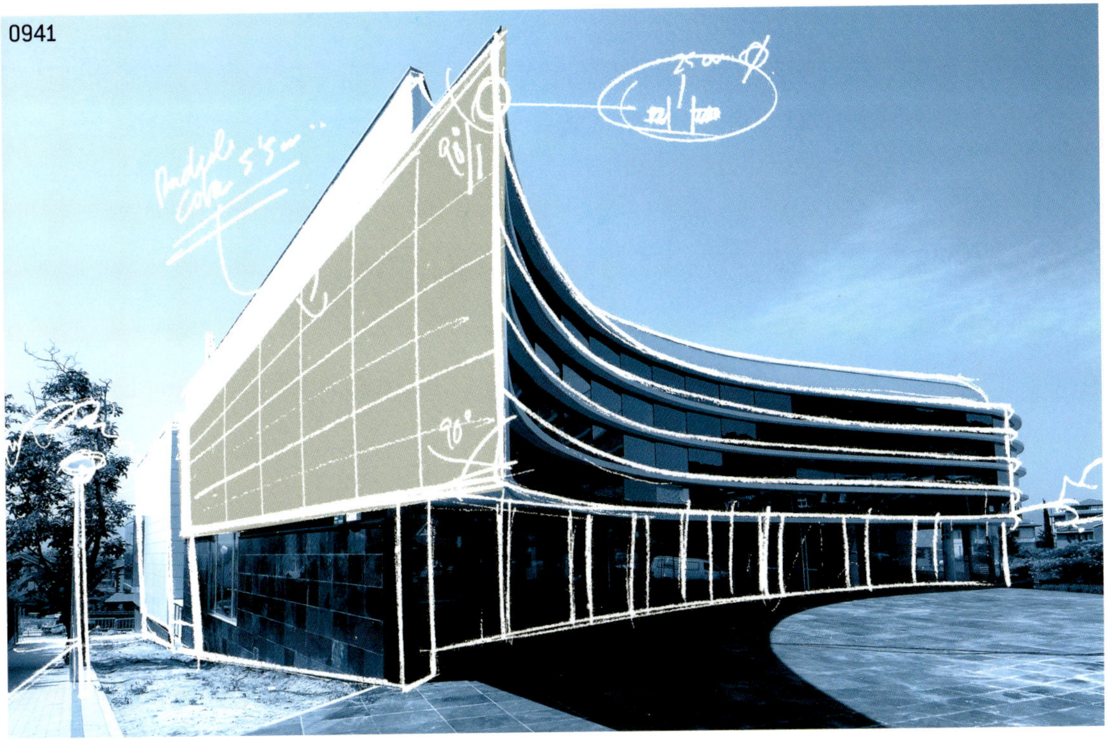

0941

0942

0943

0944

0945

0946

0947

0948

0949

0950

>

0951

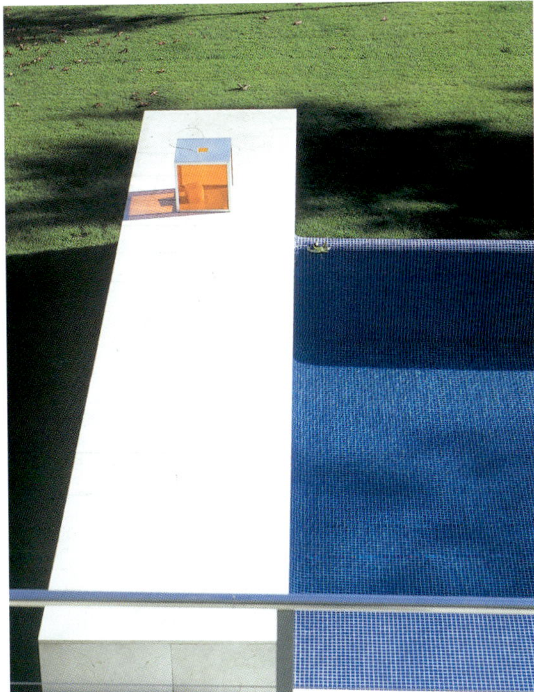

The interior walls of this residence are almost totally covered with wide travertine marble tiles. This surface combines perfectly with dark floors and ceilings and brings maximum brightness to the interior.

L'intérieur de cette habitation est presque entièrement recouvert de travertin. Cette surface s'allie à la perfection avec les sols et les plafonds obscurs et offre une luminosité optimale aux pièces.

Die Innenräume dieser Wohnung sind fast vollständig mit großflächigen Feldern aus Travertinmarmor verkleidet. Diese Oberfläche passt perfekt zu dunklen Böden und Decken und bietet den Innenräumen optimale Helligkeit.

De interieurs van deze woning zijn bijna volledig bekleed met grote kaders uit travertijn. Deze bekleding past perfect bij de donkere vloeren en plafonds en verschaft aan de interieurs de optimale helderheid.

0952

0953

0954

0955

0956

0957

0958

0959

0960

0961

0962

0963

The architects have used marble to create a calm and atemporal interior design. The large panels of marble, combined with translucent glass, form this large architectural volume.

L'utilisation du marbre a permis aux architectes de créer un espace imprégné de calme et une conception intemporelle en son intérieur. Ces grands panneaux en marbre, combinés avec des verres translucides forment ce grand volume architectural.

Durch den Einsatz von Marmor ist es den Architekten gelungen, einen Innenraum zu gestalten, der Ruhe ausstrahlt und ein zeitloses Design besitzt. Die groÀen Marmorplatten bilden zusammen mit durchscheinendem Glas dieses groÀe architektonische Volumen.

Door marmer te gebruiken, zijn de architecten erin geslaagd in het interieur een tijdloze ruimte te creëren die rust uitstraalt. Dit grote architectonische volume werd samengesteld uit grote marmeren panelen in combinatie met doorschijnend glaswerk.

0964

0965

0966

0967

0968

0969

>

0970

0971

0972

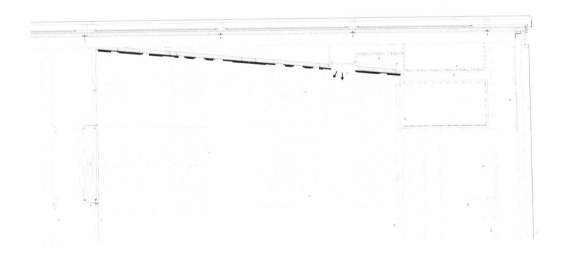

0973

0974

0975

Beadazzled, a glass-encrusted wallpaper, is the first of its kind. The synthetic material that is made from is one of the most hard-wearing and flexible options for covering walls, and comes in different geometric patterns.

Conçu avec des incrustations de verre, le revêtement Beadazzled est le premier de son genre. Il est constitué de matériau synthétique grâce auquel il s'avère être un des éléments les plus durables et flexibles pour recouvrir un mur. Il existe différents modèles géométriques.

Die Beadazzled Verkleidung mit Glasinkrustierungen ist die erste dieser Art. Der Kunststoff, aus dem sie hergestellt ist, macht sie zu einer der dauerhaftesten und flexibelsten Optionen, mit denen eine Wand bedeckt werden kann. Sie ist in verschiedenen geometrischen Mustern erhältlich.

De bekleding Beadazzled, uitgevoerd met glazen inlegwerk, is de eerste in zijn soort. Dankzij het synthetische materiaal is het een van de meest duurzame en flexibele opties voor muurbekledingen. Het is bovendien beschikbaar in verscheidene geometrische patronen.

0976

0977

0978

0979

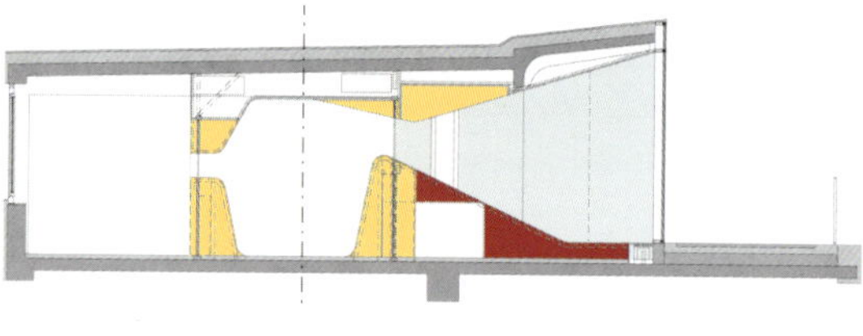

0980

0981

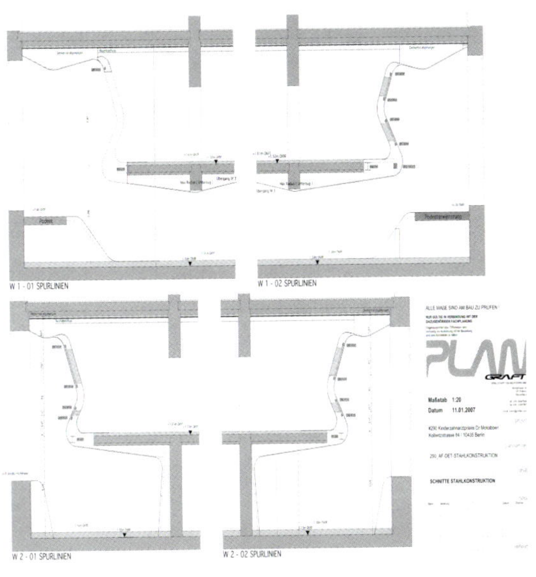
W 1 - 01 SPURLINIEN
W 1 - 02 SPURLINIEN
W 2 - 01 SPURLINIEN
W 2 - 02 SPURLINIEN
ALLE MAßE SIND AM BAU ZU PRÜFEN !
PLAN
GRAFT
Maßstab 1:20
Datum 11.01.2007
SCHNITTE STAHLKONSTRUKTION

0982

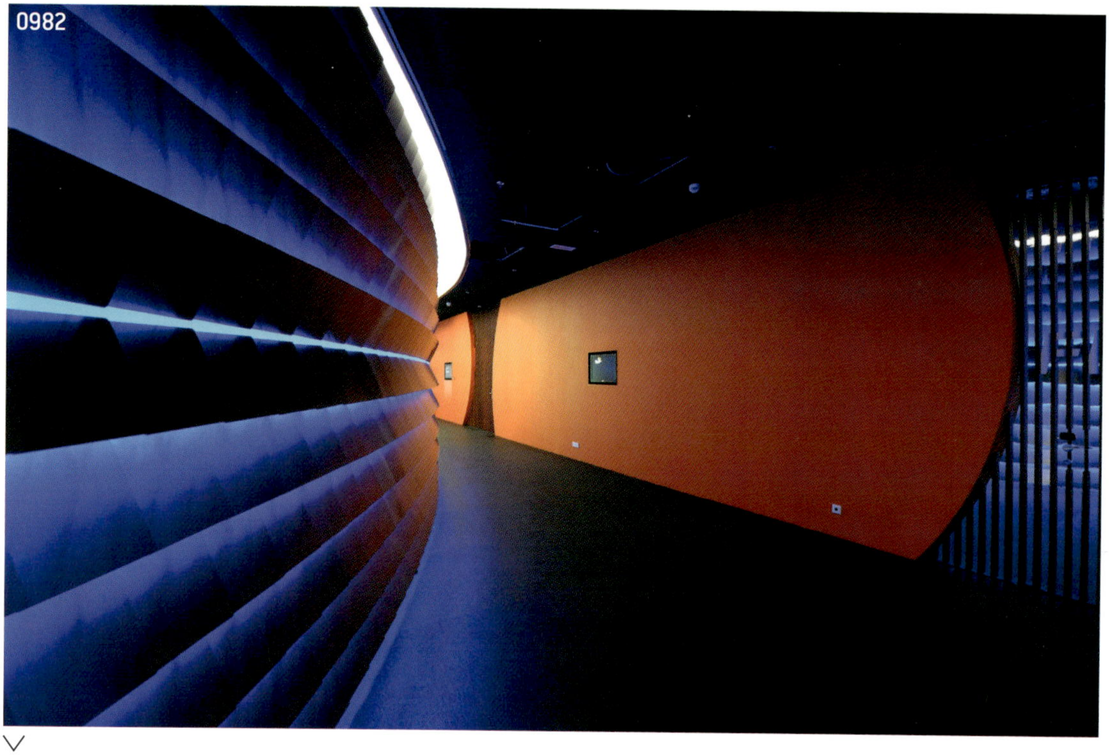

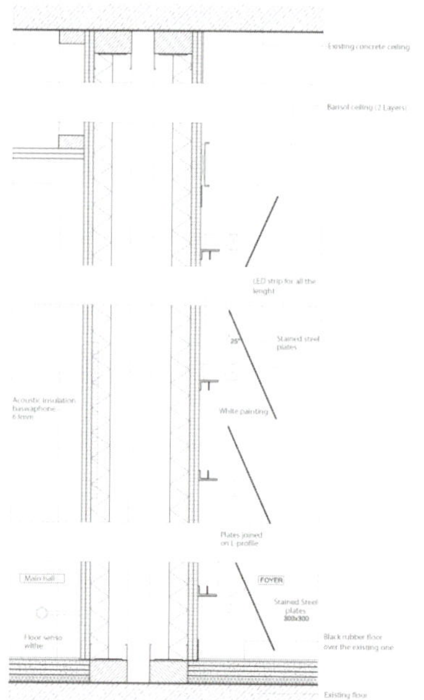

Existing concrete ceiling
Barrisol ceiling (2 Layers)
LED strip for all the lenght
25°
Stained steel plates
Acoustic insulation
White painting
Plates joined on L profile
Main hall
FOYER
Stained Steel plates 300x300
Black rubber floor over the existing one
Existing floor

0983

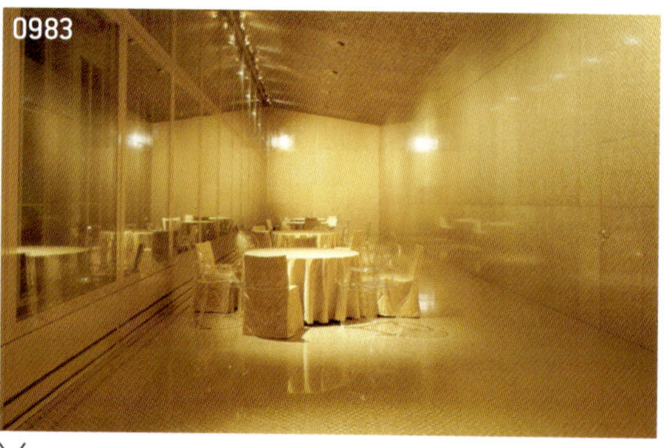

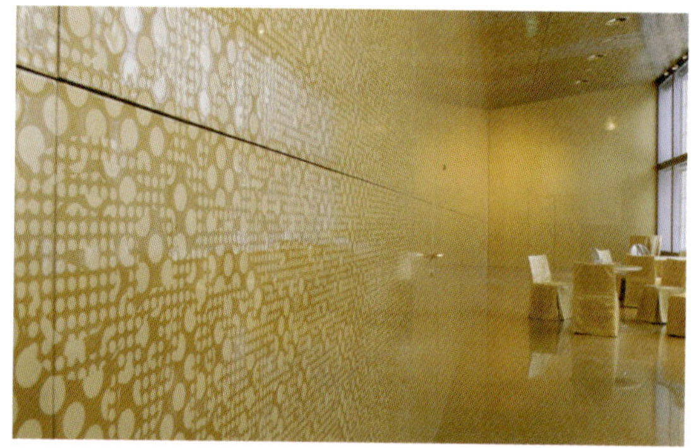

0984

The padded polyurethane and imitation leather panels used in this loft apartment serve a threefold function: the door for the children's bedroom, covering for a hidden shelving unit, and acoustic insulation for the living area, in addition to providing color.

Les panneaux capitonnés en polyuréthane et skaï que l'on a installé dans ce loft remplissent trois fonctions : ils font office de porte pour la chambre des enfants, recouvrent des étagères cachées et servent d'isolant acoustique pour le salon, en plus d'apporter de la couleur.

Die in diesem *loft* eingebauten, mit Polyurethan und Skai gepolsterten Paneele erfüllen eine dreifache Aufgabe: Sie dienen als Tür des Kinderschlafzimmers, verkleiden ein verdecktes Regal und isolieren akustisch das Wohnzimmer, indem sie diesem auÀerdem viel Farbe verleihen.

De gewatteerde panelen uit polyurethaan en skai die in deze *loft* geïnstalleerd werden, vervullen een drievoudige functie: ze dienen als deur voor de slaapkamers van de kinderen, ze bekleden een verborgen rek en zorgen voor een kleurrijke akoestische isolatie van het salon.

>

0985

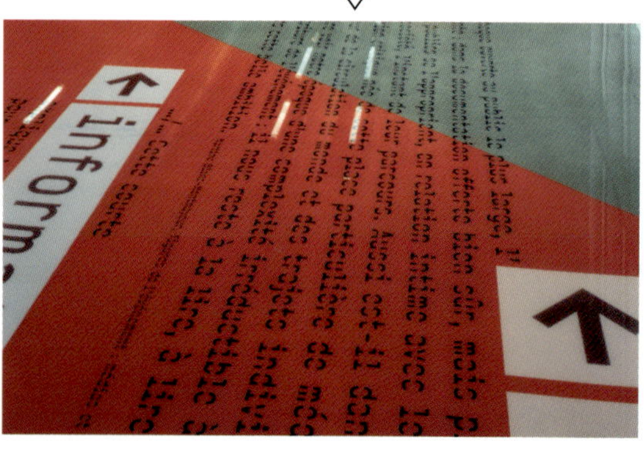

0986

0987

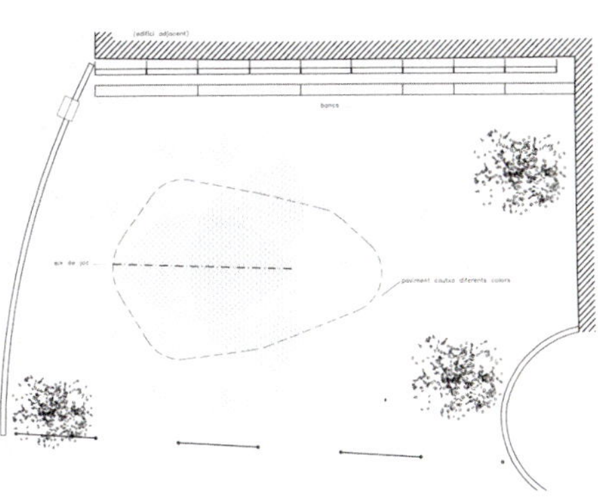
(edifici adjacent)
bancs
eix de joc
paviment cautxú diferents colors

0988

0989

0990

0991

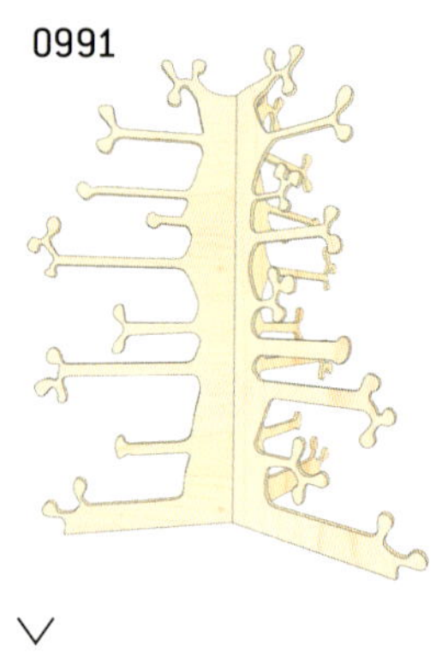

0992

0993

L'Annexe at the BHV is a new space designed by Matali Crasset for the BHV Belle Epine store. It is a 2,900 m² space for young people to practice leisure activities, hold workshops and exchange ideas. For this reason, electric and acid colors have been selected that change to create a new stage.

L'Annexe du BHV est un nouvel espace conçu par Matali Crasset pour le magasin BHV de Belle Epine. Il s'agit de 2 900 m² consacrés à la jeunesse au sein desquels ont lieu des activités de loisir, des ateliers et des échanges d'idées. Voilà pourquoi le choix s'est porté sur des couleurs électriques et acides, qui changent, pour marquer un nouvel espace scénique.

L'Annexe at the BHV ist ein neuer, von Matali Crasset für den BHV Belle Epine Laden entworfener Bereich. Dabei handelt es sich um 2.900 m² für die Jugend, in denen Freizeitaktivitäten, Workshops und Ideenaustauschmöglichkeiten vereint sind. Aus diesem Grund wurden sich verändernde elektrische und Säurefarben ausgewählt, um einen neuen szenischen Bereich zu kennzeichnen.

L'Annexe at the BHV is een nieuwe ruimte die door Matali Crasset ontworpen werd voor de winkel BHV Belle Epine. Het gaat hier om een ruimte van 2.900 m², bestemd voor de jeugd, waarin vrijetijdsactiviteiten, workshops en de uitwisseling van ideeën verenigd worden. Daarom werd voor de afbakening van de nieuwe toneelruimte dan ook gekozen voor felle kleuren.

0994

0995

0996

0997

0998

0999

1000

PHOTO CREDITS > CRÉDITS PHOTOGRAPHIQUES
FOTONACHWEIS > FOTOVERANTWOORDING

© Adam Radosavljevic | Dreamstime.com 0633
© Aida Ricciardiello | Dreamstime.com 0839
© Alex Bramwell | Dreamstime.com 0452
© Algimantas Balezentis | Dreamstime.com 0872
© Ana Vasileva | Dreamstime.com 0712
© Andreasg | Dreamstime.com 0798
© Andrei Radzkou | Dreamstime.com 0084
© Andrés Rodríguez | Dreamstime.com 0051, 0624, 0688
© Andris Piebalgs | Dreamstime.com 0080
© Anthony Aneese Totah Jr | Dreamstime.com 0864, 0866
© António Nunes | Dreamstime.com 0445
© Baloncici | Dreamstime.com 0109, 0110, 0111, 0112
© Benis Arapovic/.shock | Dreamstime.com 0123
© Bertrandb | Dreamstime.com 0450
© Bosenok | Dreamstime.com 0060
© Branislav Senic | Dreamstime.com 0046, 0063
© Brooke Whatnall | Dreamstime.com 0824
© Colleen Coombe | Dreamstime.com 0444, 0464
© Daniël Leppens | Dreamstime.com 0594
© Dan Wallace | Dreamstime.com 0874
© Darryl Brooks | Dreamstime.com 0117
© Davidmarty... | Dreamstime.com 0054
© David Morgan | Dreamstime.com 0099
© Deborah Benbrook | Dreamstime.com 0713
© Dejan LjamiÀ| Dreamstime.com 0460
© Denis Kartavenko | Dreamstime.com 0458
© Drbouz | Dreamstime.com 0066
© Elena Elisseeva | Dreamstime.com 0052
© Ene | Dreamstime.com 0709
© Erik De Graaf | Dreamstime.com 0815, 0867, 0873
© Erik Reis | Dreamstime.com 0598
© Fallsview | Dreamstime.com 0875
© Feeman_4_life | Dreamstime.com 0078
© Fred Goldstein | Dreamstime.com 0059
© Frode Krogstad | Dreamstime.com 0070
© Galina Barskaya | Dreamstime.com 0045, 0057, 0686
© Gemenacom | Dreamstime.com 0113
© George Mayer | Dreamstime.com 0205, 0617
© Gira | Dreamstime.com 0447
© Goran Bogicevic | Dreamstime.com 0865
© Gordon Ball | Dreamstime.com 0226
© Hannu Liivaar | Dreamstime.com 0706
© Ian Francis | Dreamstime.com 0595
© Igorr | Dreamstime.com 0116
© Igor Terekhov | Dreamstime.com 0108
© Ilja Mašík | Dreamstime.com 0708
© Isabel Poulin | Dreamstime.com 0726
© Italianestro | Dreamstime.com 0071
© Jasmin Krpan | Dreamstime.com 0096
© Jelena Popic | Dreamstime.com 0765
© Jian Zhang | Dreamstime.com 0710
© Joan Coll Jcvstock | Dreamstime.com 0087, 0454
© Joanne Zh | Dreamstime.com 0040, 0042, 0075, 0082
© Joe Gough | Dreamstime.com 0121
© Jorge Salcedo | Dreamstime.com 0050
© Jose Gil | Dreamstime.com 0044
© Josef Muellek/Digitalpress | Dreamstime.com 0130
© Jozef Sedmak | Dreamstime.com 0761
© Juanjo Tugores | Dreamstime.com 0451
© Judy Ben Joud | Dreamstime.com 0048
© Justin Sailor | Dreamstime.com 0695, 0701
© Kai Koehler | Dreamstime.com 0632
© Kai Zhang | Dreamstime.com 0704
© Ken Toh | Dreamstime.com 0124
© Kheng Guan Toh | Dreamstime.com 0068, 0069
© Knud Nielsen | Dreamstime.com 0463
© Koh Sze Kiat | Dreamstime.com 0592
© Krzyssagit | Dreamstime.com 0083
© Krzysztof Korolonek | Dreamstime.com 0053
© Lance Bellers | Dreamstime.com 0055
© Lars Christensen | Dreamstime.com 0461
© Lawrence Wee | Dreamstime.com 0073
© Lennyfdzz | Dreamstime.com 0076
© Loft Publications 0100, 0999
© Lucabertolli | Dreamstime.com 0127
© Lucy Cherniak | Dreamstime.com 0079
© Marjan Veljanoski | Dreamstime.com 0058
© Maxim Petrichuk | Dreamstime.com 0077
© Melinda Fawver | Dreamstime.com 0043
© Micha Rosenwirth | Dreamstime.com 0620
© Michael Kempf | Dreamstime.com 0627
© Mikhail Olykainen | Dreamstime.com 0958
© Mirage1 | Dreamstime.com 0074
© Mohamed Badawi | Dreamstime.com 0129
© Natalia Guseva | Dreamstime.com 0061
© Natalia Vasina Vladimirovna | Dreamstime.com 0453
© Nick Stubbs | Dreamstime.com 0103, 0448
© Nikolay Okhitin | Dreamstime.com 0459
© Norman Chan | Dreamstime.com 0119
© Oleg Fedorenko | Dreamstime.com 0707
© Pavalache Stelian | Dreamstime.com 0128
© Pavel Losevsky | Dreamstime.com 0576, 0715
© Peter Albrektsen | Dreamstime.com 0067
© Petr Vaclavek | Dreamstime.com 0023
© Phartisan | Dreamstime.com 0891
© Photawa | Dreamstime.com 0065
© Photoblueice | Dreamstime.com 0090
© Photoclicks | Dreamstime.com 0870
© Pindiyath100 | Dreamstime.com 0684
© Piotr Antonów | Dreamstime.com 0126
© Pontus Edenberg | Dreamstime.com 0228
© Radomír Režný | Dreamstime.com 0577
© Ragne Kabanova | Dreamstime.com 0104, 0877
© Rangerx | Dreamstime.com 0049
© Risto Hunt | Dreamstime.com 0876
© Robert Lerich | Dreamstime.com 0449
© Rod He | Dreamstime.com 0118
© Rognar | Dreamstime.com 0269
© Ron Maandag | Dreamstime.com 0596
© Ruigouveia | Dreamstime.com 0629
© Ryby | Dreamstime.com 0115
© Saporob | Dreamstime.com 0462
© Sebastian Czapnik | Dreamstime.com 0455, 0456, 0634
© Serdarbasak | Dreamstime.com 0125
© Simba3003 | Dreamstime.com 0843
© Simon Schmidt | Dreamstime.com 0711
© Sparkia | Dreamstime.com 0056
© Startouche... | Dreamstime.com 0070
© Stephen Coburn | Dreamstime.com 0101
© Steve Lovegrove | Dreamstime.com 0086
© Steven Jones | Dreamstime.com 0578
© Stratum | Dreamstime.com 0206
© Svlumagraphica | Dreamstime.com 0081
© Thorsten | Dreamstime.com 0120
© Tomasz Markowski | Dreamstime.com 0047
© Tom Dowd | Dreamstime.com 0457
© Tupungato | Dreamstime.com 0868
© Vangelis | Dreamstime.com 0062
© Vego | Dreamstime.com 0609
© Victor Zastol`skiy | Dreamstime.com 0274, 0625
© Videowokar... | Dreamstime.com 0085
© Vinicius Tupinamba | Dreamstime.com 0988
© V J Matthew | Dreamstime.com 0869
© Vuk Vukoslavovic | Dreamstime.com 0122
© Vvoronov | Dreamstime.com 0132
© William Howell | Dreamstime.com 0131, 0871
© Yali Shi | Dreamstime.com 0064
© Youssouf Cader | Dreamstime.com 0446
© Yulia Saponova | Dreamstime.com 0106
© Yuri Strakhov | Dreamstime.com 0034
© Zhang Lei | Dreamstime.com 0626

Chris Bosse 0365
© Chris Bosse 0365, 0385

Chris Bosse, students from UTS
© Chris Bosse 0380

Christian de Portzamparc
© Atelier Christian de Portzamparc, Kamel Khalfi, Nicolas Borel 0781

Casagrande Laboratory
© Casagrande Laboratory 0754

Claude Cormier Architectes Paysagistes
© Claude Cormier Architectes Paysagistes 0388, 0880

Claus en Kaan Architecten
© Claus en Kaan Architecten 0763
© Satoshi Asakawa 0769

CLE Architects Limited
© CLE Architects Limited 0019

Co-labarchitects
© S. Lewis, G. McLuskey, N. Andriotis 0294

Coop Himmelb(l)au
© Coop Himmelb(l)au 0012, 0832
© Hélène Binet, Ari Marcopoulos 0826

Cossmann_de Bruyn
© Nicole Zimmermann 0292, 0945

Cricursa
© Cricursa 0830

Dal Pian Arquitetos Associados
© Dal Pian Arquitectos 0481, 0550

Dalibos Studis
© Miquel Tres 0951

Damglass
© Damglass 0727

Daniel Bonilla Arquitectos
© Daniel Bonilla Arquitectos 0714

Daniela Moderini, Laura Zampieri, Ippolito Pizetti
© Daniela Moderini, Laura Zampieri, Ippolito Pizetti 0531

Dardelet
© Dardelet 0492

David Randall Hertz/SEA - Studio of Enviromental Architecture
© Jeurgen Nogai 0304, 0339

De Amicis Architetti
© De Amicis Architetti 0546

Delta Vorm Groep
© Frank Colder, Picture7 0475, 0519, 0522, 0524

DeMaria Design Associates
© Andre Movsesyan, Christian Kienapfel 0438

Denton Corker Marshall & Robert Owen
© Denton Corker Marshall & Robert Owen 0393

Denzer & Poensgen
© Denzer & Poensgen, Marmagen 0823

Desalto
© Desalto 0214

Despang Architekten
© Despang Architekten 0027, 0658, 0699, 0740, 0766, 0767, 900

Die Baupiloten
© Jan Bitter 0992

DO+CE
© DO+CE 0218

Dominique Perrault Architects
© ADAGP, A. Morin 0570

Donaldson & Warm Architects
© Martin Farquharson 0553

Dosmasuno Arquitectos
© Miguel de Guzmán 0857

Douglas Teiger/Abramson Teiger Architects
© Richard Barnes Photography 0293

Dovre
© Dovre 0163, 0164

DP Architects, Ministry of Design, Colin Seah
© Design Hotels 0006

Driendl Architects
© Driendl Architects 0703

Duravit
© Duravit 0247

Ecosistema Urbano
© Emilio P. Doiztua 0434, 0437

EDAW
© David Lloyd, Dixi Carrillo y Frank Chow/EDAW, Hai River Administration Bureau 0261
© Dixi Carrillo/EDWA, Peter Matthews 0551

EEA-Erick van Egeraat Associated Architects
© Christian Richters 0305, 0838

EHDD Architecture
© Doug Snower 0404
© EHDD Architecture 0321

EMBT – Enric Miralles + Benedetta Tagliabue
© Duccio Malagamba 0676

Emilio Llobat Guarino
© Emilio Llobat Guarino 0254, 0786

Enric Ruiz-Geli
© Luis Ros 0318, 0664

Equip Xavier Claramunt
© Ascer 0937

Eric Owen Moss Architects
© Tom Bonner 0697

Erin Moor
© Gary Tarleton 0423, 0427

Estudio Lamela Arquitectos, Richard Rogers Partnership
© Manuel Renau 0030, 0277, 0681, 0696

Europizarras
© Europizarras 0648

FAR frohn&rojas
© FAR frohn&rojas 0311, 0313

Faulkner & Chapman Landscape Design
© Shania Sheguedyn 0491

Felipe Assadi + Francisca Pulido
© Guy Wenborne 0935

Fermator
© Fermator 0631, 0635, 0636, 0637, 0638, 0642, 0639

Fermín Vázquez/b720 Arquitectos
© Rafael Vargas 0804

Fibo Leuchten-Schmiedeeisen
© Fibo Leuchten-Schmiedeeisen 0144

Filippo Bombace
© Luigi Filetici 0230

FOA-Foreign Office Architecture
© Francisco Andeyro García, Alejandro García González 0094
© Kim Jae-kyung 0739

Forjas Artísticas "El Francés"
© Forjas Artísticas "El Francés" 0194, 0195, 0602, 0878

Foscarini
© Foscarini 0265, 0267

Fougeron Architects
© Richard Barnes 0021

Francis Soler Architecte
© Francis Soler Architecte 0389

Francis Vermonden
© Francis Vermonden 0498

Frank Gehry
© Adrian Tyler 0353

Future Systems
© Søren Aagaard Photography 0785

GAD- Global Architectural Development
© Ali Bekman 0745
© Ali Bekman, Ozlem Ercil 0770, 0929

Galán + Lubascher Arquitectos
© Galán + Lubascher Arquitectos 0855

García Ruiz Arquitectos
© Pedro Mmahamud 0240

Gary Chang/EDGE (HK) Ltd
© Almond Chu 0237

GCA Arquitectes Associats
© Jordi Miralles 0359, 0909

Germán del Sol
© Guy Wemborne 0588, 0589
© Felipe Camus 0672

Giovanni Vaccarini
© Alessandro Ciampi 0657

GMP-Von Gerkan, Marg und Partner Architekten
© Ben Mcmillan, Christian Gahl 0343
© Christian Gahl 0853
© GMP-Von Gerkan, Marg und Partner Architekten 0378, 0379
© Heiner Leiska 0860
© Marcus Bredt 0309, 0683

Gora Art & Landscape
© Åke E:son Lindman 0331, 0337, 0680

Graft
© Andi Albert Photographie 0981
© Graft 0384
© Hiepler Brunier Architekturfotografie 0979

Graftworks architecture + design
© David Joseph 0387

Green Fortune
© Green Fortune 0500

Greenmeme
© Greenmeme 0501

Gregotti Associati International Spa
© Donato di Bello 0926, 0966

Griffin Enright Architects
© Benny Chan 0366
© Griffin Enright Architects 0383, 0386

Grimshaw Architects
© Shannon Macgrath 0687

Groep Delta Architectuur
© Groep Delta Architectuur 0534

Grollmitz-Zappe
© Kirsti Kriegel 0246

GROSS. MAX. Landscape Architects
© GROSS. MAX., Mark Dion 0523, 0527

Gudmundur Jonsson Arkitektkontor
© Gudmundur Jonsson Arkitektkontor 0252

Guillermo Hevia
© Cristián Barahona, Guillermo Hevia 0800

Gustafson Porter
© Gustafson Porter 0469

Gwenael Nicolas/Curiosity
© Daici Ano 0233

Hascher und Jehle Architektur
© Svenha Bockhop 0802

Henning Larsen Architects
© Adam Mørk 0001, 0580
© Henning Larsen Architects 0015
© Reinhard Görner 0319

Hideki Yoshimatsu + Archipro Architects
© Archipro Architects 0730

Hild und K Architekten
© Hild und K Architekten 0271

Hiroaki Ohtani
© Hiroaki Ohtani 0630
© Kouji Okatomo 0509

Hobby A.Schuster & Maul, Gerold Peham
© Marc Haader 0435

Hofman Dujardin Architecten
© Matthijs von Roon 0994

HOK- Hellmuth, Obata + Kassabaum
© HOK- Hellmuth, Obata + Kassabaum 0028

Holzbox
© Holzbox 0440

Hutterreimann + Cejka Landschaftsarchitekten, Jens Schmahl/A Lab Architektur
© Christo Libuda, Franziska Poreski, Hutterreimann + Cejka 0593, 0965

Hwam 165
© Hwam 0165, 0166, 0167

Ian Ayers, Francesc Zamora
© Francesc Zamora 0989, 0990

Ibarra Rosano Design Architects
© Ibarra Rosano Design Architects 0138

IGV
© IGV 0640, 0641, 0643

India Mahdavi, Javier Sánchez/JS[a]
© Undine Pröhl 0811

Invicta
© Invicta 0159

Isthmus Group
© Simon Devitt 0263

Jaime Varon, Abraham Metta, Álex Metta/Migdal Arquitectos
© Paul Czitrom Baus, Werner Huthmacher 0604, 0834

James Corner Field Operations, Diller Scofidio+Renfro
© James Corner Field Operations, Diller Scofidio+Renfro 0507

Jan Søndergaard, KHR Arkitekter AS
© Ib Sørensen 0039

Jarmund/Vigsnæs architects
© Nils Petter Dale 0677

Jasarevic Architekten
© Alen Jasarevic, Angelika Bardehle, Nursen Ozlukurt 0924, 0960

Jaume Valor
© Eugeni Pons 0913

Jean Marc Ibos Myrto Vitart
© Georges Fessy 0840
© Georges Fessy, Philippe Ruault 0985

Jeff Brock, Belén Moneo/Moneo Brock Studio
© Luis Asín, Jeff Brock 0969

Jeffrey Beers International
© Peter Paige 0004

Jennifer Siegal/Office of Mobile Design
© Jennifer Siegal/Office of Mobile Design 0428

Jensen & Skodvin Arkitektkontor AS
© Jensen & Skodvin Arkitektkontor 0583, 0690, 0736, 0907

Jeremy Edmiston, Douglas Gauthier / System Architects
© Jeremy Edmiston, Douglas Gauthier / System Architects 0360, 0432, 0433

Jestico + Whiles
© Ales Jungmann 0002
© Jestico + Whiles 0621, 0835

JKMM Architects
© Arno de la Chapelle, Jussi Tiainen, Kimmo Räisänen 0741

JML arquitectura del agua
© Stephane Llorca 0474, 0476, 0468, 0472, 0488

Johan Cubillos/Hierro Ornamental
© Johan Cubillos/Hierro Ornamental 0139, 0190

John Cunningham Architects, Landworks Studio, Office DA
© Landworks Studio 0541

John Friedman Alice Kimm Architects
© Benny Chan / Fotoworks 0325, 0408

John Portman & Associates
© Michael Portman 0607, 0678, 0812

Johnson Chou
Volker Seding Photography 0244

Johnston Marklee & Associates
© Eric Staudenmaier 0779

Jordi Garcés
© Jordi Miralles 0499, 0775

Jorge Armando Rodríguez Bello
© Jorge Armando Rodríguez Bello 0762

Josep Lluís Mateo/MAP Architectes
©Beat Marugg 0911
©Infinite Light, Beat Marugg 0910

Jouin Manku
© Eric Laignel 0266, 0297, 0605, 0608, 0882, 0953

JS[a] diseñodesarrollo
© Luis Gordoa, Jair Navarrete 0603

Juan Carlos Doblado
© Alex Kornhuber 0930
© Elsa Ramírez 0932, 0948

Juan Domingo Santos
© Amparo Garrido, Francisco Román, Valentín García, Fernando Alda 0773, 0933
© Fernando Alda, Valentín García, Estudio jds 0923

Juan Pablo Corvalán/Supersudaka
© Supersudaka.com 0748

Jun Itami
© Shigeyuki Morishita 0669

Jungles Landscape Architecture
© Lenny Provo 0489

Kabalab
© Kabalab 0215, 0216

Kalfire
© Kalfire 0168

Kashef Mahboob Chowdhury/Urbana
© Kashef Mahboob Chowdhury 0771

Kazunori Fujimoto Architect
© Kaori Ichikawa 0772, 0837

Kengo Kuma & Associates
© Daici Ano 0650, 0649, 0848
© Mitsumasa Fujitsuka 0495, 0691, 0738, 0881

Kieran Timberlake Associates
© Barry Halkin 0298, 0424
© Kieran Timberlake Associates 0310

Kim Herforth Nielsen, Bo Boje Larsen, Kim Christiansen/3XN
© Adam Mørk 0016

Kiyoshi Sey Takeyama + AMORPHE
© Koichi Torimura 0517

Klein Dytham Architecture
© Katsuhisa Kida 0301, 0845, 0852

Kochi Architects Studio
© Daicio Ano 0614
© Kazuysu Kochi, Daici Ano 0611
© Kazuysu Kochi 0919
© Nobumitsu Watanabe 0613

Konstantin Grcic Industrial Design
© Stockhölm Furniture Fair 0014

Koselicka Landschaftsarchitektur
© Koselicka Landschaftsarchitektur 0530

KPMB Architects
© Eduard Heuber/Arch Photo, Marc Cramer, Tom Arban/Tom Arban Photography 0018, 0037

KPMB Architects, GBCA Architects
© Eduard Heuber/Arch Photo, Tom Arban/Tom Arban Photography 0017, 0038

Kramm & Strigl
© Dieter Leistner, Kramm Strigl 0375, 0391

La Dallman Architects
© Kevin J. Miyazaki 0022, 0329

LAB Architecture Studio, Bates Smart Architects
© Andrew Hoobs, Adrian Lander, Peter Clarke, Trevor Main 0581, 0782, 0833

LABFAC, Finn Geipel et Nicolas Michelin
© Agence Nicolas Michelin & Associés 0559
© François Bergeret 0563

Lanbacher
© Lanbacher 0600

Landau & Kindelbacher Architekten Innerarchitekten
© Christian Hacker 0946

LAND-I Archicolture
© Roberto Capecci, Raffaella Sini 0552

Landworks Studio
© Landworks Studio 0526

Lazzarini Pickering Architetti
© Matteo Piazza 0295, 0808

Leger Wanaselja Architecture
© César Rubio, Karl Wanaselja 0398
© Leger Wanaselja Architecture 0401

Lehrer Architects
© Marvin Rand 0809

Lema Mobili
© Lema Mobili 0219, 0220

Lemonpack
© Lemonpack 0026

Levin Monsigny Landscape Architects
© Claas Dreppenstedt 0516

Lichtblau + Wagner Architekten
© Bruno Klomfar 0029

Lippmann Associates
© Lippmann Associates 0912

Lluís Clotet, Ignasi Paricio/Clotet, Paricio i Associats
© Lluís Casals 0908

Lomakka
© Lomakka 0286, 0287, 0288, 0291

Lorenzo Castro
© Guillermo Quintero, Sergio García, Ana María Pradilla, Lorenzo Castro 0483

Luca Lancini/Fujy
© Miguel de Guzmán 0358, 0400

Luis de Garrido
© David Campos, Habitat Futura 0357
© Luis de Garrido 0409
© Maite Piera 0414

Maki and Associates
© Shinkenchiku-sha, Toshiharu Kitajima 0915

Makoto Tanijiri/Suppose Design Office
© Makoto Tanijiri/Suppose Design Office 0390

Manuel Cerdá/MPC Arquitectura
© Joan Roig 0817

Manuel Cervantes Cespedes/CC Arquitectos
© Luis Gordoa 0041, 0931, 0967

Manuelle Gautrand
© Manuelle Gautrand 0350
© Philippe Ruault, Platform 0335

Marcel Wanders, Karin Krautgartner, Bisazza
© Alberto Ferrero 0241

María Victoria Besonías, Guillermo de Almeida, Luciano Kruk/BAK
© Daniela Mac Adden 0776, 0920

Mario Botta Architetto
© Enrico Cano 0963

Mark Dziewulski
© Keith Cronin 0257

Markus Wespi Jérôme de Meuron Architekten
© Markus Wespi Jérôme de Meuron Architekten 0757

Martí Manyà
© Xavier Martí, Neus Homs 0140, 0141, 0156, 0623

Martín Gómez Arquitectos
© Daniela Mac Adden 0747

Martin Liefheber + Associates/Breathe Architects
© Martin Liefhebber 0399

Masamichi Udagawa & Sigi Moeslinger/Antenna Design
© Ryuzo Masunaga 0372

MA-Sistemas S.L.
© MA-Sistemas S.L. 0302, 0565

Massimiliano Fuksas Architetto
© Archivio Massimiliano Fuksas Architetto 0675
© Maurizio Marcato 0020, 0343
© Moreno Maggi 0784, 0847, 0850, 0854
© Phillipe Ruault 0564, 0567

Matali Crasset
© Patrick Gries 0991, 0993

Mattinson Associates
© Carlos Dominguez, Mattinson Associates 0702

Maya Romanoff
© Maya Romanoff 0883, 0886, 0888, 0889, 0890, 0894, 0896, 0897, 0898, 0901, 0974, 0975, 0973

Mc Gregor & Partners
© Mc Gregor & Partners 0394

McIntosh Poris Associates
© Kevin Bauman 0229

Metalunic
© Metalunic 0098

Michael Singer Studio
© Michael Singer Studio 0862

Michelle Kaufmann Designs
© John Swain 0352, 0403
© Michelle Kaufmann Designs 0425

Mikael Bergquist Arkitektkontor
© Åke E:son Lindman 0760

Min ffl Day
© Larry Gawell 0885

Minsuk Cho + Kisu Park/Mass Studies
© Yong-Kwan Kim 0513

Miquel Xirau
© Àlex Sánchez Vidiella 0143, 0147, 0148, 0187
© Miquel Xirau 0150, 0151, 0152, 0153, 0154, 0155, 0191, 0196, 0198, 0199

Miró Rivera Architects
© Paul Finkel/Piston Design 0721

MITHUN architects+designers+planners
© JH 0421

MoHen Design International
© MoHen Design International 0234

Molteni
© Molteni 0211

Mount Fuji Architects Studio
© Mount Fuji Architects Studio 0585, 0742

MOVE/DARAQ Import
© MOVE/DARAQ Import 0222

Murphy/Jahn Architects
© Andreas Keller 0851
© Doug Snower 0685, 0797
© H.G. Esch 0575

MVRDV
© Rob't Hart 0819, 0859

Nicholas Grimshaw & Partners
© Nicholas Grimshaw & Partners 0338

Nicola Tremacoldi/NM arquitecte
© Adrià Goula 0314

Nicos Kalogirou
© Nicos Kalogirou 0756

NIPpaysage
© NIPpaysage 0479, 0542, 0543

NMDA-Neil M. Denari Architects
© NMDA-Neil M. Denari Architects 0333, 0355, 0436

Notson Acustica
© Notson Acustica 0289, 0290

Nurmela-Raimoranta-Tasa Arkkitehdit
© Jyriki Tasa, Jussi Tiainen 0665

Obie G. Bowman
© Obie G. Bowman, Robert Foothorap 0324

Obra Architects
© Obra Architects 0200

Odden Rodrigues Architects
© Robert Frich/Acorn Photo Agency 0667

Odos Architects
© Odos Architects, Ros Kavanagh 0158

Ofis Arhitekti
© Tomaz Gregoric 0303

Olgga Architects
© Olgga Architects 0430

Omnidecor
© Omnidecor 0224, 0722, 0723, 0841

One Plus Partnership
© Gabriel Leung 0232, 0236, 0239, 0243
© Law Ling Kit, Virginia Lung 0005, 0262

ONL-Kas Oosterhuis, ONL-Oosterhuis_Lénárd
© Jeroen Bos/ONL- Oosterhuis_Lénárd 0674
© ONL- Oosterhuis_Lénárd 0348, 0351
© Walter Fogel, Festo AG & Co. KG, ONL 0371, 0374

Orlando Busarello, Dilva Cândida, Daniela Slomp Busarello
© Slomp & Busarello Architects 0528

Óscar Tusquets Blanca
© Gunnar Knetchel, Rafael Vargas 0914

Oslund and Associates
© George Heinrich 0545

Pablo Fernández Lorenzo, Pablo Redondo Díez
© Pablo Fernández Lorenzo, Pablo Redondo Díez 0221

Pagani+ Di Mauro Architetti
© Andrea Corbellini 0653

Paolo Cesaretti
© Paolo Cesaretti 0705

Paolo L. Bürgi/ Studio Bürgi
© Paolo L. Bürgi/ Studio Bürgi 0480

Pascal Arquitectos
© Víctor Benítez 0789, 0961, 0962

Patrick Blanc
© Patrick Blanc 0508

Patrick Marsilli
© Benjamin Thoby 0353
© Patrick Marsilli 0299, 0322

Paul Bernier Architecte
© Paul Bernier, Vittorio Viera 0752

Paul Cocksedge Studio
© Richard Brine 0368

Paul de Ruiter
© Paul de Ruiter 0842
© Pieter Kers 0092
© Rien van Rijthoven, Herman van Doorn 0089
© Rob 't Hart and Pieter Kers 0091, 0814

Paul Morgan Architects
© Peter Bennetts 0751
© John Gollings 0803, 0928

Pelli Clarke Pelli Architects
© Pelli Clarke Pelli Architects 0402, 0406

Pete O'Shea ASLA FAAR/Siteworks Studio
© Pete O'Shea ASLA FAAR/Siteworks Studio 0465, 0466, 0467

Peter Marino
© Peter Marino, Takashi Orii, Vincent Kapp 0373

Petr Hájek/HSH architekti
© Ester Havlová 0731, 0916

Pich-Aguilera
© Pich-Aguilera 0411

Plajer & Franz
© www.diephotodesigner.de 0349, 0502

Plan 01 Architects
© Stéphane Chalmeau, Frédéric Delangle 0679

PTW Architects
© PTW Architects 0397

PTW Architects, ARUP, China State Construction Design International (CCDI)
© PTW + CSCEC 0327

Pugh + Scarpa Architects
© Marvin Rand 0794, 0934
© Pugh + Scarpa Architects 0377

Pushak
© Pushak 0496

PWP Landscape Architecture
© PWP Landscape Architecture 0255, 0548

R&Sie (n)
© R&Sie(n) 0518, 0568, 0569

Radius Design
© Radius Design 0171

Rais
© Rais 0170

RAU
© Kusters fotografie 0420

Ray Kappe + DU Architects
© Ray Kappe 0405

RB Arkitektur AB
© RB Arkitektur AB 0231

RCR Aranda Pigem Vilalta Arquitectes
© Hisao Suzuki 0903

Realarchitektur
© Martin Widerberg 0204

Renzo Piano Building Workshop
© Ishida Shunji 0718
© Renzo Piano Building Workshop 0336

Ricardo Cabrera/Artesano Iron Works
© Artesano Iron Works 0149

Richard Rogers Partnership, Alonso Balaguer & Arquitectos Asociados, GCA Arquitectes Associats
© Gogortza & Llorella 0902

Richardson Sadeki
© Andrew Bordwin 0013

Rintala Eggertsson Architects
© Sami Rintala 0396

Romain Brenas & Rémy Casteu
© Romain Brenas & Rémy Casteu 0308

Ron Arad Associates
© Design Hotels 0003, 0381

Room 11 Studio
© Jasmin Latona 0316

Rosa Grena Kliass Arquitectura Paisagística
© Nelson Kon 0587

Rotzler Krebs Partner
© Rotzler Krebs Partner 0535, 0574

RozO architectes
© RozO architectes 0326

Rush & Wright Associates
© Peter Clarke 0520
© Derek Swalwell, Peter Bennetts 0544

Saia Barbarese Topouzanov Architectes
© Vladimir Topouzanov 0661

Saloni Cerámica
© Saloni Cerámica 0105, 0719, 0787, 0936, 0940, 0941, 0944

Sambuichi Architects
© Hiroyuki Hirai 0413

Samyn and Partners, Architects & Engineers
© Ch. Bastin, J. Evrard, Samyn and Partners, Architects & Engineers 0566

Santa-Rita Architects
© Joa˘o Santa-Rita, Joa˘o de Castro 0558, 0591

Santi Fuchs/Arte-Sano
© Santi Fuchs/Arte-Sano 0157, 0197

Santiago Calatrava
© Auditorio de Tenerife, José Ramón Oller 0764

Satoshi Okada Architects
© Satoshi Okada Architects 0533

Sauerbruch Hutton Architects
© Bitter & Bredt Fotografie 0332
© Gerrit Engel 0673

Scapelab
© Miran Kambic˘ 0482, 0549

Scarsi Bernardo S.n.c.
© Virginia Scarsi 0133, 0134, 0145, 0182, 0183, 0184, 0185, 0186, 0188, 0189

Schotten & Hansen
© Schotten & Hansen 892

Schwarz Design
© Schwarz Design 0275, 0278, 0280, 0281, 0282, 0284, 0662, 0689, 0725

Sebastián Irarrázaval
© Carlos Eguiguren 0410

Seno & Siffredi/Colpi di Martello
© Seno G. Carlo/Colpi di Martello 0137, 0146

Sevasa
© CriSamar®STEP 0025

SHEDKM
© Mark Braund, Miles Pearson and Dave King of SHEDKM 0560, 0561

SHH Architects
© SHH Architects 0732

Shuhei Endo Architect Institute
© Toshiraru Kitajima 0334
© Yoshiharu Matsumura 0670, 0671

Site Office Landscape Architecture
© Trevor Mein 0584, 0921

SKAARA Arkitekter AS
© Espen Grønli 0801
© Frank Tolpinrud 0749

SLA Landskabsarkitekter
© Frode Birk Nielsen 0484
© SLA, Jens Lindhe, Lars Bahl, Torben Petersen 0470
© Torben Petersen 0540

Smarch
© Beat Mathys, Claudio Moser, Dominique Uldry, Thomas Jantscher 0573

SOY Source Architectural Design Office
© Hiroshi Yokoyama 0768, 0925

Spigo Group
© Spigo Group 0283, 0285

Spillmann Echsle Architekten
© www.freitag.com 0382

Spittelwerk
© Paul Ott, 821, 0827, 0983, 1000
© Spittelwerk 1000

Stefan Eberstadt
© Stefan Eberstadt 0426

Stefan Sterf Architekten
© Isabella Scheel 0668

Stein Halvorsen as sivilarkitekter MNAL
© Kim Müller 0795, 0968

Stelle Architects
© Jeff Heatley 0599

Stephen Taylor Architects
© David Grandorge 0660

Stephen Varady Architecture
© Stephen Varady Architecture 0655

Steven Holl Architects
© Andy Ryan 0846, 0849, 0858

Strobl Architekten
© Josefine Unterhauser 0306

Studio 63 Architecture & Design
© Rimini Fiera-SIA Guest 0009
© Yael Pincus 0363, 0364

Studio 804
© Studio 804 0412

Studio Daniel Libeskind
© Bitter Bredt 0035, 0268, 0276, 0810, 0816, 0825

Studio Giovanni D'Ambrosio
© Peter Mylonas 0792, 0947, 0971

Studio Granda Architects
© Sigurgeir Sigurjónsson 0586

Studio NL-D
© Hans Werlemann/Hectic Pictures 312

Stûv
© Stûv 0169, 0173, 0173, 0174, 0175, 0176, 0177, 0180

Tadao Ando
© Mitsuo Matsuoka 0717

TAF Arkitektkontor
© TAF Arkitektkontor 0606

Taylor Cullity Lethlean
© Ben Wrigley, Carla Gottgens 0547

TEAM Landschaftsarchitekten
© Hansjorg Walter 0486

Teresa Sapey Estudio de Arquitectura
© Pablo Orcajo 0562

Tham & Videgård Hansson Arkitekter
© Åke E:son Lindman 0088, 0733, 0734, 0856, 0986

The Apartment Creative Agency
© Michael Weber 0238

The Paul Hogarth Company
© Laganside Corporation, The Paul Hogarth Company 0264

Theo Hotz Archtitekten + Planer AG
© Rolf Gähwiler 0036

Thilo Folkerts, SPAX Architects
© Sébastien Secchi 0471

Thyssenkrupp Elevadores
© Thyssenkrupp Elevadores 0644, 0645, 0646

Tino & Ricardo Barbosa/Barbosa Space Projects
© Marce Sedano 0136

Titus Bernhard Architekten
© Titus Bernhard Architekten 0320

Todd Saunders/Saunders Architecture
© Todd Saunders/Saunders Architecture 0397

Tom Allisma Productions
© Tom Allisma Productions 0212, 0213

Tonwerk
© Tonwerk 0178, 0179

Tony Trobe/TT Architecture
© Tony Trobe 0033

Topos Atelier
© Xavier Antunes 0515, 0654, 0646, 899

TOPOTEK 1 landscape architects
© Hanns Joosten 0529

Toscoquattro
© Toscoquattro 0242

Toyo Ito & Architects Associates, JML Arquitectura del Agua
© Stéphane Llorca 0555

Toyo Ito & Architects Associates, TAISEI Design PAE
© Toyo Ito & Architects Associates, TAISEI Design PAE 0805

Treehouse Company
© Chris Tubbs 0511

Turenscape
© Kongijan Yu, Cao Yang 0477, 0556

UN Studio van Berkel & Bos
© Brigida Gonzalez, Christian Richters 0783, 0917
© Christian Richters 0341, 0342, 0616, 0818, 0828, 0836, 0844, 0918, 0972

United Visual Artists, Onepointsix
© United Visual Artists 0354

Unopiù
© Unopiù 0192, 0193

Urbanus Architecture & Design
© Yan Meng, Jiu Chen 0557

Vāstu Shilpā Consultants
© Vāstu Shilpā Consultants 0422

Venhoeven CS
© Venhoeven CS 0493

Vicente Guallart/Guallart Architects
© Laura Cantarella 0514, 0777, 0970

Víctor Cañas, Joan Roca/Aquart
© Jordi Miralles 0097, 0720, 0780, 0955

Vidal y Asociados Arquitectos
© Ignacio Álvarez Monteserín 0998

Voorsanger Architects
© Thomas Damgaard 0503

Vyniluse
© Vyniluse 0980

West 8 Urban Design & Landscape Architecture
© West 8 Urban Design & Landscape Architecture 0490

West&Partner
© West&Partner 0525

Wilkinson Eyre Architects
© Helene Binet 0682
© Wilkinson Eyre Architects 0317

Wingårdh Arkitektkontor AB
© James Silverman 0497
© Ulf Celander 0571, 0572

Winn Wittman architecture
© Cassey Duna, Thomas McConnell 0315

Wood Marsh Architects
© Peter Bennetts 0778, 0906, 0949

Ximena Muñoz, Mónica Labra, Rodrigo Gajardo, Paulina Villalobos, Stefano Benaglia/theANEMIX
© www.kerbe.co.uk, Ximena Muñox 0370, 0369

Zwarts & Jansma Architects
© DigiDaan 0345, 0347
© Zwarts & Jansma Architects 0347